The Servant-Leader Within

A Transformative Path

To Tom + Mary —

Lovely to meet you and to
know of your commitment
to servant-leadership.

Warm regards,

Larry Spears

July, 2004

The Servant-Leader Within

A Transformative Path

ROBERT K. GREENLEAF

EDITED BY
HAMILTON BEAZLEY
JULIE BEGGS
AND
LARRY C. SPEARS

Paulist Press
New York/Mahwah, N.J.

Other Books by Robert K. Greenleaf

Servant Leadership, 25th Anniversary Edition, 2002 (Paulist Press)
The Power of Servant-Leadership, 1998
On Becoming a Servant-Leader, 1996
Seeker and Servant, 1996
Servant Leadership, 1977

Book design by Bookcomp, Inc.
Cover design by Morris Berman Studio

Library of Congress Cataloging-in-Publication Data

Greenleaf, Robert K.
    The servant-leader within : a transformative path / by Robert K. Greenleaf ; edited by Hamilton Beazley, Julie Beggs, and Larry C. Spears.
      p. cm.
Includes bibliographical references and index.
    ISBN 0-8091-4219-8 (alk. paper)
    1. Leadership. 2. Associations, institutions, etc. 3. Organizational change. 4. Organizational effectiveness. I. Beazley, Hamilton, 1943– II. Beggs, Julie. III. Spears, Larry C., 1955– IV. Title.
    HM1261 .G74 2003
    303.3'4—dc22

2003015908

Published by Paulist Press
997 Macarthur Boulevard
Mahwah, New Jersey 07430

www.paulistpress.com

Printed and bound in the
United States of America

CONTENTS

ABOUT THE AUTHOR

Robert K. Greenleaf (1904–90)

Robert K. Greenleaf spent most of his organizational life in the field of management, research, development, and education at AT&T. Just before his retirement as director of management research there, he held a joint appointment as visiting lecturer at MIT's Sloan School of Management and at the Harvard Business School. In addition, he held teaching positions at both Dartmouth College and the University of Virginia.

He was a consultant to universities, businesses, foundations, and churches during the tumultuous 1960s and 1970s. His consultancies included Ohio University, MIT, Ford Foundation, R. K. Mellon Foundation, Lilly Endowment, and the American Foundation for Management Research. His eclectic and wide-ranging curiosity, reading, and contemplation provided an unusual background for observing these institutions.

As a lifelong student of organization (i.e., how things get done), he distilled these observations in a series of essays, books, and videotapes on the theme of "The Servant as Leader," the objective of which is to stimulate thought and action for building a better, more caring society.

FOREWORD

Hamilton Beazley

Robert K. Greenleaf coined the term *servant-leadership* in 1970 and applied it to business and educational institutions in his seminal essay, "The Servant as Leader." Three decades later, servant-leadership continues to fascinate us with its promise, its paradoxes, and its intuitive attractiveness. But does it work in the real world? Is servant-leadership quixotic and idealistic? Or is it powerful and transformative? Greenleaf himself posed the question in "The Servant as Leader," "Can the two roles [of servant and leader] be fused in one real person, in all levels of status or calling? If so, can that person live and be productive in the real world of the present?"

After thirty years of experience with servant-leadership, the answer to Greenleaf's question has emerged with startling clarity. It is, "Yes." Servant-leadership is powerful and transformative—especially in the turbulent change of the new century, for which it is particularly well-suited. In business, servant-leadership principles characterize many of *Fortune* magazine's "100 Best Companies to Work For," creating enviable organizations with impressive operating statistics. In education, servant-leadership has led to new pedagogy, new learning, and new organizations devoted to its practice. In all its applications, servant-leadership achieves what is apparently impossible: bringing transformative experiences to the realm of the ordinary, to the everyday events that, cumulatively, define our lives and shape our experiences.

Nothing in the Industrial Age prepared us for the new era of technological revolution and shattering change, for the leap from managerial despot to team leader, for the global reach and unprecedented power of interactive networks of electronics and human

1

beings. Out of this chaos of understanding are emerging a few truths—still inchoate and still hard to believe. These simple truths applicable to management and leadership in the new century revolve around cooperation, collaboration, and service. They are captured in the concept of servant-leadership, and they are the new laws of survival. Those who adhere to these principles will flourish; those who reject them will perish. Greenleaf has become the Darwin of the twenty-first century, not because he created the concept of servant-leadership, but because he has described its effect in the real world of business.

Both business and education are buffeted by the same forces that are reordering the world, and both are struggling to find a hidden path through the shifting maze created by technology shock and its aftershocks. Although servant-leadership relies on a natural inclination to serve, its development in students and leaders requires instruction, facilitation, and support. Greenleaf's definitive work on how servant-leadership can be developed in a university (and in businesses and other institutions) is his parable, *Teacher as Servant*.

The Servant-Leader Within combines in one volume that parable and two of his essays, "Life's Choices and Markers" and the original version of "The Servant as Leader" (written in 1970 for a student audience). Each provides a different but complementary perspective on servant-leadership and its relationship to the art of teaching and the act of learning. For this edition, the editors have added commentary designed to make the parable and the essays even more useful to those interested in the teaching and practice of servant-leadership. *Teacher as Servant* is being reissued in this form in response to the growing demand from business executives and academic institutions for information on teaching servant-leadership to students, faculty, and staff in the case of academic institutions and to executives, managers, and workers in the case of business entities.

Servant-leadership belongs to a class of leadership philosophies that have the power to bring about dramatic and profound transformations in individuals, their organizations, and the society in which they live. Like other such philosophies, servant-leadership rests on eternal truths, is driven by deep human needs, and is grounded in existential realities. It resonates with the human psyche because it is directly related to our humanity—to what we are as human beings—and because it fascinates and challenges us with its simplicity and difficulty, its demands and revelations, its promises and potentialities.

Teacher as Servant is unique in its exploration of the means by which servant-leadership can be taught, that is, can be understood, experienced, and practiced in a structured environment created for that purpose. It is clear from Greenleaf's writings—and from his contention that faculty in the 1970s were not answering the students' pleas for more meaningful educational experiences—that the teaching of servant-leadership requires a practice component as well as formal instruction because servant-leadership is largely experiential; it is intellectual only in its foundations. As a result, servant-leadership is taught in the broadest and most inclusive sense of that word. In fact, it is more "caught than taught," and so the role modeling used to illustrate its principles and the environment designed to facilitate its learning are critical elements for those interested in teaching servant-leadership. Research on university servant-led living units and servant-leadership companies provides convincing evidence that servant-leadership *can* be taught. *Teacher as Servant* illustrates the organizational culture through which it can be learned and experienced and the role modeling necessary to teach it.

In addition to its pedagogical qualities, *Teacher as Servant* is significant because it suggests the results that can be expected from a coordinated effort to teach servant-leadership at a university and, by implication, in business organizations. Greenleaf uses a fictional university residence hall, Jefferson House, presided over by a wise physics professor named Dr. Billings as the vehicle for this description of outcomes. The purpose of a parable, of course, is to teach, which may be one of the reasons Greenleaf chose this term to describe *Teacher as Servant*. The book translates the concepts of his essays into fictional practice. In the first seventy-five pages and the last twenty-five pages of the book, Greenleaf shows the workings of Jefferson House and the efforts of its residents to master the art of servant-leadership. The remainder of the book consists of quasi-essays on other applications. So the heart—the meat—of the book is contained in these hundred pages. Greenleaf says as much by suggesting that if the reader will peruse these pages, he or she "will have the gist of it." These hundred pages are fascinating in another way as well: they have proven to be both a blueprint for—and a prophetic look at—three residence halls devoted to servant-leadership that were created in American universities twenty years after Greenleaf wrote his parable.

Fulfilling the Prophecy

The University of South Florida in Tampa opened the first servant-leadership house in America in the academic year 1996–97, and Butler University in Indianapolis opened the second such house the following year. These bold experiments in teaching servant-leadership provide an opportunity to observe, *in situ*, operationalization of Greenleaf's servant-leadership concept in a university environment, with ramifications for other organizational settings as well. Through readings, guest speakers, discussions, consensus decision making, service projects, and the hands-on management of their residence halls and, of course, their lives, the students of these houses learn what it means to be servant-leaders—not in the abstract, but in the rough-and-tumble of daily life.

Hampton House at Butler University was started in the fall of 1997 from a transformed sorority house. It began its practice of servant-leadership in the fall of 1998. In the fall of 1998 when I studied it, the house consisted of twenty-nine students—nineteen women and ten men—who ranged in grade level from sophomores to seniors. Only the women were permitted to live in the house because of an agreement with a sorority, which owned the building and had leased it to the university. The men had access to the house, however, on a twenty-four-hour basis. In accordance with Greenleaf's design, a rotating board of servants replaced the traditional hierarchy of officers.

My first visit to Hampton House, in which I joined the students for one of their evening meetings, began with a remarkable experience. By design, these students had not yet read *Teacher as Servant*, and so while they had been exposed to the principles of servant-leadership and the house structure that Greenleaf had envisioned, they had no direct experience with the scenes he had described in the pages of his book. I sat in the living room of Hampton House in the circle the students had formed, listening intently to what they were saying. What I witnessed was an eerie replication of the essence of the fictional scenes at Greenleaf's Jefferson House. I felt as if I were watching a play in which well-rehearsed actors were portraying Greenleaf's students as they met and talked about servant-leadership and their house experience. The pages of the book had come dramatically to life. So I began my study of servant-leadership houses fascinated by them.

As my conversations with the students continued, fascination turned to awe. I began to observe at greater and greater depth what Greenleaf had predicted when he created the students of Jefferson House. On the basis of observations, surveys, and interviews, I learned more about the Hampton House students and their counterparts at the University of South Florida's Leadership House. While the houses at the two universities differed in certain important ways, they did not vary so much that the experience was substantially different for the two sets of students in terms of what they learned about servant-leadership. These differences suggest that quite a wide range of options exists in constructing environments that facilitate the growth of servant-leaders. The results of these two far-sighted experiments speak of exceptional promise. If the self-reports of the students and observations of their advisers are accurate, it appears that the students do begin the journey to servant-leadership in these houses, tasting its first fruits and, for the most part, wanting more.

Building Relationships

The lived experience of these students in the servant-leadership houses suggests a common theme, one that is expressed in many different permutations but that can be summarized as follows: *each of us is intimately connected to the other, and in recognizing that connection, we are moved to greater service; to a more profound understanding, appreciation, and tolerance of one another; to an honest self-examination of our own attitudes and behavior; and to the building of community. What is most important in life are the relationships we establish and maintain with other people.*

This shared lesson of the servant-leadership houses is manifested in a variety of attitudes and behaviors, some of which are described in the following paragraphs.

Appreciating Diversity, Accepting Differences

One student observed, "The house mirrors life—complex, rewarding, disappointing, frustrating. People fail to fulfill their promises, forget, procrastinate, try to avoid responsibility some days just as they embrace it others. Some shy away from participation while others want it. It's all about the difficulty of understanding and accepting others—and coming to see them as less-than-perfect-but-good-enough, as human beings who are flawed and talented at the same time. People who are different from me, but just like me."

Consensus decision making, which honors individual differences and conflicting viewpoints, is a new experience for many students, and it leads them to a greater appreciation of the advantage of diversity in background and viewpoints. One student said, "I came to realize that I can learn from people who are completely unlike me. In fact, I can learn something from anyone. I have been able to get beyond the personality types I might not usually associate with and get to know them." Another ventured, "We've learned to *listen* to one another as an active discipline, not a passive activity. I learned to listen objectively to another opinion without shooting it down first. I also learned that my way is not always the right way. I had never really listened before. I had just tried to be heard."

Knowing One's Self: Introspection and Self-Examination

"Servant-leadership," wrote one student, "invites discussion about what is important in our lives at the moment and for the long haul—what should be our personal goals and priorities and aims—and this is not a discussion that is often raised in a residence hall [or in a corporate office]. I have learned to be more introspective and to seek knowledge about my strengths and weaknesses. In the process, I've learned humility, which is really understanding that other people's needs and beliefs also have validity and should be respected." Another admitted, "I developed a willingness to be criticized, to examine my own behavior in light of the larger goals of the group. I've learned that I'm not perfect and can't be perfect and that it's all right."

Serving Others

The meaning of serving others and of being served were important aspects of the learning that occurred among the students in the servant-leadership houses. "Real servant-leadership," concluded one student, "is in the small acts of kindness that we do rather than necessarily the big charity event or service project. Service assumes a larger role in our whole lives, in everything we do, and we understand that even small things can be important. Just because things don't seem important doesn't mean they aren't. Little things can make a difference. Tutoring someone, for example, might have a great impact on their lives. I have a better idea of how to serve others as a result of living here." Another said, "I used to think of serving others in dramatic terms like working at a soup kitchen or a big clothes drive for the poor. Now, I realize that I can serve by living my life. You can serve in even the smallest things. If you are helping someone, you are serving."

Greenleaf was clear in *Teacher as Servant* that the motto of Jefferson House was "to serve and be served by." He was emphatic that the obligation to serve also carried an obligation to be served. This lesson is not lost on the members of the real servant-leadership houses. Said one student, "I learned how to accept help. Most people in the house are givers and not takers. Here we learn that it's okay to ask for help or to take it when it's offered."

Leading

The students of the servant-leadership houses learn that true leaders do not always have to lead, but can allow others to lead when it is more appropriate. At such moments, leaders don the role of followers. One student reported, "Sometimes you have to be a follower before you can lead and that isn't always easy. You finally develop a sense of when you should lead and when you should follow." Another said, "Before leading, you learn to ask yourself, 'Why am I leading them? Should I be leading them? What's best for them?' As a result of these questions and of living in the house, I am more hesitant to try to lead them than I would have been in the past."

One of the most gratifying aspects of the servant-leadership house experience is that the students take their commitment to servant-leadership into the university community and into other organizations. This multiplier effect increases their influence out of proportion to their numbers.

Creating Community

Perhaps the most moving result of the servant-leadership houses is the sense of community that develops and that encourages a new appreciation of the value of difference and a concomitant respect for diversity. This sense of commonality—of shared purpose and values—creates a supportive atmosphere for accepting others and for experimenting with new behaviors. The vision of servant-leadership unites the house and makes possible internal debates that can be quite fierce and yet constructive as the students grapple with the meaning of servant-leadership in their house and their lives. This sense of community fires the commitment to living servant-leadership and to helping others live it as well. One student said, "We are so used to succeeding, to following instructions, to figuring out the path to success and walking it that Hampton House came as a surprise. There was no formula, and that changed everything. We had to begin to act and lead through understanding rather than by technique or trick. For those of us who are accomplished leaders, who understand the system and how to milk it, this experience was something entirely new. It was frightening at first and later thrilling."

Symbiosis: Business and Education

Teacher as Servant has important implications for business. In the parable, business leaders tutor students over the summer in the appropriate use of power, speak to students about leading and serving, and provide opportunities for students to join them after college in transforming the institutions they serve. Business and education have mutual interests in furthering servant-leadership on campus. By supporting servant-leadership houses and servant-leadership education, businesses ensure a source of servant-leaders for their next generation of leaders. By turning to business, universities allow their students to profit from the wisdom of practicing servant-leaders who command the institutions that shape society. When the two work together, they provide the invaluable spark that lights the fire of serving in the collegian so that, in maturity, it might be transferred, burning brightly, to business institutions.

One of the lessons of the servant-leadership houses is that they do prepare effective leaders whose influence reaches beyond the house to other organizations on campus and then to the community beyond. This ability to lead well in the new environment is precisely what business organizations require—and need to transfer to their employees. Universities provide a means of understanding how servant-leadership can be taught and can serve as living laboratories for the development of more effective means of educating servant-leaders. Businesses and universities have a symbiotic relationship that both need to exploit in the most productive sense of the word. Neither, really, can afford to do without the other.

Answering the Call

My experience with the servant-leadership houses has convinced me that the critical period of self-discovery that characterizes the college experience can be tapped to shepherd remarkable personal growth leading to the development of servant-leaders and to transformed lives. My sadness in making this observation comes from realizing how few institutions have taken advantage of this opportunity. Even those that have done so have failed to support the houses with sufficient resources to ensure their growth. Without some form of institutionalization of the houses coupled with enthusiastic and focused university support, the future of servant-leadership houses is in jeopardy. Without adequate resources and a dedicated faculty specifically committed to the houses, they cannot fulfill their potential. It would be a national tragedy if we, in our myopia, neutralize the great foresight of those who devoted themselves and their energies to the creation of these remarkable servant-leadership houses. If we cannot, as educators and businesspeople, support servant-leadership in our universities, we will have failed in our most fundamental duty to our youth, our country, and ourselves. We will not have served them; we will not have led.

Can you imagine describing a place to parents or to the public or to the nation in which young people could learn to appreciate the value of individual differences, embrace diversity as a means of growing in wisdom and insight, and accept differences of opinion as empowering and enriching rather than toxic and destructive? Can you imagine a place where students learn to commit themselves to serving others, to listening devotedly, to building community, to learning humility, and to leading well? Can you imagine a place where the young come to understand the meaningfulness of human relationships, the holism of life that connects us all, and the awesome responsibilities we have to ourselves and to each other? Can you imagine such a place? And yet three such places exist, including a new servant-leadership house that just opened in the semester in which this foreword was written.

Why are there only three?

Why have we not answered the same call to servant-leadership as have the students in these houses: to serve and be served by them? Why have we failed to grasp and then support their dreams for a more meaningful life based in service? Why have we failed to *lead them* by offering them what they, in their youth, may intuitively sense they want but we, in our wisdom, should explicitly know they should have: the opportunity to serve first, and, in serving, to make the conscious choice to lead so that others might become freer, happier, and more likely to become servant-leaders themselves?

Servant-leadership is a state of mind, a philosophy of life, a way of being. It is at once an art and a calling. Servant-leadership is transformative because it reorders the manner in which people view themselves in relation to the world. Servant-leadership remains conceptual until it is applied. Its power is discovered in the crucible of real-life experiences that include mistakes and losses as well as right actions and victories. Its rewards remain undiscovered until they are experienced.

As educators, we hold this gift in our hands—the gift of servant-leadership offered to a generation of college students. The time has come to act generously and decisively by offering this gift of a service-based life to our young people who are seeking it. The time has come for us to become servant-leaders ourselves, to support the creation of servant-leadership houses across the campuses of our nation, and to spread the word about the benefits of such houses.

We are called to do no less.

INTRODUCTION

Understanding the Growing Impact of Servant-Leadership

LARRY C. SPEARS

The servant-leader is servant first. It begins with the natural feeling that one wants to serve. Then conscious choice brings one to aspire to lead. The best test is: do those served grow as persons; do they, while being served, become healthier, wiser, freer, more autonomous, more likely themselves to become servants?

—ROBERT K. GREENLEAF

The work of leadership education today takes place in a world that is increasingly glutted with information and yet starved for wisdom. While Robert K. Greenleaf's writings were based on organizational life in a different era, he nevertheless articulated a belief that resonates ever more clearly with each passing year. In so doing, Greenleaf transcended the old arena of leadership techniques and has helped to move our thinking toward true leadership wisdom.

The servant-leader concept continues to grow in its influence and impact. In fact, we have witnessed an unparalleled explosion of interest and practice of servant-leadership in the past decade. In many ways, it can truly be said that the times are only now beginning to catch up with Robert Greenleaf's visionary call to servant-leadership.

Servant-leadership, now in its fourth decade as a specific leadership and service concept, continues to create a quiet revolution in workplaces around the world. This introduction is intended to provide a broad overview of the growing influence this unique concept of servant-leadership is having on people and their workplaces.

Today, we are rapidly seeing that traditional, autocratic, and hierarchical modes of leadership are yielding to a newer model—one based on teamwork and community, one that seeks to involve others in decision making, one strongly based in ethical and caring behavior, and one that is attempting to enhance the personal growth of workers while improving the caring and quality of our many institutions. This emerging approach to leadership and service is called *servant-leadership*.

The words *servant* and *leader* are usually thought of as being opposites. When two opposites are brought together in a creative and meaningful way, a paradox emerges. And so the words *servant* and *leader* have been brought together to create the paradoxical idea of servant-leadership. The basic idea of servant-leadership is both logical and intuitive. Since the time of the Industrial Revolution, managers have tended to view people as objects; institutions have considered workers as cogs within a machine. In the past few decades we have witnessed a shift in that long-held view. Standard practices are rapidly shifting toward the ideas put forward by Robert Greenleaf, Stephen Covey, Peter Senge, Max DePree, Margaret Wheatley, Peter Block, Ken Blanchard, and many others who suggest that there is a better way to manage our organizations in the twenty-first century.

There is also a much greater recognition of the need for a more team-oriented approach to leadership and management. Robert Greenleaf's writings on the subject of servant-leadership helped to get this movement started, and his views have had a profound and growing effect on many.

Robert K. Greenleaf

> Despite all the buzz about modern leadership techniques, no one knows better than Greenleaf what really matters.
> — *Working Woman* magazine

The term *servant-leadership* was first coined in a 1970 essay by Robert K. Greenleaf (1904–90) entitled "The Servant as Leader." Greenleaf, born in Terre Haute, Indiana, spent most of his organizational life in the field of management research, development, and education at AT&T. Following a forty-year career at AT&T, Greenleaf enjoyed a second career that lasted twenty-five years, during which time he served as an influential consultant to a number of major institutions, including Ohio University, MIT, Ford Foundation, R. K. Mellon Foundation, the Mead Corporation, the American Foundation for Management Research, and Lilly Endowment Inc. In 1964 Greenleaf also founded the Center for Applied Ethics, which was renamed the Robert K. Greenleaf Center in 1985 and is now headquartered in Indianapolis.

As a lifelong student of how things get done in organizations, Greenleaf distilled his observations in a series of essays and books on the theme of "The Servant as Leader"—the objective of which was to stimulate thought and action for building a better, more caring society.

The Servant-as-Leader Idea

The idea of the servant as leader came partly out of Greenleaf's half century of experience in working to shape large institutions. However, the event that crystallized Greenleaf's thinking came in the 1960s, when he read Hermann Hesse's short novel *Journey to the East*—an account of a mythical journey by a group of people on a spiritual quest.

After reading this story, Greenleaf concluded that the central meaning of it was that the great leader is first experienced as a servant to others, and that this simple fact is central to his or her greatness. True leadership emerges from those whose primary motivation is a deep desire to help others.

In 1970, at the age of sixty-six, Greenleaf published "The Servant as Leader," the first of a dozen essays and books on servant-leadership. Since that time, more than a half million copies of his books and essays have been sold worldwide. Slowly but surely, Greenleaf's servant-leadership writings have made a deep, lasting impression on leaders, educators, and many others who are concerned with issues of leadership, management, service, and personal growth.

What Is Servant-Leadership?

In all of his works, Greenleaf discusses the need for a better kind of leadership model, a model that puts serving others—including employees, customers, and community—as the number one priority. Servant-leadership emphasizes increased service to others, a holistic approach to work, promoting a sense of community, and the sharing of power in decision making.

Who *is* a servant-leader? Greenleaf said that the servant-leader is one who is a servant first. In "The Servant as Leader" he wrote, "It begins with the natural feeling that one wants to serve, to serve first. Then conscious choice brings one to aspire to lead. The difference manifests itself in the care taken by the servant—first to make sure that other people's highest priority needs are being served. The best test is: do those served grow as persons; do they, while being served, become healthier, wiser, freer, more autonomous, more likely themselves to become servants?"

It is important to stress that servant-leadership is *not* a "quick-fix" approach. Nor is it something that can be quickly instilled within an institution. At its core, servant-leadership is a long-term, transformational approach to life and work—in essence, a way of being—that has the potential for creating positive change throughout our society.

Ten Characteristics of the Servant-Leader

Servant leadership deals with the reality of power in everyday life—its legitimacy, the ethical restraints upon it and the beneficial results that can be attained through the appropriate use of power.

— *New York Times*

After some years of carefully considering Greenleaf's original writings, I have identified a set of ten characteristics of the servant-leader that I view as being of critical importance to the development of servant-leaders:

1. *Listening:* Leaders have traditionally been valued for their communication and decision-making skills. While these are also

important skills for the servant-leader, they need to be reinforced by a deep commitment to listening intently to others. The servant-leader seeks to identify the will of a group and helps clarify that will. He or she seeks to listen receptively to what is being said (and not said!). Listening also encompasses getting in touch with one's own inner voice and seeking to understand what one's body, spirit, and mind are communicating. Listening, coupled with regular periods of reflection, is essential to the growth of the servant-leader.

2. *Empathy:* The servant-leader strives to understand and empathize with others. People need to be accepted and recognized for their special and unique spirits. One assumes the good intentions of co-workers and does not reject them as people, even while refusing to accept their behavior or performance. The most successful servant-leaders are those who have become skilled empathetic listeners.

3. *Healing:* Learning to heal is a powerful force for transformation and integration. One of the great strengths of servant-leadership is the potential for healing one's self and others. Many people have broken spirits and have suffered from a variety of emotional hurts. Although this is a part of being human, servant-leaders recognize that they have an opportunity to "help make whole" those with whom they come in contact. In "The Servant as Leader" Greenleaf writes: "There is something subtle communicated to one who is being served and led if, implicit in the compact between servant-leader and led, is the understanding that the search for wholeness is something they share."

4. *Awareness:* General awareness, and especially self-awareness, strengthens the servant-leader. Making a commitment to foster awareness can be scary—you never know what you may discover! Awareness also aids one in understanding issues involving ethics and values. It lends itself to being able to view most situations from a more integrated, holistic position. As Greenleaf observed: "Awareness is not a giver of solace—it is just the opposite. It is a disturber and an awakener. Able leaders are usually sharply awake and reasonably disturbed. They are not seekers after solace. They have their own inner serenity."

5. *Persuasion:* Another characteristic of servant-leaders is a reliance on persuasion, rather than using one's positional authority,

in making decisions within an organization. The servant-leader seeks to convince others, rather than coerce compliance. This particular element offers one of the clearest distinctions between the traditional authoritarian model and that of servant-leadership. The servant-leader is effective at building consensus within groups. This emphasis on persuasion over coercion probably has its roots within the beliefs of the Religious Society of Friends (Quakers), the denomination with which Robert Greenleaf himself was most closely allied.

6. *Conceptualization:* Servant-leaders seek to nurture their abilities to "dream great dreams." The ability to look at a problem (or an organization) from a conceptualizing perspective means that one must think beyond day-to-day realities. For many managers this is a characteristic that requires discipline and practice. The traditional manager is focused on the need to achieve short-term operational goals. The manager who wishes to also be a servant-leader must stretch his or her thinking to encompass broader-based conceptual thinking. Within organizations, conceptualization is also the proper role of boards of trustees or directors. Unfortunately, boards can sometimes become involved in the day-to-day operations (something that should always be discouraged!) and fail to provide the visionary concept for an institution. Trustees need to be mostly conceptual in their orientation, staffs need to be mostly operational in their perspective, and the most effective CEOs and leaders probably need to develop both perspectives. Servant-leaders are called to seek a delicate balance between conceptual thinking and a day-to-day, focused approach.

7. *Foresight:* Closely related to conceptualization, the ability to foresee the likely outcome of a situation is hard to define, but easy to identify. One knows it when one sees it. Foresight is a characteristic that enables the servant-leader to understand the lessons from the past, the realities of the present, and the likely consequences of a decision for the future. It is also deeply rooted within the intuitive mind. As such, one can conjecture that foresight is the one servant-leader characteristic with which one may be born. All other characteristics can be consciously developed. There hasn't been a great deal written on foresight. It remains a largely unexplored area in leadership studies, but one most deserving of careful attention.

8. *Stewardship:* Peter Block (author of *Stewardship* and *The Empowered Manager*) has defined stewardship as "holding something in trust for another." Robert Greenleaf's view of all institutions was one in which CEOs, staffs, and trustees all played significant roles in holding their institutions in trust for the greater good of society. Servant-leadership, like stewardship, assumes first and foremost a commitment to serving the needs of others. It also emphasizes the use of openness and persuasion rather than control.

9. *Commitment to the growth of people:* Servant-leaders believe that people have an intrinsic value beyond their tangible contributions as workers. As such, the servant-leader is deeply committed to the growth of each and every individual within his or her institution. The servant-leader recognizes the tremendous responsibility to do everything within his or her power to nurture the personal, professional, and spiritual growth of employees. In practice, this can include (but is not limited to) concrete actions such as making available funds for personal and professional development, taking a personal interest in the ideas and suggestions from everyone, encouraging worker involvement in decision making, and actively assisting laid-off workers to find other employment.

10. *Building community:* The servant-leader senses that much has been lost in recent human history as a result of the shift from local communities to large institutions as the primary shaper of human lives. This awareness causes the servant-leader to seek to identify some means for building community among those who work within a given institution. Servant-leadership suggests that true community can be created among those who work in businesses and other institutions. Greenleaf said: "All that is needed to rebuild community as a viable life form for large numbers of people is for enough servant-leaders to show the way, not by mass movements, but by each servant-leader demonstrating his own unlimited liability for a quite specific community-related group."

These ten characteristics of servant-leadership are by no means exhaustive. However, I believe that the ones listed serve to communicate the power and promise that this concept offers to those who are open to its invitation and challenge.

Tracing the Growing Impact of Servant-Leadership

Servant leadership has emerged as one of the dominant philosophies being discussed in the world today.

— *Indianapolis Business Journal*

Servant-Leadership as an Institutional Model

Servant-leadership principles are being applied in significant ways in
a half dozen major areas. The first area has to do with servant-leadership as an institutional philosophy and model. Servant-leadership
crosses all boundaries and is being applied by a wide variety of people
working with for-profit businesses; not-for-profit corporations; and
churches, universities, health care organizations, and foundations.

In recent years, a number of institutions have jettisoned their
hierarchical decision making and replaced it with a servant-leader
approach. Servant-leadership advocates a group-oriented approach
to analysis and decision making as a means of strengthening institutions and improving society. It also emphasizes the power of persuasion and seeking consensus, over the old top-down form of
leadership. Some people have likened this to turning the hierarchical
pyramid upside down. Servant-leadership holds that the primary purpose of a business should be to create a positive impact on its employees and community, rather than using profit as the sole motive.

Many individuals within institutions have adopted servant-
leadership as a guiding philosophy. An increasing number of companies have adopted servant-leadership as part of their corporate
philosophy or as a foundation for their mission statement. Among
these are the Toro Company (Minneapolis, Minnesota), Synovus
Financial Corporation (Columbus, Georgia), ServiceMaster Company (Downers Grove, Illinois), The Men's Wearhouse (Fremont,
California), Southwest Airlines (Dallas, Texas), and TDIndustries
(Dallas, Texas).

TDIndustries (TD), one of the earliest practitioners of servant-
leadership in the corporate setting, is a Dallas-based heating and
plumbing contracting firm that has consistently ranked in the top ten
of *Fortune* magazine's "100 Best Companies to Work for in America." TD's founder, Jack Lowe Sr., came upon "The Servant as

Leader" essay in the early 1970s and began to distribute copies of it to his employees. They were invited to read through the essay and then to gather in small groups to discuss its meaning. The belief that managers should serve their employees became an important value for TDIndustries.

Thirty years later, Jack Lowe Jr. continues to use servant-leadership as the guiding philosophy for TD. Even today, any TDPartner who supervises at least one person must go through training in servant-leadership. In addition, all new employees continue to receive a copy of "The Servant as Leader" essay; and TD has developed elaborate training modules designed to encourage the understanding and practice of servant-leadership.

Some businesses have begun to view servant-leadership as an important framework that is helpful (and necessary) for ensuring the long-term effects of related management and leadership approaches such as continuous quality improvement and systems thinking. It is suggested that institutions which want to create meaningful change may be best served in starting with servant-leadership as the foundational understanding and then building on it through any number of related approaches.

Servant-leadership has influenced many noted writers, thinkers, and leaders. Max DePree, former chairman of the Herman Miller Company and author of *Leadership Is an Art* and *Leadership Jazz*, has said, "The servanthood of leadership needs to be felt, understood, believed, and practiced." And Peter Senge, author of *The Fifth Discipline*, has said that he tells people "not to bother reading any other book about leadership until you first read Robert Greenleaf's book, *Servant-Leadership*. I believe it is the most singular and useful statement on leadership I've come across." In recent years, a growing number of leaders and readers have "rediscovered" Robert Greenleaf's own writings through books by DePree, Senge, Covey, Wheatley, Autry, and many other popular writers.

Education and Training of Not-for-Profit Trustees

A second major application of servant-leadership is its pivotal role as the theoretical and ethical basis for "trustee education." Greenleaf wrote extensively on servant-leadership as it applies to the roles of boards of directors and trustees within institutions. His essays on these applications are widely distributed among directors of for-profit and nonprofit organizations. In his essay "Trustees as Servants" Greenleaf urged trustees to ask themselves two central questions: "Whom do you serve?" and "For what purpose?"

Servant-leadership suggests that boards of trustees need to undergo a radical shift in how they approach their roles. Trustees who seek to act as servant-leaders can help to create institutions of great depth and quality. Over the past decade, one of America's largest grant-making foundations (Lilly Endowment Inc.) has sought to encourage the development of programs designed to educate and train not-for-profit boards of trustees to function as servant-leaders.

Community Leadership Programs

The third application of servant-leadership concerns its deepening role in community leadership organizations across the country. A growing number of community leadership groups are using Greenleaf Center resources as part of their own education and training efforts. Some have been doing so for more than fifteen years.

M. Scott Peck, who has written about the importance of building true community, says the following in *A World Waiting to Be Born:* "In his work on servant-leadership, Greenleaf posited that the world will be saved if it can develop just three truly well-managed, large institutions—one in the private sector, one in the public sector, and one in the nonprofit sector. He believed—and I know—that such excellence in management will be achieved through an organizational culture of civility routinely utilizing the mode of community."

Service-Learning Programs

The fourth application involves servant-leadership and experiential education. During the past twenty-five years experiential education programs of all sorts have sprung up in virtually every college and university—and, increasingly, in secondary schools, too. Experiential education, or "learning by doing," is now a part of most students' educational experience.

Around 1980, a number of educators began to write about the linkage between the servant-leader concept and experiential learning under a new term called "service-learning." It is service-learning that has become a major focus for experiential education programs in the past few years.

The National Society for Experiential Education (NSEE) has adopted service-learning as one of its major program areas. NSEE has published a massive three-volume work called *Combining Service and Learning*, which brings together many articles and papers about service-learning—several dozen of which discuss servant-leadership as the philosophical basis for experiential learning programs.

Leadership Education

The fifth application of servant-leadership concerns its use in both formal and informal education and training programs. This is taking place through leadership and management courses in colleges and universities, as well as through corporate training programs. A number of undergraduate and graduate courses on management and leadership incorporate servant-leadership within their course curricula. Several colleges and universities now offer specific courses on servant-leadership. Also, a number of noted leadership authors, including Peter Block, Ken Blanchard, Max DePree, and Peter Senge, have all acclaimed the servant-leader concept as an overarching framework that is compatible with, and enhancing of, other leadership and management models such as total quality management, systems thinking, and community building.

In the area of corporate education and training programs, dozens of management and leadership consultants now utilize servant-leadership materials as part of their ongoing work with corporations. Some of these companies have included Starbucks, the Mead Corporation, and U.S. Cellular. A number of consultants and educators are now touting the benefits to be gained in building a total quality management approach upon a servant-leadership foundation. Through internal training and education, institutions are discovering that servant-leadership can truly improve how business is developed and conducted, while still successfully turning a profit.

Personal Transformation

The sixth application of servant-leadership involves its use in programs relating to personal growth and transformation. Servant-leadership operates at both the institutional and personal levels. For individuals it offers a means to personal growth—spiritually, professionally, emotionally, and intellectually. It has ties to the ideas of M. Scott Peck (*The Road Less Traveled*), Parker Palmer (*The Active Life*), Ann McGee-Cooper (*You Don't Have to Go Home from Work Exhausted!*), and others who have written on expanding human potential. A particular strength of servant-leadership is that it encourages everyone to actively seek opportunities to both serve and lead others, thereby setting up the potential for raising the quality of life throughout society.

Servant-Leadership and Multiculturalism

For some people, the word *servant* prompts an immediate negative connotation, due to the oppression that many people—particularly women and people of color—have historically endured. For some, it may take a while to accept the positive usage of this word *servant*. However, those who are willing to dig a little deeper come to understand the inherent spiritual nature of what is intended by the pairing of *servant* and *leader.* The startling paradox of the term *servant-leadership* often serves to prompt new insights.

In an article entitled "Pluralistic Reflections on Servant-Leadership," Juana Bordas has written: "Many women, minorities and people of color have long traditions of servant-leadership in their cultures. Servant-leadership has very old roots in many of the indigenous cultures. Cultures that were holistic, cooperative, communal, intuitive and spiritual. These cultures centered on being guardians of the future and respecting the ancestors who walked before."

Women leaders and authors are now writing and speaking about servant-leadership as a twenty-first-century leadership philosophy that is most appropriate for both women and men to embrace. Patsy Sampson, former president of Stephens College in Columbia,

Missouri, is one such person. In an essay on women and servant-leadership she writes: "So-called (service-oriented) feminine characteristics are exactly those which are consonant with the very best qualities of servant-leadership."

A Growing Movement

> Servant-leadership works like the consensus building that the Japanese are famous for. Yes, it takes a while on the front end; everyone's view is solicited, though everyone also understands that his view may not ultimately prevail. But once the consensus is forged, watch out: With everybody on board, your so called implementation proceeds wham-bam.
>
> —*Fortune* magazine

Interest in the philosophy and practice of servant-leadership is now at an all-time high. Hundreds of articles on servant-leadership have appeared in various magazines, journals, and newspapers over the past few years. Many books on the general subject of leadership have been published that have referenced servant-leadership as the pre-eminent leadership model for the twenty-first century. And, there is a growing body of literature available on the understanding and practice of servant-leadership.

The Greenleaf Center for Servant-Leadership is an international, not-for-profit educational organization that seeks to encourage the understanding and practice of servant-leadership. The center's mission is to fundamentally improve the caring and quality of all institutions through a servant-leader approach to leadership, structure, and decision making.

In recent years, the Greenleaf Center has experienced tremendous growth and expansion. Its growing programs include the following: the worldwide sales of more than 120 books, essays, and videotapes on servant-leadership; a membership program; workshops, retreats, institutes, and seminars; and an annual International Conference on Servant-Leadership. A number of notable Greenleaf Center members have spoken at our annual conferences, including James Autry, Peter Block, Max DePree, Stephen Covey, Meg

Wheatley, M. Scott Peck, and Peter Senge, to name but a few. These and other conference speakers have spoken of the tremendous impact that the servant-leader concept has played in the development of his or her own understanding of what it means to be a leader.

Paradox and Pathway

The Greenleaf Center's logo is a variation on the geometrical figure called a "mobius strip." A mobius strip, pictured here, is a one-sided surface constructed from a rectangle by holding one end fixed, rotating the opposite end through 180 degrees, and applying it to the first end—thereby giving the appearance of a two-sided figure. It thus appears to have a front side that merges into a back side, and then back again into the front.

The mobius strip symbolizes, in visual terms, the servant-leader concept—a merging of servanthood into leadership and back into servanthood again, in a fluid and continuous pattern. It also reflects the Greenleaf Center's own role as an institution seeking to both serve and lead others who are interested in leadership and service issues.

Life is full of curious and meaningful paradoxes. Servant-leadership is one such paradox that has slowly but surely gained hundreds of thousands of adherents over the past quarter century. The seeds that have been planted have begun to sprout in many institutions, as well as in the hearts of many who long to improve the human condition. Servant-leadership is providing a framework from which many thousands of known and unknown individuals are helping to improve how we treat those who do the work within our many institutions. Servant-leadership truly offers hope and guidance for a new era in human development, and for the creation of better, more caring institutions.

For more information on servant-leadership resources and programs contact:

The Greenleaf Center for Servant-Leadership
921 E. 86th Street, Suite 200
Indianapolis, IN 46240
Phone: 317-259-1241
Fax: 317-259-0560
Website: www.greenleaf.org

THE SERVANT AS LEADER

(Original 1970 edition)

The following version of "The Servant as Leader" is the original 1970 edition that Robert K. Greenleaf first published. This version was in print from 1970 to 1973. Careful readers of the original version will note that one of the student leaders Greenleaf chose to quote was a very young Hillary Rodham (later Senator Hillary Rodham Clinton), from her 1969 commencement address as president of the student body at Wellesley College. This quote and many other quotes from students of the time were removed and replaced with new material when Greenleaf did a major revision of the essay in 1973.

The revised edition of "The Servant as Leader" is the one that has been in print since 1973. Since that time more than a quarter of a million copies of it have been sold around the world. Robert K. Greenleaf probably never dreamed that his essay would influence several generations of servant-leaders and spark worldwide interest in servant-leadership.

Special thanks go to Harriet Lowe, whose longstanding encouragement to republish the original edition of "The Servant Leader" helps to make this possible.

The Greenleaf Center is pleased to be able to put back into print the original 1970 version of "The Servant as Leader." Those readers who are interested in obtaining a copy of the revised 1973 version of the essay can do so by contacting the Greenleaf Center for Servant-Leadership.

—THE EDITORS

Part 1

THE SERVANT AS LEADER

This piece began with seminars for students of Prescott College in October 1968. Since then it has gone through several drafts with generous comments from friends, including students. It is put in print now not as a final or complete statement, but as a record of thinking in transition, drawn more from experience and searching than from scholarship, and with the hope that some who read it will respond with gleanings from their own experience with serving and leading.

Behind what is said here is a twofold concern: first for the individual in society and his or her bent to deal with the massive problems of our times wholly in terms of systems, ideologies, and movements. These have their place, but they are not basic because they do not make themselves. What is basic is the incremental thrust of an individual who has the ability to serve and lead.

My second concern is for the individual as a serving person and for the tendency of such people to deny wholeness and creative fulfillment for themselves by failing to lead when they could lead.

Overarching these is a concern for the total process of education and its seeming indifference to the individual as servant and leader, as a person and in society, on the assumption that intellectual preparation favors his or her optimal growth in these ways when, in fact, quite the reverse may be true.

Part of the problem is that *serve* and *lead* are overused words with negative connotations like obsequious, self-righteous, patronize, dominate, manipulate, exploit. But they are also good words and I can find no others that carry as well the meaning I would like to convey. Not everything that is old and worn, or even corrupt, can be thrown away. Some of it has to be rebuilt and used again. So it is, it seems to me, with the words *serve* and *lead*.

—Robert K. Greenleaf

HERMANN HESSE'S STORY, *Journey to the East*, tells of a band of men, each having his own goal, on a mythical journey to the East. With them is the servant Leo, who does their menial chores, sustains them with his spirit and his song, and, by the quality of his presence, lifts them above what they otherwise would be. All goes well until Leo disappears. Then the group falls into disarray and the journey finally is abandoned. They cannot make it without the servant Leo. The narrator, one of the party, after some years of wandering finds Leo and is taken into the Order that had sponsored the journey to the East. He discovers that Leo is the titular head of the Order, its guiding spirit, a great and noble leader.

Leo portrays at once two roles that are often seen as antithetical in our culture: the servant who, by acting with integrity and spirit, builds trust and lifts people and helps them grow, *and* the leader who is trusted and who shapes others' destinies by going out ahead to show the way.

Can these two roles merge in *one real person*—for all manner of men and women, in all levels of status and calling? If so, can that person live and be productive in the real world of the present? For some time I have said yes to the first question. My sense of the present leads me now to say yes to both questions. This paper is an attempt to explain why and to suggest how.

The 1970s

Ours are revolutionary times. Not so much for the extent of turbulence and disruption as because of the emergence of a significant number of thoughtful and aware people who see more clearly the world as it is and are not satisfied with it. They challenge both the pervasive acceptance of injustice and the sharp disparity between the quality of society that they know is reasonable and possible with our available resources, and, on the other hand, the actual performance of the whole range of institutions that exist to serve society.

Many are taking a fresh look at the issues of power and authority, and some are beginning to learn, however haltingly, to relate to one another in less coercive and more creatively supporting ways. A new moral principle may be emerging which holds that the only authority deserving of one's allegiance is that which is freely and knowingly granted by the led to the leader in response to, and in proportion to, the clearly evident servant stature of the leader. Those who choose to follow this principle will not casually accept the authority of existing institutions. Rather, they will freely respond only to individuals who are chosen as leaders because they are proven and trusted as servants. To the extent that this principle prevails, the only truly viable institutions will be those that are predominantly servant led. And with this we hope there will be an openness of style in which leaders will be natural people acting naturally, mortal people subject to error and deserving forgiveness like everybody else.

Moral principles do not emerge from theory, but from testing and experience. Theories are later built to encase and explain the working principles. The new principle of the servant as leader is more likely to emerge in practice in those segments of society where the concern is most intensely felt for justice (rather than order), for the performance (rather than the form) of our institutions, and for the appropriateness (rather than the result) of power and authority.

Currently this intensity of feeling is greatest among the students of our colleges and universities, but it is not yet clear that the necessary disciplined testing by experience, the hard sweating out of the how-to-do, will be done at this level. The test of experience runs the risk of failure, I believe, because the institutions where our students live and learn today are not generally ready to grow with students and support them.

Conversely, then, I believe this test of experience will succeed if and when our colleges and universities move from their present theoretical concern about life and change to become institutional model builders for the future. I do not see this yet under way. But some of the signs are encouraging. Let us listen.

Two students at Le Moyne College, Reginald Burton and Priscilla Hayes, responded to an early draft of this paper in these words: "every individual has ultimate control over his destiny and, thus, has the influence and the ability to mold the destinies of persons associating with him. . . . Leaders . . . are manifestations of the community, of community relations, and of community problems. The nature of their ability allows them to expand their influence, in many cases, to national and international levels. . . . It is not the individual who decides that he is a leader or will become a leader, but the community that places him in that particular role. . . . The individual's choice is only whether or not he will accept the responsibility given him by the community. . . . Leaders are ordinary people who, through the needs of the community, emerge as 'special' people. Through certain events and situations, they acquire extraordinary and compelling powers that attract followers. It is the community's responsibility to control that power while at the same time supporting that leader who is voicing the opinions of the community."

These words state a part of the leadership equation. The other part is the will and the personal strength to opt for leadership as a meaningful lifestyle, toward which an individual may progress by conscious preparation. But Mr. Burton and Ms. Hayes have defined the more important part for these times. We must face the problem: the natural leader, called upon like Cincinnatus, is too rare to be embraced as the total solution, and yet the self-chosen leader, who does not see himself or herself as of the people, will ultimately be unacceptable, no matter how able he or she is.

Either way, the leader is trusted because he or she chances losing leadership by taking the initiating risks to venture for the common good, because he or she insists on the hard choices required to build and rebuild institutions within a social framework of radically expanded justice, and because he or she helps others sort out the destructive influences (the nihilistic, the hedonistic, the pathological) from the sane, the moral, the building forces and attitudes that ennoble human life. Effective servant-leaders who move in these ways emerge strong and speak with authority when the values and goals of those who go with them are truly served by their actions.

Let us hear more from the students. Hillary Rodham, president of the student body at Wellesley College, said in her 1969 commencement address, "Too long our leaders have viewed politics as the art of the possible, and the challenge now is to practice politics as the art of making what appears to be impossible possible.

"If the experiment in human living doesn't work in this country, in this age, it's not going to work anywhere. . . . The goal of it must be human liberation, a liberation enabling each of us to fulfill our capacities so as to be free to create within and around ourselves. . . . We are, all of us, exploring a world that none of us understands, and attempting to create within that uncertainty. But there are some things we feel, feeling that a prevailing acquisitive and competitive corporate life, including—tragically—the universities, is not the way of life for us. We're searching for a more immediate, ecstatic, and penetrating mode of living."

It is not the obligation of society to deliver to anybody this more immediate, ecstatic, and penetrating mode of living. And those who pursue it too narrowly may lose their way. What we may achieve is more likely to be something unasked, that we experience for brief moments because, much like Leo, we achieve an inner serenity that enables us, with our own internal resources, to create within and around ourselves in a way that projects a radiance of trust and confidence into the wider society. Our acts may lift us above where we would otherwise be, and, in significant ways, we may take on the task of making the impossible possible. The result will not be a perfect society—because the view of what is possible, as well as of the impossible that might be made possible, will continually expand. As long as people are capable of visions they will be dissatisfied.

Professor B. D. Napier, dean of the chapel and professor of religion at Stanford University, offers an example of the effect on the environment of those who, in an imperfect society, manage to "create within and around themselves." He comments on David Harris, then age twenty-one, one of the better known of the recent student protest leaders, on the occasion of Harris's resignation as president of the student body of Stanford. "I don't know what Dave's reasons are for resigning and maybe that's beside the point. His ASSU administration has taken its toll on him and, I think in the long run beneficially, on official Stanford. But he's been there long enough to see his real stature, his authentic greatness. How often do you see a man who, in being himself, can help you be and find yourself; in whom you can detect no deviousness at all; whose compassion is no less compassion for being unsentimental; who cares like hell about the world he lives in and can somehow go on loving and believing in the people who inhabit it, even while he protests the ways we go on lousing it up? For all of his sharp, unremitting criticism—in part, of course, because of it—all of us, and all of Stanford, and the whole college and university scene in America are better for having him where he's been." What more could one ask a man to accomplish by age twenty-one? A leader by example, a very special kind of person.

The students consider the building of trust as the central issue for leadership by means of service. Hillary Rodham summed it up this way: "Trust. This is the one word that, when I asked our class what it was they wanted me to say for them, everyone came up to me and said, 'Talk about *trust*, talk about the lack of trust both for us and the way they feel about others, talk about the *trust bust*.'"

Enough trust to hold a society together, so that the impossible can be made possible, will not issue, full-blown, simply because it is demanded. Those who strongly feel the need must do the hard work, the disciplined serving and leading that are necessary to bring it about. To put it another way: the young people who have brought the revolution thus far must accept its implications: they must produce, in their generation, new ways of building trust that are viable under the new conditions that are already emerging as a result of their initiative. Builders must emerge from among the critics if the present ferment is to produce a better society.

The youth revolution will probably move inexorably in ways that are inexplicable, painful, and disruptive. The issue here is not to justify or to condemn it. We accept the state of flux as something that *is*, and that is not going away simply because a lot of people don't like it. But we do expect also that the present turbulence will supply opportunities for advance, along with possibilities for disaster.

What direction will the movement take? Much depends on how determined today's young are to come to grips with the age-old problem of how to live in a human society. I say this because so many of them, having made their awesome decision for autonomy and independence from tradition, and having taken their firm stand *against* injustice and hypocrisy, find it hard to convert themselves into affirmative builders of a better society. How many of them will seek their personal fulfillment by making the hard choices, and by undertaking the rigorous preparation that building a better society requires? It all depends on what kind of leaders emerge and how they—we—respond to them.

I dare no predictions on the shape and structure of the society that will emerge from the present ferment. But I do know that there will be institutions and there will be leaders.

There will probably be many far-reaching consequences of the contemporary revolution. But here I want to deal only with that part of the future that affords opportunities for the servant as leader. I am concerned that enough of those who are servants rise to the opportunity and qualify to lead.

The servant-leader is not necessarily the most popular among his or her contemporaries. The "popular" leader type will very likely gravitate to easier alternatives. When Leo laid down the conditions for entering the Order they were tough and hard to take. My thesis, that more young servants should emerge as leaders, is not a popular one. It is much more comfortable to go with a less demanding point of view about what is expected of one *now*. There are several undemanding, plausibly argued alternatives from which to choose. Among them is the assumption that since the effort to reform existing institutions has not brought perfection, the remedy is to destroy them completely so that fresh new perfect ones can grow. Not much thought seems to be given to the problem of where the new seed will come from or who the gardener to tend them will be.

Serving stands in sharp contrast to this kind of thinking. It requires that the concerned individual accept the problems he or she sees in the world as his or her own personal task, as a means of achieving his or her own integrity. He or she sees the external manifestation of this internal achievement as beginning with caring for individual persons, in ways that require dedication and skill and that help them grow and become healthier, stronger, and more autonomous. The servant will move from this to larger spheres of influence, leading and showing the way to larger groups—institutions, perhaps vast culture-shaping institutions. One consequence of the contemporary revolution, as I see it, is that there will not be enough trust in any other kind of leader to make a viable society possible. This poses the challenge of the 1970s.

Serving (and leading as so defined) is not popular, because it is exacting and hard to attain. But it is highly rewarding and fulfilling when it is done well. The society-building voices that advocate it and are contending to be heard are speaking with more caution. They have more respect for the integrity of those who might hear, and consequently they are more difficult to hear. But they must be heard, because only they hold out the adventurous pursuit of a dream as the path to wholeness. Criticism has its place, but as a total preoccupation it is sterile. If, in a time of crisis, too many potential builders are taken in by a complete absorption with dissecting the wrong and by a zeal for instant perfection, then the future of this civilization is dark indeed. The danger, perhaps, is to hear the analyst too much and the artist too little.

Albert Camus stands apart from other great artists of his time, in my view, and deserves the title of *moralist*, because of his unrelenting demand that each of us confront the exacting terms of our own existence, and, like Sisyphus, *accept his or her rock and find his or her happiness in dealing with it.* Camus sums up the relevance of his position to our concern for the servant as leader in the last paragraph of his last published lecture, entitled "Create Dangerously."

> One may long, as I do, for a gentler flame, a respite, a pause for musing. But perhaps there is no other peace for the artist than what he finds in the heat of combat. "Every wall is a door," Emerson correctly said. Let us not look for the door, and the way out, anywhere but in the wall against which we are living. Instead, let us seek the respite where it is—in the very thick of battle. For in my opinion, and this is where I shall close, it *is* there. Great ideas, it has been said, come into the world as gently as doves. Perhaps, then, if we listen attentively, we shall hear, amid the uproar of empires and nations, a faint flutter of wings, the gentle stirring of life and hope. Some will say that this hope lies in a nation; others, in a man. I believe rather that it is awakened, revived, nourished by millions of solitary individuals whose deeds and works every day negate frontiers and the crudest implications of history. As a result, there shines forth fleetingly the ever-threatened truth that each and every man, on the foundations of his own sufferings and joys, builds for them all.

One is asked, then, to accept the human condition, its sufferings and its joys, and to work with its imperfections as the foundation upon which the individual will build his or her wholeness through adventurous creative achievement. For the person with creative potential, there is no wholeness except in using it. As Camus explained, however, the going is rough and the respite is brief. It is significant that he would title his last university lecture "Create Dangerously."

What follows, as I have said, is written more out of experience and out of searching than as the product of scholarship. It is intended for those who accept *their* damned rock—the human condition—and accept that other people have rocks as well, and that, except for a few extreme deviants who will be restrained, *all* will live in societies and accommodate to each other.

This is written for those who want to serve and are resolved to be led only by servants, and who will respond to the opportunity to lead, if given, to the end that an increment of trust will be put into an imperfect society that is currently very short of it. It is for those who see integrity not just as affirming right thoughts and avoiding error, but as requiring *them* to be inventive, venturesome, risking the initiative to find better ways, *and* doing the hard and sometimes dangerous work that brings the impossible to reality.

If one may make an easy generalization about people, there are those who are visionaries, and there are those who see a vision but have their feet on the ground. This set of little essays has been written for the latter.

Who Is the Enemy?

Who is the enemy? Who is holding back more rapid movement to the better society that is reasonably possible with available resources? Who is responsible for the mediocre performance of so many of our institutions? Who is standing in the way of a larger consensus on the definition of the better society and paths to reaching it?

Not evil people. Not stupid people. Not apathetic people. Not the "system." Not the protesters, the disrupters, the revolutionaries, the reactionaries.

Granting that fewer evil, stupid, or apathetic people or a better "system" might make the job easier, their removal would not change matters, not for long. The better society will come, if it comes, with plenty of evil, stupid, apathetic people around and with an imperfect, ponderous, inertia-charged "system" as the vehicle for change. Liquidate the offending people, radically alter or destroy the system, and in less than a generation they will all be back. It is not in the nature of things that a society can be cleaned up once and for all according to an ideal plan. And even if it were possible, who would want to live in an aseptic world? Evil, stupidity, apathy, the "system" are not the enemy even though society-building forces will be contending with them all the time. The healthy society, like the healthy body, is not the one that has taken the most medicine. It is the one in which the internal health-building forces are in the best shape.

The *real* enemy is fuzzy thinking on the part of good, intelligent, vital people, and their failure to lead. Too many settle for being critics and experts. There is too much intellectual wheel spinning, too much retreat into "research," too little preparation for and willingness to undertake the hard, and sometimes corrupting, tasks of building better institutions in an imperfect world, too little disposition to see "the problem" as residing *in here* and not *out there*.

In short, the enemy is servants who have the potential to lead but do not lead.

Who Is the Servant-Leader?

The story of Leo could be misleading by portraying him as servant first and later as leader. He was really the leader all the time. Because, in the first part of the story, his formal role was servant, his leadership contribution was not seen. When he disappeared the mission collapsed, not because the ostensible servant had gone but because they had lost their leader. Leo, in these two merged roles, is symbolically the *whole man. The true servant must lead in order to be a complete person!*

The servant quality probably emerges when one is quite young, and is shaped more by example than by precept. Who are one's heroes? Are they true servants of others or are they self-serving people?

The really critical question is, what distinguishes the servant of others from the self-serving person? Great injustice and destruction have been wrought by so-called good people who presumed to be serving others. The best test, and difficult to administer, is: do those being served grow as persons; do they become healthier, wiser, freer, more autonomous while being served? Since so many people seem afraid to grow, the true servant-leader who brings it about is an extraordinary person, a Leo.

The leader facet of the servant-leader, the disposition to take the risks to initiate, to provide the ideology and the structure, and, in so doing, go out ahead to show the way, seems a conscious choice that is made when the issues of identity are faced in the late teens or early twenties. What follows then?—another crucial question.

One does not "learn" to be a leader the way one learns most things that are taught in college. Like anything else that is acquired, one will do better with a mentor or a coach than without one. But academic learning, unfortunately the main concern of the university, does not usually provide the kind of support that growth in leadership ability requires. An occasional teacher does become a great mentor for potential leaders; but, at present, one cannot depend on finding such a mentor and those young people who choose to grow as leaders are largely on their own.

The servant prepares himself or herself to lead by a process of growth through experience guided by a self-image as a builder and within a conceptual framework that suggests the strengths that will emerge if allowed.

Leaders are not trained; they evolve. A step-by-step conscious striving will produce something, of course. But a contrived synthetic person is not as likely to reach that level of servant-leader as will one who has evolved with his or her own natural rhythm. Yet one must consciously try and hope for a natural congruence.

There are processes, techniques, and knowledge sources that provide the *expertise* of the special field in which the leader works. The mastery of these takes time and hard work and the possession of them makes one an expert or a critic but not necessarily a leader. *Leadership overarches expertise*, and it cannot be reduced to a style.

A leader is not an identifiable style of person. Charismatic people sometimes lead well. Those who seem dull and pedestrian sometimes lead well. In an age of candor, charisma is suspect of being manipulative and may be a liability.

Effective leadership defies categorization, but one is risked—four words: direction, values, competence (including judgment), and spirit. Their meaning will emerge in later sections.

Ultimately, every established leader has his or her own ideas about the art (and it is truly an art). What is suggested here is a set of entering propositions that have withstood considerable testing. They are offered as suggestive only and are presented as a series of short essays, some elaborated more than others, but not as an integrated thesis. This will make it easier for the reader to select which, if any of them, to allow into the arena of his or her own inward confrontation.

Origins of the Dominating Leader

The first consultant of record on leadership was a man named Jethro. Jethro was the father-in-law of Moses. He came to visit Moses, who was the leader of the people of Israel in the wilderness. He found Moses wearing himself out on the job and gave him advice (in the eighteenth chapter of Exodus):

> You shall represent the people before God, and bring their cases to God; and you shall teach them the statutes and the decisions, and make them know the way they must walk and what they must do. Moreover choose able men from all the people, such as fear God, men who are trustworthy and who hate a bribe; and place such men over the people as rulers of thousands, of hundreds, of fifties, and of tens. And let them judge the people at all times; every great matter they shall bring to you, but any small matter they shall decide themselves; so it will be easier for you, and they will bear the burden with you. If you do this, and God so commands you, you will then be able to endure, and all this people also will go to their place in peace.

This is the earliest statement of the hierarchical principle of organization. This principle sets the leader at the top of the organizational pyramid. He is the man who speaks to God (which makes him the ultimate authority because, presumably, nobody else speaks to God). Below him the hierarchy spreads out until finally the little people have their little problems decided by the little rulers of tens. This basic principle of organization entered human knowledge over 3,000 years ago and still dominates everything that is organized— armies, churches, governments, universities, businesses. It has stood all of these years virtually unchallenged, as the laws of Euclid stood as self-evident truths for so many centuries. Mathematicians finally broke out of this slavery to the "law." Modern organization theorists are growing restless with Jethro's formulation but it has not yet been effectively challenged. The institutional world that most of today's college students will enter will still be dominated by Jethro's thinking.

A close examination of Jethro's principle reveals that it does not assume Moses in the role of servant. Clearly he is the dominating leader, dedicated though he may be to his job, and this arrangement seems designed primarily to assure his survival in that job. For the people, it is a design to provide justice (insofar as rulers are capable of rendering it). All that is promised is that Moses will endure and "this people will go to their place in peace."—This may have been a great promise in biblical times, but not for today.

To date, Jethro's ideas have not been replaced, in practice, by anything better. And most institutional life is locked so tightly with these assumptions that perhaps nothing less than the jolt administered by the modern young revolutionaries will open the way for better ideas. This is the great opportunity of this college generation—to go beyond the attack on the system and produce the better ideas, demonstrate their effectiveness by carrying them into the leadership of the forthcoming society, and become the future builders of trust.

Everything Begins with the Initiative of an Individual

The forces for good or evil in the world are propelled by the thoughts, attitudes, and actions of individual beings. What happens to our values, and therefore to the quality of our civilization, in the future will be shaped by the conception, born of inspiration, of individuals. Perhaps only a few will receive this inspiration (insight) and the rest will learn from them. The very essence of leadership, going out ahead to show the way, derives from more than usual openness to inspiration, to insight. Why would anybody accept the leadership of another except that the other sees more clearly where it is best to go? Perhaps this is the current problem: too many who presume to lead do not see more clearly and, in defense of their inadequacy, they all the more strongly assert Jethro's principle and argue that the "system" must be preserved—a fatal error in this day of candor.

But the leader needs more than inspiration, more than insight. He or she has to take the risk to say, "I will go; come with me!" The leader has to initiate, push, provide the ideas and the structure, and take the risk of failure along with the chance of success. This is partly what the element of *spirit* is about; spirit sustains the leader as he or she takes the risk of saying, "I will go; follow me!" when he or she knows that the path is uncertain, even dangerous.

Paul Goodman, speaking through a character in *Making Do*, has said, "If there is no community for you, young man, young man, make it yourself."

What Are You Trying to Do?

What are you trying to do?—one of the easiest to ask and most difficult to answer of questions.

A mark of leaders, an attribute that puts them in a position to show the way for others, is that they are better than most at pointing the direction. As long as they are leading, they always have a goal. It may be a goal arrived at by group consensus, or the leader, acting on inspiration, may simply have said, "Let's go this way." But the leader *always* knows what it is and can articulate it for any who are unsure. By clearly stating and restating the goal the leader gives certainty and purpose to others who may have difficulty in achieving it for themselves.

The dictionary defines *goal* rather broadly. It is used here in the special sense of the overarching purpose, the big dream, the visionary concept, the ultimate consummation that one approaches but never really achieves. It is something presently out of reach; it is something to strive for, to move toward, or become. It is so stated that it excites the imagination and challenges people to work for something they do not yet know how to do, something they can be proud of as they move toward it.

Every achievement starts with a goal. But not just any old goal and not just anybody stating it. The starter of the goal must elicit trust, especially if it is a high-risk or visionary goal, because those who follow must accept the risk along with the leader. Direction, a goal, from a leader does not elicit trust unless one has confidence in his or her values and competence (including judgment) and unless he or she has a sustaining spirit (*entheos*) that will support the tenacious pursuit of that goal.

Important as goals are as the base point of leadership, the faltering of leadership today is not so much for want of goals as for the lack of trust because the evidence of values, competence, and spirit is lacking. This is a candid, cynical age. People rightly want to know, "What are your plans? Can you really do it? It is a big risk, can I trust you?" And not enough who presume to lead measure up.

Listening and Understanding

Persons who achieve important leadership roles often are not good listeners. By nature, because they are disposed to lead, they may be too assertive. If they wish to become good listeners they may have to learn it as a conscious discipline. And it is terribly important that they do learn because one cannot *serve* as one leads, and sometimes one cannot lead well, without being a good listener. It is an absurdly simple rule, but the fact is that one misses some things one needs to know if one does not listen in a really discriminating way.

Listening is much more than just keeping quiet, although one must keep quiet in order to listen. Listening begins with attention and the search for understanding, both the outward manifestation and the inward conviction of really searching to understand. This must be communicated by the way one attends and the way one responds.

The good listener remembers what the other person expresses (words, mood, expression) and refrains from piecemeal value judgments. The good listener keeps himself or herself in a position to assess the relationship between the facts, attitudes, opinions, and feelings being expressed and therefore is able to respond to the total expression of the other person. Listening is a discipline that improves face-to-face relations, it saves time in the process of communicating, and it "lifts" both the listener and the one listened to. Listening does not make one a servant or a leader but it is likely to be an attribute of the servant-leader.

Listeners learn about people in ways that modify—first, the listener's attitudes, then his or her behavior, and finally the attitudes and behavior of others. Listening is equally important to a mother relating to her children as to a head of state. Sometimes the heat can be taken out of a child's temper tantrum with just a few seconds of intense listening. Listening is basically an attitude—really wanting to understand. It is also a technique. But the technique without the attitude is phoney.

Language and Imagination

A prime requirement of leadership is goal setting or goal finding. In any kind of group enterprise the person who can *articulate* the consensus idea is *the* leader, even though someone else may be designated as leader and it may be someone else's idea. This is partly a matter of insight—concept. One can *act* on a concept that one can't articulate. But to lead, one must articulate, one must have the language.

But language is deceptive—it is not a solid, unchanging thing. And it just does not go in a straight line from speaker to listener as water goes through a funnel.

Alfred North Whitehead once said, "No language can be anything but elliptical, requiring a leap of imagination to understand its meaning in its relevance to immediate experience." Nothing is meaningful until it is related to the hearer's own experience. One may hear the words, one may even remember them and repeat them, as a computer does in the retrieval process. But *meaning*, a growth in experience as a result of receiving the communication, requires that the hearer supply the imaginative link, from the listener's fund of experience, to the abstract language symbols the speaker has used. As a leader (including teacher, coach, administrator) one must have facility in tempting the hearer into that leap of imagination that connects the verbal concept to the hearer's own experience. The limitation on language, to the communicator, is that the *hearer* must make that leap of imagination. One of the great communicating arts is to say just enough to facilitate that leap. Many attempts to communicate are nullified by saying too much.

The physicist and philosopher Percy Bridgman takes another view of it when he says, "no linguistic structure is capable of reproducing the full complexity of experience. . . . The only feasible way of dealing with this is to push a particular verbal line of attack as far as it can go, and then switch to another verbal level which we might abandon when we have to. . . . Many people . . . insist on a single self-consistent verbal scheme into which they try to force all experience. In doing this they create a purely verbal world in which they can live a pretty autonomous existence, fortified by the ability of many of their fellows to live in the same verbal world." This, of course, is what makes a cult—a group of people who thus isolate themselves from the evolving mainstream by staying within their own closed verbal world and forfeit the opportunity to lead others. One of the great tragedies is when a proven able leader becomes trapped in one of these closed verbal worlds and loses his or her ability to lead.

Most of us at one time or another, some of us a good deal of the time, would *really* like to communicate, *really* get through to a significant level of meaning in the hearer's experience. It can be terribly important. The best test of whether we are communicating at this depth is to ask ourselves, first, are we really listening? Are we listening to the one we want to communicate to? Is our basic attitude, as we approach the confrontation, one of wanting to understand? Remember that great line from the Prayer of St. Francis, "Lord, grant that I may not seek so much to be understood as to understand."

One must not be afraid of a little silence. Some find silence awkward or oppressive. But a relaxed approach to dialogue will include the welcoming of some silence. It is often a devastating question to ask oneself, but it is sometimes important to ask it—"In saying what I have in mind will I really improve on the silence?"

Withdrawal—Finding One's Optimum

Leadership in any of its dimensions from the home to the world community can be pressure ridden and very taxing—emotionally and physically. Two kinds of people go for leadership: those who are so constituted physically and emotionally that they like pressure, seek it out, and perform best when they are totally intense, and those who do not like pressure, do not thrive under it, but who want to lead and are willing to endure the pressure in order to have the opportunity. The former welcome a happy exhaustion and the latter are constantly in defense against that state. For both the art of withdrawal is useful. To the former it is a change of pace; to the latter it is a defense against an unpleasant state. The former may be the more natural leader; the latter needs a tactic to survive. The art of withdrawal serves them both.

The ability to withdraw and reorient oneself, if only for a moment, presumes that one has learned the art of systematic neglect, to sort out the more important from the less important—and the important from the urgent—and attend to the more important, even though there may be penalties and censure for the neglect. One may govern one's life by the law of the optimum (optimum being that pace and set of choices that give one the best performance over a life span)—bearing in mind that there are always emergencies and the optimum includes carrying an unused reserve of energy in all periods of normal demand so that one has the resilience to cope with the emergency.

Pacing oneself by appropriate withdrawal is one of the best approaches to making optimal use of one's resources. The servant-as-leader must constantly ask himself or herself, how can I *use* myself to serve best?

Acceptance and Empathy

A college president once said, "Educators may be rejected by their students and they must not object to this. But they may never, under any circumstances, regardless of what the students do, reject a single student."

We have known this a long time in the family. For a family to be a family, no one can ever be rejected. Robert Frost in his poem "The Death of the Hired Man" states the problem in a conversation on the farmhouse porch between the farmer and his wife about the shiftless hired man, Silas, who has come back to their place to die. The farmer is irritated about this because Silas was lured away from his farm in the middle of the last haying season. The wife says this is the only home he has. They are drawn into a discussion of what a home is. The husband gives his view:

> Home is the place where when you have
> to go there they have to take you in!

This is the male view, the symbolic masculine—hard, rational, uncompromising.

The wife gives the symbolic feminine reply—gentle, feeling, accepting. What is a home? She says,

> I should have called it something you
> somehow haven't to deserve.

Some women are hard and uncompromising and some men are gentle and accepting. What Robert Frost has portrayed for us here are the masculine and feminine *principles*.

Because of the vagaries of human nature, the halt, the lame, half-made creatures that we all are, the great leader (whether it is the mother in her home or the head of a vast organization) would say what the wife said about home in Robert Frost's poem. The interest in and affection for his or her followers which a leader has, and it is a mark of true greatness when it is genuine, is clearly something the followers haven't to deserve. Great leaders, including "little" people, may have gruff, demanding, uncompromising exteriors. But deep down inside, the great ones have an unqualified acceptance of those who go with their leadership.

Acceptance requires a tolerance of imperfection. Anybody could lead perfect people—if there were any. But there aren't *any* perfect people. And the parents who try to raise perfect children are certain to raise neurotics.

It is part of the enigma of human nature that the "typical" person—immature, stumbling, inept, lazy—is capable of great dedication and heroism *if* he or she is wisely led. Many otherwise able people are disqualified to lead because they cannot work with and through the half-people who are all there are. The secret of institution building is to be able to weld a team of such people by lifting them up to grow taller than they would otherwise be.

Individuals grow taller when they are accepted for what they are and are led by the ablest and strongest and ethically soundest people. (Ethical in the sense of being sensitive to what helps people grow taller and more autonomous and disposed to act on that knowledge.) Leaders who fully accept those who go with them are more likely to be trusted.

Know the Unknowable—
Beyond Conscious Rationality

The requirements of leadership impose some intellectual demands that are not measured by academic intelligence ratings. The two are not mutually exclusive but they are different things. The leader needs two intellectual abilities that are usually not formally assessed in an academic way: he or she needs to *have a sense for the unknowable* and be able to *foresee the unforeseeable*. The leader knows some things and foresees some things which those he is presuming to lead do not know or foresee as clearly. This is partly what gives leaders their "lead," what puts them out ahead and qualifies them to show the way. This is why geniuses must sometimes accept the leadership of those who are mainly wise.

Until quite recently many would attribute these qualities of knowing the unknowable and foreseeing the unforeseeable to mystical or supernatural gifts—and some still do. Now it is possible at least to speculate about them within a framework of natural law. The electrical body field theory suggests the possibility of an interconnection between fields and could explain telepathy. Some are willing to speculate on the possibility of memory traces being physical entities, thus providing a basis for explaining clairvoyance. In far-out theorizing every mind, at the unconscious level, has access to every "bit" of information that is or ever was. Those among us who seem to have unusual access to these "data banks" are called "sensitives." What we now call intuitive insight may be the survivor of an earlier much greater sensitivity. What we now normally have of intuition may bring us much nearer the optimal balance between conscious and unconscious rationalities. Much of this is highly speculative but it is within bounds of what some scientific minds are willing to ponder within the framework of what is known about natural phenomena. Information recall under hypnosis is suggestive of what is potentially available from the unconscious.

What is the relevance of this somewhat fanciful theory to the issue at hand, the thought processes of a leader? One contemporary student of decision making put it this way: "If, on a practical decision in the world of affairs, you are waiting for *all* of the information for a good decision, it never comes." There always is a little more information that one might have if one waited longer or worked harder to get it—but the delay and the cost are not warranted. On an important decision one rarely has 100 percent of the information needed for a good decision no matter how much one spends or how long one waits. And if one waits too long he or she has a different problem and has to start all over. This is the terrible dilemma of the hesitant decision maker.

As a practical matter, on most important decisions there is an information gap. That is why we have leaders. If all the information for all of the decisions were always available we would have a computer-run society and decision makers, leaders—people to do this—would not be necessary. But there usually is an information gap between the solid information in hand and what is needed. The art of leadership rests, in part, on the ability to bridge that gap by intuition. The person who is better at this than most is likely to emerge as the leader because he or she can *serve*, can contribute something of great value. Others will depend on the leader to go out ahead and show the way because his or her judgment will be better than most. Leaders, therefore, must be more creative than most, and creativity is largely discovery, a push into the uncharted and the unknown. Every once in a while a leader finds himself or herself needing to think like a scientist, an artist, or a poet. And his or her thought processes may be just as fanciful as theirs.

Intuition is a feel for patterns, the ability to generalize based on what has happened previously. Wise leaders know when to bet on these intuitive leads, but they always know that they are betting on percentages—their hunches are not seen as eternal truths.

Two separate "anxiety" processes may be involved in a leader's intuitive decision, an important aspect of which is timing, the decision to decide. One is the anxiety of holding the decision until as much information as possible is in. The other is the anxiety of making the decision when there really isn't enough information—which, on critical decisions, is usually the case. All of this is complicated by pressures building up from those who "want an answer." Again, trust is at the root of it. Has the leader a really good information base (both hard data and sensitivity to feelings and needs of people) and a reputation for consistently good decisions that people respect? Can he or she defuse the anxiety of a lot of people who want more certainty than exists in the situation?

Intuition in a leader is more valued, and therefore more trusted, at the conceptual level. An intuitive answer to an immediate situation can be a gimmick and conceptually defective. Overarching conceptual insight that gives a sounder framework for decisions (so important, for instance, in foreign policy) is the great gift. But even there, courage to act on insight and take immediate losses in the interest of long-term sound actions may be the greater virtue. It gets down, in the end, to humility. Is the leader really a servant?

Foresight—the Central Ethic of Leadership

The common assumption about the word *now* is that it is this instant moment of clock time—*now*. In usage we qualify this a little by saying *right* now, meaning this instant, or *about* now, allowing a little leeway. Sometimes we say, "I'm going to do it now," which means, "I'm going to start soon and do it in the near future," or "I have just now done it," meaning that I did it in the recent past. The dictionary admits all of these variations of usage.

Let us liken *now* to the spread of light from a narrowly focused beam. There is a bright intense center, this moment of clock time, and a diminishing intensity, theoretically out to infinity on either side. As viewed here, *now* includes all of this—all of history and all of the future. As one approaches the central focus, the light intensifies as this moment of clock time is approached. All of it *is now* but some parts are more *now* than others, and this central focus that marks this instant of clock time moves along as the clock ticks. *This is not the way it is!* It is simply an analogy to suggest a way of looking at *now* for those who wish better to see the unforeseeable—a mark of a leader.

Prescience, or foresight, is a better than average guess about *what* is going to happen *when* in the future. It begins with a state of mind about *now*, something like that suggested by the light analogy. What is there in the present moment of clock time is merely the intense focus that is connected with what has gone on in the past and what will happen in the future. The prescient individual has a sort of "moving average" mentality (to borrow a statistician's term) in which past, present, and future are one, bracketed together and moving along as the clock ticks. The process is continuous.

Machiavelli, writing about how to be a prince, put it this way, "Thus it happens in matters of state; for knowing afar off (which it is only given a prudent man to do) the evils that are brewing, they are easily cured. But when, for want of such knowledge, they are allowed to grow so that everyone can recognize them, there is no longer any remedy to be found."

The shape of some future events can be calculated from trend data. But, as with a practical decision mentioned earlier, there is usually an information gap that has to be bridged, and one must cultivate the conditions that favor intuition. This is what Machiavelli meant when he said that "knowing afar off (which it is only given a prudent man to do) the evils that are brewing, they are easily cured." The prudent man is the man who constantly thinks of "now" as the moving concept in which past, present moment, and future are one organic unity. And this requires living by a sort of rhythm that encourages a high level of intuitive insight about the whole gamut of events from the indefinite past, through the present moment, to the indefinite future. One is at once, in every moment of time, historian, contemporary analyst, and prophet—not three separate roles. This is what the practicing leader is, every day of his or her life.

Living this way is partly a matter of *faith*. Stress is a condition of most of modern life, and, if one is a servant-leader and carrying the burdens of other people—going out ahead to show the way—one takes the rough and tumble (and it really is rough and tumble in some leader roles), in the belief that, if one enters a situation prepared with the necessary experience and knowledge at the conscious level, *in the situation* the intuitive insight necessary for one's optimal performance will be forthcoming. Is there any other way, in the turbulent world of affairs (including the typical home), for one to maintain serenity in the face of uncertainty? One follows the steps of the creative process which require that one stay with the conscious analytical process as far as it will carry him or her and then withdraw, release the analytical pressure, if only for a moment, in full confidence that a resolving insight will come. The concern with past and future is gradually attenuated as this span of concern goes forward or backward from the instant moment. The ability to do this is the essential structural dynamic of leadership.

Foresight is seen as a wholly rational process, the product of a constantly running internal computer that deals with intersecting series and random inputs and is vastly more complicated than anything technology has yet produced. It is regarding the events of the instant moment and constantly comparing them with a series of projections made in the past and at the same time projecting future events—with diminishing certainty as projected time runs out into the indefinite future.

The failure of a leader to foresee may be viewed as an *ethical* failure, because a serious ethical compromise today (when the usual judgment on ethical inadequacy is made) is sometimes the result of a failure at an earlier date to foresee today's events and take the right actions when there was freedom to act. The action that society labels "unethical" in the present moment is often really one of no choice. By this standard a lot of guilty people are walking around with an air of innocence that they would not have if society were able always to pin the label *unethical* on the failure to foresee and the consequent failure to act constructively when there was freedom to act.

Foresight is the "lead" that the leader has. Once leaders lose this lead and events start to force their hand, they are leaders in name only. They are not leading; they are reacting to immediate events and they probably will not long be leaders. There are abundant current examples of loss of leadership that stem from a failure to foresee what reasonably could have been foreseen and from failure to act on that knowledge while the leader had freedom to act.

There is a wealth of experience available on how to achieve this perspective of foresight, but only one aspect is mentioned here. Required is that one live a sort of schizoid life. One is always at two levels of consciousness: one is in the real world—concerned, responsible, effective, value-oriented. One is also detached, riding above it, seeing today's events, and seeing oneself deeply involved in today's events, in the perspective of a long sweep of history and projected into the indefinite future. Such a split enables one better to foresee the unforeseeable. Also, from one level of consciousness, each of us acts resolutely from moment to moment on a set of assumptions that then governs our life. Simultaneously, from another level, the adequacy of these assumptions is examined, in action, with the aim of future revision and improvement. How else can one live and act in the real world with a clear conscience?

Awareness and Perception

Framing all of this is awareness, opening wide the doors of perception so as to take in more of what is available of sensory experience and other signals from the environment than people usually take in. It is not hard to do and it makes life more interesting; certainly it strengthens one's effectiveness as a leader. When one is aware, there is more than the usual alertness, there is more intense contact with the immediate situation, and a lot more is stored away in the unconscious computer to produce intuitive insights in the future when needed.

William Blake has said, "If the doors of perception were cleansed, everything will appear to man as it is, infinite." Those who have gotten their doors of perception open wide enough often enough know that this statement of Blake's is not mere poetic exaggeration. Most of us move about with very narrow perception—sight, sound, smell, tactile—and we miss most of the grandeur that is in the minutest thing, the smallest experience. We also miss leadership opportunities. There is danger, however. Some people cannot take what they see when the doors of perception are open too wide, and they had better test their tolerance for awareness gradually. A qualification for leadership is that one can tolerate a sustained wide span of awareness so that he or she better "sees it as it is."

The opening of awareness stocks both the conscious and unconscious minds with a richness of resources for future need. But it does more than that: it is value building and value clarifying and it armors one to meet the stress of life by helping build serenity in the face of stress and uncertainty. The cultivation of awareness gives one the basis for detachment, the ability to stand aside and see oneself in perspective in the context of one's own experience, amid the ever present dangers, threats, and alarms. Then one sees one's own peculiar assortment of obligations and responsibilities in a way that permits one to sort out the urgent from the important and perhaps deal with the important. Awareness is *not* a giver of solace—it is just the opposite. It is a disturber and an awakener. Able leaders are usually sharply awake and reasonably disturbed. They are not seekers after solace. They have their own inner serenity.

A leader must have more of an armor of confidence in facing the unknown—more than those who accept his or her leadership. This is partly anticipation and preparation but it is also belief that in the stress of real-life situations one can compose oneself in a way that permits the creative process to operate—and this is what makes dynamic, visionary leadership possible.

This is told dramatically in one of the great stories of the human spirit—the story of Jesus when confronted with the woman taken in adultery. In this story Jesus is seen as a man, like all of us, with extraordinary prophetic insight of the kind we all have some of. He is a leader; He has a goal—to bring, among other things, more compassion to the lives of people.

In this scene the woman is cast down before Him by the mob that is challenging Jesus' leadership. They cry, "The *law* says she shall be stoned, what do *you* say?" Jesus must make a decision; He must give the *right* answer, right in the situation, and one that sustains His leadership toward His goal. The situation is deliberately stressed by His challengers. What does He do?

He sits there writing in the sand—a withdrawal device. In the pressure of the moment, having assessed the situation rationally, He assumes the attitude of withdrawal that will allow creative insight to function.

He could have taken another course; He could have regaled the mob with rational arguments about the superiority of compassion over torture. A pretty good logical argument can be made for it. What would the result have been had He taken that course?

He did not choose to do that. He chose instead to withdraw and cut the stress—right in the event itself—in order to open His *awareness* to creative insight. And a great one came, one that has kept the story of the incident alive for 2,000 years—"Let him that is without sin among you cast the first stone."

Persuasion—Sometimes One Person at a Time

Leaders work in wondrous ways. Some assume great institutional burdens, others quietly deal with one individual at a time. Such a man was John Woolman, an American Quaker who lived through the middle years of the eighteenth century. He is known to the world of scholarship for his journal, a literary classic. But in the area of our interest, leadership, he is the man who almost singlehandedly rid the Society of Friends (Quakers) of slaves.

It is difficult now to imagine the Quakers as slaveholders, as indeed it is difficult now to imagine anyone being a slaveholder. One wonders how the society of 200 years hence will view "what man has made of man" in our generation. We may look pretty bad.

But the eighteenth-century American Quakers were, many of them, affluent, conservative slaveholders and John Woolman, as a young man, chose as his goal the ridding of his beloved Society of the practice of slavery. Thirty of his adult years (he lived to age fifty-two) were largely devoted to this. By 1770, nearly a hundred years before the Civil War, no Quakers held slaves.

His method was unique. He didn't raise a big storm about it or start a protest movement. No moral stigma was heaped on the Quaker slaveholders.

Although John Woolman was not a strong man physically, he

accomplished his mission by journeys up and down the East Coast by foot or horseback visiting slaveholders—over a period of many years. The approach was not to censure the slaveholders because Woolman thought slaveholding was wrong (although he did emphatically think it was wrong). Rather, the burden of his approach was to raise questions: What does the owning of slaves do to you as a moral person? What kind of an institution are you binding over to your children? Person by person, inch by inch, by persistently returning and revisiting and pressing his gentle argument over a period of thirty years, the scourge of slavery was eliminated from this Society, the first religious group in America formally to denounce and forbid slavery among its members. One wonders what would have been the result if there had been fifty John Woolmans, or even five, traveling the length and breadth of the Colonies in the eighteenth century *persuading* people one by one with gentle, nonjudgmental argument that a wrong should be righted by individual voluntary action. Perhaps we would not have had the war with its 600,000 casualties and the impoverishment of the South and with the resultant vexing social problem that is at fever heat a hundred years later with no end in sight. We know now, in the perspective of history, that just a slight alleviation of the tension in the 1850s might have avoided the war. A few John Woolmans, just a *few*, might have made the difference. Leadership by persuasion has the virtue of change by convincement rather than coercion. Its advantages are obvious.

John Woolman exerted his leadership in an age that must have looked as dark to him as ours does to us today. We may easily write off his effort as a suggestion for today on the assumption that the Quakers were ethically conditioned for this approach. All individuals are so conditioned, to some extent—enough to gamble on.

One Action at a Time—
The Way Some Great Things Get Done

Two things about Thomas Jefferson are of interest in this context. First, as a young man he had the good fortune to find a mentor, George Wythe, a Williamsburg lawyer whose original house still stands in the restored village. George Wythe was a substantial man of his times, a signer of the Declaration of Independence and a member of the Constitutional Convention. But his chief claim to fame is as Thomas Jefferson's mentor. It was probably the influence of mentor on protégé, as Jefferson studied law in Wythe's office, that moved Jefferson toward his place in history and somewhat away from his natural disposition to settle down at Monticello as an eccentric Virginia scholar (which he remained, partly, despite Wythe's influence). The point of mentioning George Wythe is that old people may have a part to play in helping the potential servant-as-leader to emerge at his or her optimal best.

Perhaps the most significant aspect of Jefferson, more important in history than the Declaration of Independence or Jefferson's later term as president, was what he did during the war. With the publication of the Declaration, the war was on and Jefferson was famous. He was importuned on all sides to take important roles in the war. But he turned them all down. *He knew who he was* and he was resolved to be his own man. He chose his own role. He went back to Virginia and didn't leave the state for the duration of the war.

Jefferson believed the war would be won by the Colonies, that there would be a new nation and that that nation would need a new system of law to set it on the course that he had dreamed for it in the Declaration of Independence. So he went back to Monticello, got himself elected to the Virginia legislature, and proceeded to write new statutes embodying the new principles of law for the new nation. He set out, against the determined opposition of his conservative colleagues, to get these enacted into Virginia law. It was an uphill fight. He would go to Williamsburg and wrestle with his colleagues until he was slowed to a halt. Then he would get on his horse and ride back to Monticello to rekindle his spirit and write some more statutes. Armed with these he would go back to Williamsburg and take another run at it. He wrote 150 statutes in that period and got fifty of them enacted into law, the most notable being separation of church and state. For many years Virginia legislators were digging into the remaining hundred as new urgent problems made their consideration advisable.

When the Constitution was drafted some years later Jefferson wasn't even around; he was in France as our ambassador. He didn't have to be around. He had done his work and made his contribution in the statutes already operating in Virginia. Such are the wondrous ways in which leaders do their work—when they know who they are and resolve to be their own persons and will accept making their way to their goal by one action at a time with a lot of frustration along the way.

Knowing who one is, establishing one's identity, is essential for leadership, but it is not leadership itself. Knowing who one is before one becomes a leader is more likely to elicit trust than if one seeks to be a leader as a means of establishing one's identity.

Healing and Serving

Twelve ministers and theologians of all faiths and twelve psychiatrists of all faiths had convened for a two-day off-the-record seminar on the one-word theme of *healing*. The chair, a psychiatrist, opened the seminar with this question, "We are all healers, whether we are ministers or doctors. Why are we in this business? What is our motivation?" There followed only ten minutes of intense discussion and they were all agreed, doctors and ministers, Catholics, Jews, and Protestants. "For our own healing," they said.

This is an interesting word, *healing*, with its meaning, "to make whole." The example above suggests that one really never makes it. It is always something sought. Perhaps, as with the minister and the doctor, the servant-leader might also acknowledge that his or her own healing is his or her motivation. There is something subtle communicated to one who is being served and led if, implicit in the compact between servant-leader and led, is the understanding that the search for wholeness is something they share.

Alcoholics Anonymous is regarded by some who know as recovering more alcoholics from this dreadful illness than all other approaches combined. Legend has it that the founding meeting to incorporate the organization was held in the office of a noted philanthropist, a very wealthy man. In the course of the discussion of the principles that would guide the new organization, the philanthropist made a statement something like this: "From my experience I think I know about the things that can be done with money and the things that cannot be done with money. What you in AA want to do cannot be done with money. You must be poor. You must not use money to do your work." There was more conversation but this advice profoundly influenced the course of AA. A fundamental principle that has guided the work of AA over the years was born at that meeting: they will be poor; no one but an alcoholic can contribute money to AA's modest budget; AA will own no real property; the essential work of AA, one recovered alcoholic helping another toward recovery, will not be done for money.

In an affluent age with burgeoning professionalism and institutionalism, AA stands as a clear sentinel that gold does not always glitter, that the need for a person to heal himself or herself may be an adequate motive to serve, and that an unpaid amateur with dedication to service may excel the most gifted (and expensive) professional.

Institutions

Unless we turn back the clock, get rid of 190 million people in this country, and become a nation of isolated, subsistence farmers and hermits living in caves, we are all going to live with and be deeply involved in institutions.

At the center of every institution is the notion of compromise. The nature of any institution that goes beyond the very small mutual self-help arrangement or something exceptional like AA, is that it employs people to render a service to other people—usually a larger number. The first compromise is that the institution must meet the requirements of those who work for it. For instance, a university must set up the conditions that attract a faculty and must operate so as to serve their needs. In addition, governments pass laws, communities impose customs, donors or other funding agencies have wishes. All of these may combine to shape the services offered students—and the result is a compromise that may not be the very best for the student.

Then there are many students, each one having unique needs. Even if the university were not limited by other commitments, it probably could not adjust completely to every student's need. Some compromise would be necessary.

Thus in the nature of any institution is compromise. And a fatal error for the leader is to see his or her role as largely the mediator of the compromise, the keeper of peace. Clearly a leader must do some of this. But there is a larger role—to excite and stretch the institution with demanding goals, larger goals than the machinery of compromise would postulate. The larger role includes reaching to make the impossible possible, insistently demanding it at times, and venturing to challenge mediocrity and injustice.

The leader maintains some detachment from the action so that he or she can see the whole of it. In a large institution a leader has the services of a staff that does the detailed analytical studies of what is going on. These resources help him or her see and foresee better than can those who see only part of the whole.

The leader must be in communication with *all* those involved. In a large institution this requires a system. But *every single person* must hear and be heard, and must feel that the communication channel is adequate.

An able leader who uses these resources and is trusted can build an esprit de corps, maintain an ethical climate, and sustain an institutional performance that is accepted as better than any individual or segment of the institution can achieve for itself. For the many who can accept some compromise with having things wholly their own way, a strong, well-led institution will take them farther faster than they could go on their own. For most people, over a life span, some compromise with the requirements of institutions is the price of optimal achievement.

The quality of a modern society is determined largely by the quality of its institutions, and institution building is the process by which a highly organized society moves along. Forward movement generally results from the "pull" of a pacesetter. Something or somebody moves out ahead and the rest emulate the model. Retrogression is inevitable when there is no pull from a pacesetter.

Who will be the pacesetter in institution building that marks a substantial movement toward the better society that is reasonable and possible with available resources? The *university* is nominated because there resides the largest share of good, intelligent, vital people who *could* make the university an institutional model for all of society—the pacesetter.

The university, as an institution, is currently the most troubled, the most fragile, and the least certain of its goals. By reversing this and becoming the strongest, the most serene, and the surest footed, the university could become the pacesetter for the next great social advance. Although the university has the resources, the autonomy, and the know-how to do this, at this writing it seems one of those impossible things. Yet some university must do this, the impossible, for its own self-preservation and for the preservation of all universities.

The university *must* become the institution-building model because nearly half the university-age people in the United States are now college or university students, and the influence of the university, through its students, on the shape of society is enormous. Furthermore, the university is currently imposing a stereotyped academic education on this large group of young people for whom such an approach is suitable for an estimated 15 percent or less. And this must be changed.

Opinions differ as to how moral the present generation of young people is, but their zeal for honesty and for the reduction of injustice is at an exceptional level. Their restlessness, sometimes destructively manifested, is the principal current driving force for institutional integrity in the university. They are crying out to be led, but there is not much response. Mostly they are experiencing a defensive reaction. It is no wonder that some of them seem "difficult."

Adlai Stevenson's "It is time to talk sense to the American people" in 1952 was wasted on that generation. But it would not be wasted now, in the universities, with this student generation. Saul Bellow in an interview commented simply, "Somehow I feel that truth is very attractive to a tremendous number of people." There is nowhere any greater need for dependable servants to emerge as great leaders and say it like it is than among those who guide the destinies of contemporary American universities.

Trustees

The only prediction made in these essays is that in the future society (if one survives) there will be institutions and there will be leaders.

Institutions need two kinds of leaders: those who are inside and carry the active day-to-day roles, and those who stand outside but are intimately concerned and who, with the benefit of some detachment, oversee the active leaders. These are the *trustees*.

The trustee is what the title implies, a person in whom ultimate trust is placed. Because institutions inevitably harbor conflict, the trustees are the court of last resort if an issue arises that cannot be resolved by the active parties. If tangible assets are involved, they legally hold them and are responsible to all interested parties for their good use. They have a prime concern for goals and for progress toward goals. They make their influence felt more by knowing and asking questions than by authority, although they usually have authority and can use it if need be. If, as is usual, there are several trustees, their chair has a special obligation to see that the trustees as a group sustain a common purpose and are influential in helping the institution maintain consistent high-level performance toward its goals. The chair is not simply the presider over meetings, but must serve and lead the trustees as a group and act as their major contact with the active inside leadership. Although trustees usually leave the "making of news" to active persons in the enterprise, theirs is a tremendously important leadership opportunity.

Unfortunately, trustee appointments are too often used for honorary purposes, to give the institution status by having high-status trustees, to give representation to special groups and ideologies, to secure gratis counsel from persons with special talents like bankers and lawyers, or simply to comply with the legal requirements of the charter. Also the really able ones sometimes accept too many trusteeships and therefore cannot put enough time into any one of them to be effective. Consequently, in the current wave of criticism of institutions, it is no cause for wonder that one finds the suggestion that trustees be dispensed with or made entirely honorary and stripped of all power. Nor is it surprising that other constituencies sometimes maneuver to render trustees powerless.

Trustees carry a critical leadership role that cannot be dispensed with. Because theirs is not the active leadership, their influence (or lack of it) is long run. But it is, in the end, absolutely determining. Therefore, the most exacting requirements of servant-leader should be placed on trustees. It matters not what is the age, color, sex, economic status, or political persuasion of the trustee. There should be only one requirement: he or she must be an able, dedicated servant-leader who will work hard to assure distinguished performance of the institution in trust. If one finds oneself a member of a trustee group where this one requirement is not substantially met by a majority of the trustees, and if one is unable to change it, one should weigh whether this particular board membership is a good use of his or her time.

So conceived, the role of trustees provides an unequaled fulfillment opportunity for those who would serve and lead. And no one step will more quickly raise the quality of the total society than a radical reconstruction of trustee bodies so that they are predominantly populated by able, dedicated servant-leaders. Two disturbing questions: Is there now enough discerning toughness strategically placed to see that this change takes place, in the event that able, dedicated servant-leaders become available in sufficient numbers to do it? Are enough high-potential young people now preparing themselves for these roles so that this change *can* be made in the event that it is possible to make it?

Power and Authority—
The Strength and the Weakness

In a complex, institution-centered society, which ours is likely to be into the indefinite future, there will be large and small concentrations of power. Sometimes it will be a servant's power of persuasion and example. Sometimes it will be coercive power used to dominate and manipulate people. The difference is that, in the former, power is used to create opportunity and alternatives so that the individual may choose and build autonomy. In the latter the individual is coerced into a predetermined path. Even if it is "good" for the person, if the individual experiences nothing else, ultimately his or her autonomy will be destroyed.

Some coercive power is overt and brutal. Some is covert and subtly manipulative. The former is open and acknowledged; the latter is insidious and hard to detect. Most of us are more coerced than we know. We need to be more alert in order to know, and we also need to acknowledge that, in an imperfect world, authority backed up by power is still necessary because we just don't know a better way. We may one day find one. It is worth searching for.

The trouble with coercive power is that it only strengthens resistance. And, if successful, its controlling effect lasts only as long as the force is strong. It is not organic. Only persuasion and the consequent voluntary acceptance are organic.

Since both kinds of power have been around for a long time, an individual will be better off if he or she is close enough to raw coercion to know what it is. One must be close to both the bitterness and goodness of life to be fully human.

The servant must be fully human. The servant-leader is functionally superior because he or she is closer to the ground and so hears things, sees things, knows things. Because of this a servant-leader is dependable and trusted. He or she knows the meaning of that line from Shakespeare's sonnet: "They that have power to hurt and will do none . . . "

Who Is the Servant?

For those who follow, and this is everyone—including those who lead—the really critical question is who is this moral person we would see as leader? Who is the servant? How does one tell a truly giving, enriching servant from the neutral person or the one whose net influence is to take away from or diminish other people?

A distinguished rabbi and scholar had just concluded a lecture on the Old Testament prophets in which he had spoken of true prophets and false prophets. A questioner asked him how one tells the difference between the true and the false prophets. The rabbi's answer was succinct and to the point, "There is no *way!*" he said.

Then he elaborated, "If there were a *way*, if one had a gauge to slip over the head of the prophet and establish without question that he is or he isn't a true prophet, there would be no human dilemma and life would not be worth living."

So it is with the servant issue. If there were a dependable *way* that would tell us, "this person enriches by his or her presence, is neutral, or takes away," life would be without challenge. Yet it is terribly important that one *know*, both about oneself and about others, whether the net effect of a person's influence on others enriches, is neutral, or diminishes and depletes.

Since there is no certain way to know this, one must turn to the artists for illumination. Such an illumination is in Hermann Hesse's idealized portrayal of the servant Leo whose servanthood comes through in his leadership. In stark modern terms it can also be found in the brutal reality of the mental hospital where Ken Kesey (in *One Flew Over the Cuckoo's Nest)* gives us Big Nurse—strong, able, dedicated, dominating, authority-ridden, manipulative, exploitative—the net effect of whose influence diminished other people, literally destroyed them. In the story she is pitted in a contest unto death with rough, gutter-bred MacMurphy, a patient, the net effect of whose influence is to build people up and make both patients and the doctor in charge of the ward grow bigger, stronger, healthier—an effort that ultimately costs MacMurphy his life. If one will study the two characters, Leo and MacMurphy, one will get a measure of the range of possibilities in the role of servant as leader.

None of us is perfect and in the test of real life few of us will come off as well as Leo or MacMurphy. Furthermore, in an imperfect world in which the imperfections seem a necessary part of the reality and in which a contemporary theologian can say, in all seriousness, "The capacity to find one's own seriousness absurd is a sign of grace," not all who lead will be servants. But it will be a better world if more of those who arrive at their mature years aware of some measure of the servant in them consciously try to lead, which means simply that, by going ahead to show the way, their enriching influence may go further than if, as servants, they accept a more passive role and miss being the whole people they might become.

Some of them will become leaders without consciously trying.

Those who try to become leaders run the risk of acquiring an artificiality that defeats the effort.

This has been written to help sharpen awareness of the opportunity and to help minimize the risk for those who try.

In Here, Not Out There

A king once asked Confucius's advice on what to do about the large number of thieves. Confucius answered, "If you, sir, were not covetous, although you should reward them to do it, they would not steal." This advice places an enormous burden on those who are favored by the rules, and it establishes how old is the notion that the servant views any problem in the world as *in here*, inside himself or herself, not *out there*. And if a flaw in the world is to be remedied, to the servant the process of change starts *in here*, in the servant, not *out there*. This is a difficult concept for that busybody, modern human being.

So it is with joy. Joy is inward; it is generated inside. It is not found outside and brought in. It is for those who accept the world as it is, part good, part bad, and who identify with the good by adding a little island of serenity to it.

Walt Whitman put it succinctly when he wrote (in the *Song of the Open Road*), "I and mine do not convince by arguments . . . we convince by our presence." And Hermann Hesse dramatized it in the powerful leadership exerted by Leo, who ostensibly only served in menial ways but who, by the quality of his inner life that was manifest in his presence, lifted men up and made the journey possible. Camus, in his final testament quoted earlier, leaves us with, "Each and every man, on the foundations of his own sufferings and joys, builds for them all."

Implications

These little essays were written in the belief that in the 1970s both serving and leading may be radically different—perhaps in ways yet to be discovered, but different from what has been before. To the extent that the quality of society, then or now, is not all that it reasonably might be (and ours is not), natural servants with potential for leadership have failed to prepare for and consequently to perform as leaders. They have chosen less creative roles. And they have suffered. And society has suffered. And so it may be in the future.

The future society may be just as mediocre as this one. It may be worse. And no amount of restructuring or changing the system or tearing it all down in the hope that something better will grow will change this. There may be a better system than the one we now have; it is hard to know. But, whatever it is, if the people to lead it well are not there, a better system will not produce a better society. Many people finding their wholeness through many and varied contributions make a good society. These essays are concerned with but one facet: able servants with potential to lead must lead. Not much else counts if this does not happen.

If an able young person is aware of his or her servant stature and leadership potential, what does that person do to prepare to lead? A few suggestions:

Begin by seeing the pervasive mediocrity in positions of influence for what it is—one individual at a time, not the "system." See the mediocre individual as not necessarily evil, but simply a person in a leadership spot who has no "lead," who does not see what needs to be done any more clearly, if as well, as the people he or she is trying to lead. Every time you see such a mediocre performer, say to yourself, "That fellow is there because a few years ago someone like me failed to prepare for that job." Don't blame the mediocre individual. Don't blame the system. Blame the right person for not being there and resolve that, a few years hence, such blame will not be heaped on you.

If you have the potential to lead, you have the ability to foresee events better than others, and, by using your "lead," by acting on your foresight while you have the freedom to act, you can provide some shelter from the shock of the unexpected for those less capable of foreseeing. This is not all that leadership is about, but it is an indispensable first condition. Why should anyone willingly follow

another except that the other better sees the path and better antici-
pates the dangers as well as the opportunities?

There is no better way to further one's ability to know the
unknowable and foresee the unforeseeable than to practice constantly on every observable event. Ask, what is going on here? What
motivates this individual? Where is this tending? What are the
future consequences? If another present action would bring a better
consequence, what would it be? In this circumstance, what is
required of one in a responsible position of leadership?

Even though you may be young and inexperienced and you are
in a school rather than in the world of affairs, open your awareness
to what is going on around you, make your own estimates and predictions, monitor the progress of events and check the accuracy of
your assumptions and store it away as your experience. Read the philosophy of leadership: Machiavelli's *The Prince*, Henry Taylor's *The
Statesman*, Alexander Leighton's *The Governing of Men*. Avoid the
how-to-do-it books; avoid any stereotyped leader model. Rather,
choose your own role, the one that best fits your nature, and allow
your own best leader style to emerge out of your own experience.

Realistically, we know that we have too few able leaders today,
and fewer still are servants. Otherwise we would not hold contemporary society to be mediocre. And even if the future holds a better
promise, a higher proportion of able, dedicated servant-leaders in
homes, schools, businesses, governments, labor unions, society may
still fall short because of the number who presume to lead who do
not measure up. Knowing this, what does the servant-leader do?
Two things. First, he or she makes the very best contribution regardless of the prevailing condition. No one person is responsible for the
whole society, only for what he or she achieves inwardly and how he
or she deals as an individual with opportunities. This is the first
approach of a servant-leader to a mediocre society.

The second possible action is to move to demythologize leadership. The prevailing myth holds that we respect the position even
though we cannot respect the ability of the person who occupies it.
This cannot be. Respect goes only to persons. What then do we do?
We ask all leaders to be honest, because honesty can be respected
even in the inferior person. Then the inferior person in a leadership

spot, be he or she a parent, teacher, judge, pastor, manager, president, or king, will admit to not seeing the path any more clearly than anybody else and ask for the help of those he or she is presuming to lead. In fact, it is better for all leaders to admit this, partly to leave those who go with them free to judge whether the leader's vision of the path is really superior, and partly because there will be times—no matter how prescient or perceptive the leader—when someone else does see the path more clearly.

The range of leadership opportunities is very wide, wide enough to provide a congenial role for every servant who wants to be a builder (and every true servant wants to be a builder because there are no neutral roles and one must be a builder in order to know that he or she is not a destroyer). These roles range all the way from the conspicuous formal leader to the legions of opportunities for inconspicuous, subtle, and informal leaders. The latter usually do not go down in history as the doers of great deeds. But their role is indispensable and the conspicuous formal leaders cannot function without their unremitting effort. The freer the institution and the more scope for autonomy and initiative given to individuals, as in the university, the more important is the role of the many informal leaders among all constituencies: students, faculty, alumni, trustees, and administration. Unless the predominant informal influence throughout these constituencies is from servant-leaders, builders, the formal leader is likely to be presiding over chaos—of which we have seen several conspicuous examples in recent years. The university must demonstrate that an institution with as much freedom and autonomy for individuals can steer a steadier course. Otherwise it will forfeit its opportunity to be a model builder for society, and other less free institutions that might emulate its example will certainly be discouraged to try.

This brings us to that critical aspect of realism that confronts the servant-leader, that of *order*. There must be some order because we know for certain that the great majority of people will choose some kind of order over chaos even if it is delivered by a brutal nonservant and even if, in the process, they lose much of their freedom. Therefore the servant-leader will beware of pursuing an idealistic path regardless of its impact on order. The big question is, what kind of order? This is the great challenge to the emerging generation of leaders: can they build better order?

Any older person who grew up in a period when values were more settled and the future seemed more secure will be disturbed by much he or she finds on close contact with young people today. But one firm note of hope comes through—loud and clear: we are at a turn of history in which young people are growing up faster, and some extraordinarily able, mature, servant-disposed men and women are emerging in their early and middle twenties. The percentage may be small; and, again, it may be larger than we think. And it is not an elite; it is all sorts of exceptional people. Most of them could be ready for some large society-shaping responsibility by the time they are thirty *if* they are encouraged to prepare for leadership as soon as their potential as builders is identified, which is possible for many of them by age eighteen or twenty. Preparation to lead need not be at the expense of vocational or scholarly preparation, but it must be the first priority. And it may take some difficult bending of resources and some unusual initiative on the part of these young people to accomplish all that should be accomplished in these critical years and give leadership preparation first priority. But whatever it takes, it must be done. For a while at least, until a better led society is assured, some other important goals should take a subordinate place.

All of this rests on the assumption that the only way to change a society (or just make it go) is to produce people, enough people, who will change it (or make it go). The urgent problems of our day— a senseless war, destruction of the environment, poverty, alienation, discrimination, overpopulation—are here because of human failure, individual failures, one person, one action at a time failures. Despite our massive education (or, alas, perhaps because of it) we are desperately short of talent everywhere. We will recover from this by growing people, one person at a time, people who have the goals, competence, values, and spirit to turn us about. We can and must turn about quickly and start solving problems faster than we create them. Large numbers of people in vast, complicated actions will be involved. But at the base it will be one person and one action at a time because there isn't anything else to work with. If we make it, and this is written in the belief that we will make it, the "system" will be whatever works best. The builders will find the useful pieces wherever they are, invent new ones when needed, all without reference to ideological coloration. "How do you get the right things done?" will be the watchword of the day—every day.

* * *

What is given here is a collection of short essays that seem to me to be relevant to the preparation of a servant to become a leader. These come from my own searching and experience and the suggestions of friends, including students. They are offered as a sharing with those who are young enough in spirit that they are still searching, and whose lifestyles may yet be shaped by conscious choices.

Five concluding observations seem important to me at the time of this writing:

- True servant-leaders are artists in the deep meaning of being open to chaos. In their own personal theologizing (and they all do it) they set a limit on the *logic of the spirit* and acknowledge a threshold beyond which all is mystery. They set this threshold closer to conscious reality than most "religious" people do. They may receive intimations, but they stand too much in awe of the mystery to carry their feeble logic beyond that threshold. Such people will listen both to the flower people and to the Birchers—not because it makes any particular sense in their rational consciousness to do so, but because *they* (the flower people and the Birchers) *are here*. And one does not ask why they are here because the answer to that question is beyond the threshold of the mystery where one does not ask. Who knows; if one *could* ask and get an answer that one could understand, their reasons for being here might be better than for most of us. It is a sobering thought. And it helps make one accepting of all conditions of people.
- Not much that is really important can be accomplished with coercive power. Headship, the holding of a titular position or possessing coercive power, is not at all synonymous with leadership. Some things individuals think they want, like the

Pyramids, can be built with coercive power. But, mostly, such power can destroy; it usually does not build things of ultimate importance to human beings. In an imperfect world we will probably have coercive power around for quite a while and everyone had best be wary lest he or she be coerced. In acknowledging the presence of coercion, we should also note that its value is inverse to its use. When our country *used* atomic power in a war when only we had it, we forfeited the opportunity to be influential in its use when several have it.

- Nothing much happens without a dream. For something great to happen, there must be a great dream.
- To refuse to examine the assumptions one lives by is immoral.
- In the end, all that matters is love and friendship.

TEACHER AS SERVANT

A Parable

Part 2

TEACHER AS SERVANT

Introduction

Teacher as Servant is a how-to-do-it book that describes the work of a university professor who cares deeply about the students of his university, not just those in his classes to whom he devotes the usual care of a conscientious teacher, but any students entering the university who respond to the suggestion that they become servants, and who are willing to invest a substantial share of their extracurricular time to developing their servant natures while they are in the university.

The story, while fictional, draws heavily on my observation of one university program that was very similar to the one described here. It was presided over by a dedicated faculty member who got himself installed as housemaster of a dormitory and, without extra compensation or other support, managed to wield a powerful influence on a group of students who responded to the servant idea. The work I observed is no longer there to be seen as a model. So we are left with the following fictional presentation of a dedicated professor who lived a good life by caring deeply about students, supported by my vivid memory of a fellow who, with the help of an equally dedicated and understanding wife, successfully did it.

In the course of consulting work with universities during my second career I was closely involved with radical students in the turbulent 1960s. I became convinced that the student complaints of that period were not irrational, misguided as some of their actions may have been (but who would have guided them?). Faculty had taken advantage of the shortage of teachers in the expansion after World War II to bargain down their obligations to teaching so that, come the 1960s, students had reason to feel that they were being used to provide pads from which teachers did their own things and students were being neglected. To be sure, teachers met their classes and graded their papers as required by their contracts. But adequate care of students requires much more than that. *Teacher as Servant* is an account of a professor who gave that much more care, and enjoyed a rich life in the doing of it.

My guess, confirmed by many soundings among university faculty and administrators, is that not more than one faculty member in 1,000 (of the half million or so faculty in postsecondary education) would seize the opportunity as the fictional Mr. Billings did. But if those 500 worked at it without extra compensation as Mr. Billings did over a substantial chunk of their careers, they could produce a flowering of high-serving people in the next generation that would make for a golden age of leadership. I believe that the joy of contributing to such an achievement would be immensely rewarding to the select 500 who take it on.

This fictional Mr. Billings is offered in support of the thesis that the ultimate test of the servant motive is what one does with one's optional time for which one is not paid. The strength of Mr. Billings's position in nurturing the servant motive in the students he influences is that he is not paid. He stands before them as a model of what he hopes they will become: true servants.

—ROBERT K. GREENLEAF

With gratitude for my mentors; those who, by their examples as servants and through their concern for my growth as a serving person, helped create this book.

Mary Ellicott Arnold
Eugene R. Bowen
N. Gordon Cosby
Donald J. Cowling
John Lovejoy Elliott
George W. Greenleaf
Gerald F. Heard
Oscar C. Helming
Abraham Joshua Heschel
D. Montgomery Reynolds
Oscar M. Taylor
Carolena Morse Wood

Prologue to the Parable

DO YOU WANT TO BE A SERVANT, Martin Hedeggar?

That question stopped me in my tracks ten years ago as I was about to enter the university. This book is an account of what happened when I said "yes." It was written now, when I am twenty-eight, because that decision profoundly influenced the course of my life. While much remains to unfold, I want to share the record of these past ten years while it is fresh in my mind and while, as I believe, it is still sharply relevant to what goes on in universities and how they might be made into the great institutions they have the opportunity to be.

I am a businessman, not a scholar or writer. I want only to pass on the substance of my experience to two groups who may be able to use some of it: young people who have a natural disposition to be servants and whose lifestyles may yet be shaped by conscious choices, and those of their elders who want to help young people to realize their potential as servants.

My experience has taught me two things that form the preface to this account:

For anything new to emerge *there must first be a dream*, an imaginative view of what might be. For something great to happen, there must be a great dream. Then venturesome persons with faith in that dream will persevere to bring it to reality.

Some ideas whose time has come will spread as in a forest fire. But most need the help of a teacher. I had the good fortune to have an extraordinary one. He dreamed a great dream of how servanthood could be nurtured in the young, and he spent his best years in bringing it to pass. I want to tell you about him.

I feel impelled to share my experience because it has given me a basis for hope that is not common among my contemporaries. Mine is not hope for a utopian or frustration-free society. My hope is rooted solely in the confidence that, as an individual person, I can be effective as servant in this world as it is: whether it seems absurd, brutal, and unjust; or beautiful, loving, and caring. And I see it both ways.

My confidence that I can be effective as servant in this world as it is anchors in my experience at Jefferson House during my four undergraduate years. The central figure in that experience was Professor of Physics Joseph D. Billings, who was housemaster of Jefferson House. Among his academic colleagues he had the reputation of a dedicated teacher, an adequate scholar, and a conscientious (if undistinguished) scientific contributor. Mr. Billings, as we knew him at Jefferson House, was a person with average charm and charisma. In working with us he was friendly, but reserved, and firm when it was called for. He led us but he did not dominate. He did not "teach" us to be servants or leaders or followers, but he stands tall as a model of all three and as a facilitator of our learning about them from our own experience.

Jefferson House is a place where students learn by doing. We discovered how to make such learning a lifelong process. As I reflect on it, the precious part is that we who participated in this experience came to feel it in our natures to love and to laugh and to live and work in community, and to reject the idea that our fellow humans are to be used, competed with, or judged. *Serve and be served by the present society* was the motto of Jefferson House. After four years of living intimately with this motto, *serve*, *lead*, and *follow*, as appropriate, became second nature to us.

And what do I mean by *servant*? As I use that word, it is not to be explicitly defined. If the record of my experience is read carefully, one will know what that word means to me.

Included in this book is what seems most important to me in the record of those four eventful years, a selection that may not be of equal interest to all readers. If one will read sections I, II, and VII, one will have the gist of it.

I. I Learn of Jefferson House

DO YOU WANT TO BE A SERVANT? This caption on a notice on the bulletin board caught my eye as I walked out of the university admissions office.

Do *I* want to be a servant? What a question to ask myself on the eve of my high school graduation and just having completed my registration to be admitted to the university in the fall. I quickened my steps as I walked down the hall.

Then something caught me and I stopped short. Do I want to be a servant? I became curious. What can this be about, and what is that notice doing in this place? I slowly turned back to satisfy my curiosity.

The first thing I noted was the signature at the bottom: Professor Joseph D. Billings (Physics), Housemaster of Jefferson House. A professor of physics asks me, do I want to be a servant? Then I read the notice slowly and carefully.

> Jefferson House is a dormitory that has been set aside for a special program for a selected group of seventy students, women and men, and about evenly divided among the four undergraduate years.
>
> The program of the house is not for credit and the students in it are from a wide range of academic interests. They share a common aim: they want to work together in acts of service, both for the immediate benefit of others and so that they can learn from experience how to be effective in serving, how to distinguish good service from poor service, and how to receive the service of others.
>
> Members of the house are urged to participate fully in the university community in a way that (1) they will enjoy the participation and (2) so that they will experience the university as a real-life situation in which they learn the skills of dealing with institutions and helping to make them effective *serving* institutions. Residents of Jefferson House view this university as offering the opportunity to prepare for the next chapter of their

experience in working with and within institutions—any sort of institution. *Serve and be served by* is our motto.

This is a disciplined undertaking, and residents of Jefferson House are asked to evaluate their commitment to the work of the house at the end of each school year as a condition for their readmission for the following year. Those applying for admission should view the obligation to the program as comparable to participation in a major sport. Those in the program are asked to give it first priority after their courses of study. Social life and other extracurricular activity will have reference to this first priority.

For further information, please ask for an appointment with Mr. Joseph D. Billings, Professor of Physics and housemaster of Jefferson House.

I read it slowly, again and again. Each time I read it more of the meaning came through. This was a thing in earnest. The notice was obviously designed to repel the casual and the undisciplined and to put a strong pull on those who were ready for a mature experience and a demanding opportunity. Not another notice remotely like this one was on the bulletin board.

I noted that out of 18,000 students there were places for seventy, probably a smaller number than would make a real try for the freshman football team. One could not do both, because Jefferson House would be first priority after one's program of courses.

It is curious, I thought, that only seventy out of 18,000 would be trying to learn, through participation in the life of this university, how to make it a more serving institution as explicit preparation for the next chapter of their lives where they would try to make other institutions more serving. I only dimly comprehended what this meant. The next chapter of my life was at least four years away, and I was under the impression that that was what my program of courses in the university would be designed for. But no, here in the work of Jefferson House I would be concerned, through my participation in the affairs of this university, to learn how to help make *this place* a more effective serving institution. Was there an implication that the university is *not* an effective servant now? If it is not, what am I doing here? It had never occurred to me that a university would *not* be an effective servant. I felt a little shaken by this line of thought. And I read the notice again.

After reading it about ten times I came back to the question at the top. Do you *want* to be a servant? The emphasis on the word *want* came through that time. I had the kind of upbringing that would not allow me to say *no*. But was I ready to say *yes*? There was nothing to do but to try to find Professor Billings. (Mr. Billings, the notice said, but the significance of that I learned later.)

Using the campus map, I found Jefferson House readily. No one was in the large, interestingly decorated living room but I heard a rustle of papers down the hall. There through an open door I saw a small office in considerable confusion, and sitting at a desk was a graying, slightly bald man of medium stature. He looked up with a smile. "Can I do anything for you?"

"I'm looking for Professor Billings," I said.

"I am Mr. Billings," he replied. "Come in," and he waved me to the only empty chair.

"I read the notice in the admissions office. What is this all about?" I asked bluntly.

"Well," he said slowly, "this is a dormitory where seventy women and men of all classes and all kinds of academic interest live At least in the fall I hope there will be seventy. One never knows. I am the housemaster, but I try not to be boss. I think of myself more as a leader. I try to be a servant-leader. That is something I am still learning. I count on the students to teach me about that. We do things together in the service of others. Some are simple things that we make with our own hands that others not as fortunate as we may need, things that they may not otherwise get. Here is a mathematical game that we make for elementary schools in this area. It may be commercially available at a reasonable price sometime, but it isn't yet. And it's an awfully effective learning device, Then, as individuals and in groups, we do specific things to help make this a better university—a more serving institution. Is there anything else I can tell you?"

It was not a sharp question. His was a gentle, friendly gaze. "Take your time," it said.

Now it was my turn, I thought. Why had I come here?

After some hesitation I said, "I read the notice and I gathered something like you said. But there is more to it. The notice said more than that."

He waited for me to go on, but I could not recall the notice nor could I frame a question.

Then he said slowly, "Yes, the notice said a great deal more than that. But that part is difficult to understand. In fact, if you should join this house, you may be graduated from here before you fully understand it. That is why I never know whether we can fill the house. And we must fill the house. The university lets us use the house this way only on the condition that we keep it filled. You see," and he spoke even more slowly, "the university does not sponsor this program; they only allow it."

"How does it happen to be, then?" I stammered.

"Because I want it to be," he said simply. "There are three priorities in my life: my family, which comes first, my teaching, and Jefferson House. While the house is third, I invest much of myself in it because part of me needs the nourishment that I find only in this house. In my teaching I try to serve only students who are interested in physics. In Jefferson House I try to serve students who are interested in serving—particularly in servant-leadership."

He fixed his gentle gaze on me and I knew then that I had to say something or leave. After waiting for me a few moments he said, "Here is a copy of the notice you read and here is my report to the university on what we did here last year. Although the university only allows this to go on, it does require an accounting. When you have read these and thought about it some more, if you are still interested, please come back and see me again."

I thanked him and left. As I walked downtown to the bus I thought about the new obligation imposed on me by reading that bulletin board notice—the obligation to decide. I did not expect this kind of problem so soon after registering for the university.

In a few days I went back to Professor Billings's office. I was bothered by the notion of being in a "servant" program. But something in me would not let me decide to turn it down.

"It is good to see you again," was his cheerful greeting of recognition. "How have you made out with your plans?"

"I have some questions," I said. "There are several arrangements listed in the university catalogue where course credit is given for supervised experience. Why is the work in Jefferson House not in that category?"

"I told you that this work was allowed but not supported by the university. I have never asked that this be considered a part of the academic program. I suspect that, if I should ask, I would be turned down. But I have not asked because I would prefer that it *not* be given academic credit. My reason for this is that I believe that what we have to do and learn in this house is best done without the motivation of academic credit. In my teaching in the Department of Physics I accept the role of credentialing. I don't see how the academic establishment could function without it. But in this house we have a different mission. Credentialing would not be useful.

"The question asked on the notice you read was, do you want to be a *servant?* One does not want to be a servant for any kind of external recognition. The motivation is intrinsic. Let me put it bluntly: we could not build the kind of community we have in this house if credit seeking were the motivation. We want only those who have a natural disposition to serve and who respond to the opportunity to work in a sharing program with others of like disposition so that they will become more effective as servants—so that, if they wish, they may become servant-leaders, and so that their future experience will be enriched.

"In the course of a year many people from outside the university will be invited to meet with us and share their wisdom and experience. None of them will be paid. We invite only those who are sufficiently interested in what we are doing that they will give of themselves and their time.

"You have asked a question that many ask. You will find some who have been in the house for several years who still ask it. But I have a vision for this house as a place that nurtures the disposition to serve which some students bring with them when they enter here.

We want only those who will work hard, without the incentive of grades and credits, to build the competence to be effective in serving, especially within the structures of our present institutions. That's a long answer to your question and it isn't easy for one to understand who has come to regard the university as a place where almost all effort is paid for in academic credits. But you said you had several questions. What else can I tell you about Jefferson House?"

"I would like to come. I don't have any other questions," was all I could say. Professor Billings gave me an application form, which I filled out right there.

In a few days I received a warm letter of acceptance from Professor Billings. In the intervening months between then and when I arrived on campus in the fall I occasionally dismissed thinking about Jefferson House by assuring myself that I wouldn't understand it until I got involved. But I had a good feeling about my decision to become a part of it.

My First Evening at Jefferson House

THERE WAS AN INFORMAL GATHERING in the large com-
mon room of Jefferson House that *first* evening after my arrival as an
entering freshman, and I will long remember it. Most were returning, but among those from the three upper classes were a few who
were also new. There was, at the start, much of the lively greeting
that would be expected among those who are old friends. Professor
Billings was circulating, sharing the greetings. In a few minutes,
seemingly without any signal from anyone, people began to settle
into chairs and on the floor in a big circle and the talking stopped.
Professor Billings took a chair inside the circle.

"Welcome to all of you," he said. "I don't have a welcoming
speech, and I believe that the old residents here can give a better
introduction to what goes on in this house than I can."

One of the obvious old-timers spoke up. "I suppose those who
are new would like to know about that."

"Why don't you tell them, Jeff?" Professor Billings said.

"Well, what you have all read gives you the essence," he said.
"This is a university dormitory and we operate under the same rules
as other dormitories. These rules are posted by the office door. But
we differ from other dormitories in that we were all initially selected
by Mr. Billings as being those who, among the applicants, would
both profit from and contribute to the program of Jefferson House.
At the end of each year each of us makes a formal written evaluation
of his or her individual performance as a participating member of
this house. Each of us is asked to discuss this evaluation with five others and to summarize their comments at the conclusion of the evaluation. A few people drop out voluntarily in this process every year.
The evaluations are then reviewed by a committee of seniors, which
has the final decision. Very seldom is anyone denied the opportunity
to return if he or she wants to. But occasionally the committee will
stipulate some conditions. This house is not for everybody, but most
of those who would not either contribute or benefit do not apply in
the first place.

"The rest of the students on this campus do not pay much
attention to us as a group but they are certainly aware of us as indi-

viduals because our level of participation in just about everything but major sports is well above average. The percentage of leadership positions held by upperclassmen in this house is several times our percentage of the total student body. What we learn about leadership in this house is carried by us into nearly every campus activity. What goes on in the projects, important as it is, is only a small part of the leadership, serving, and organizational experience of those of us who live here. Living here generates an uncommon alertness to serve by leading on this campus.

"Three major kinds of group activity go on here. First, we engage in service projects together. We differ from community service clubs in that we don't serve by giving money. We may use some money in what we do, but we serve mostly with our own energies. Some things we make with our own hands, like the mathematical teaching game for elementary schools that you've probably heard about. Then we do things of direct benefit to the university or to the community. We review everything we do. We try to find out whether the effort really helped and whether we made the best use of our time and money. We spend a lot of time trying to learn, and we learn a lot of good common sense in the process.

"The second major activity is participating with the guests who come here one or two times a week—mostly invited by Mr. Billings. These are people who make a short talk and join us in discussion. These are usually limited to one hour and they give this house a very unusual flavor. And, as you probably know, none of them is paid. They come because they believe in what goes on in this house and they want to serve by sharing with us. In the course of a year they make quite an impact on us.

"The third major activity here is that we take an unusual responsibility for the university and everything that goes on here. We came here because the university is set up to serve our educational needs. But it is an institution of fallible people and it needs our help too. There are plenty of critics, and they have their place. We try to spot those places where the university can do better and we think about how we can help. Then we do what we can do with our own effort. And we spend time analyzing and learning from that effort. Not everything we try to do succeeds. Sometimes I think we learn about as much from our failures as from our successes. Former members of this house come back and share with us their experience in the next stage of their careers and they tell us that what they learned here not only makes them more effective in dealing with the problems of other institutions (and they all have problems) but that life is much more interesting. As I encounter others on this campus who just bitch about things, I am sure that my life on this campus has been more interesting because I got caught up early in the spirit of working with Jefferson House members in doing something about the things that we feel will make this a better university."

"Well put," I heard another upperclassman say when Jeff concluded his statement.

"Thanks, Jeff," said Mr. Billings, "you said that better than I could say it. Anybody else have anything to say to help us get started off—something from the experienced ones that would help the newcomers? Mary?"

"What Jeff has said is an excellent statement of what we are up to in Jefferson House," Mary said. "However, *how* we do it is, to me, just as important—maybe more so—as what we do. This is a kind of community. It is not a love feast. We have lots of disagreement. Some of it gets unpleasant. But we work it out so life goes on.

"Part of how we do it is Mr. Billings. If you were in a freshman course over in the Physics Department, he would probably be called Professor Billings. If you were a senior major in a small seminar with him, you might call him Joe. But over here he is Mr. Billings—make no mistake about that.

"For a while I resented that. But after three years in this house I not only accept it, I like it. The success of this house (and it is successful for the great majority of us) is in part due to the total rightness of Mr. Billings's role here. And part of it is that he is *Mr.* Billings. He is not one of us. And he is not here as a professor—although I suspect that anybody in his role should be a member of the faculty.

"Although his title is housemaster, and he is responsible to the university for what happens here, he is inclined to say that he is not the boss; he is a leader. Not *the* leader (we all think we're leaders). But *a* leader, a particular kind of leader.

"You may already have heard him say that he is trying to be a servant-leader, and that we are teaching him. That isn't just a put-on or a ploy. I believe that he is able to lead us in this situation only because *he really wants to learn from us.* He often won't answer our questions (when we suspect that he really could give a good answer) because he feels that it is more important for us to go through the struggle to find the right answer than it is to find it. When we are wrestling with a problem he will make his input on a par with ours, and he can be about as spirited and persistent an arguer as anybody I know, but he is likely to do that only when his opinion is accepted as if he were one of us. If we are about to set off on something that he thinks is patently foolish, he will tell us so. And if we collide (as we sometimes do) with a rule of the university that he is bound to uphold, he can be as stern a law and order man as you will ever encounter.

"Part of the opportunity here is to study his role and to learn from it—not that we are trying to be just like he is, but because we can better understand how to be effective in a leadership role *if* we understand how someone else does it. There is a lot more about what we do here that will come out as the year progresses. My three years in this house have been three very different years. I can't prove it, but I believe that Mr. Billings's leadership has had something to do with each year's being different."

"Thank you, Mary," said Mr. Billings. "I think you understand me better than I understand myself. But, then, that is very likely to be the case with all of us. We listen carefully to one another in order to better understand ourselves. You are very generous, though. I make mistakes like everybody else. And mistakes are part of what we learn from. One of our visitors from a large business once told about the preeminent developer of managers in his company. He said that one of the secrets of this man's extraordinary record as a grower of people was that he believed that the most important lessons of the managerial art are learned from error and from suffering the conse-quences. This mentor believed this so thoroughly that if one of his promising young understudies was getting along too smoothly he would lead him deliberately into a contrived error. Then he would quietly ask him what he had learned. Error was never the occasion for a reprimand (unless it was repeated too often). It was always grasped as a learning opportunity. I do not deliberately commit, nor do I contrive errors for other people. Somehow both I and the rest of you find ourselves in enough error for our purposes. But it is important that you not look at me as some kind of model. I am carrying a role in what I hope is a normal human way, as I hope the rest of you are.

"Is there any other comment from those with experience in the house? Susan?"

"I think," said Susan, "it is important that newcomers should know that while we regard what goes on here as a 'disciplined' as opposed to a 'casual' undertaking, none of us is required to do anything, aside from behaving in a way that does not offend or interfere with others. A lot goes on here, but none of it is required activity of any of us. Some things start that are dropped because not enough people want to participate. About the only thing that happens is that Mr. Billings quietly asks how come we launch into something that nobody wants to do. 'What do we learn from this?' is a question that you will hear a lot in this place.

"There are guests here one or two evenings a week. The attendance will vary considerably depending on what else is going on and how the members of the house respond to the way the guest is billed. Sometimes I think Mr. Billings is embarrassed by poor attendance. But that does not seem to daunt him. I have sometimes wondered what he would do if we all just lost interest in what goes on here. What would you do, Mr. Billings?"

"Oh, I suppose," he said reflectively as he smiled and looked at the ceiling, "that I would begin by asking why. There would be a reason and I would try to get it out." (There was a general chuckle at this remark because "What do we learn from this?" was such a frequent question.) "But if I reached the conclusion that I could not function in a way that a worthwhile group endeavor resulted, I would take counsel with myself and my friends and see what other work I should be doing to help this be a better university—to serve its students better. If this house is not the thing I should be working on, there must be something else. I would be keenly disappointed if I failed to keep this house a viable thing. But I would survive. I would find another way to serve this university and its students, and I would be happy doing it."

Susan continued. "All of us who have been here before know it, but the newcomers ought to know how Mr. Billings happens to be in this role. We know that the university only allows this to go on—it really doesn't support this house. You aren't paid. It doesn't help your career as a professor of physics. Tell us again why you are doing this."

"It is a simple story," replied Mr. Billings. "As an undergraduate, I attended a university that was organized around the house plan, with a housemaster in each house. The master of my house was a classics scholar, an interest quite different from mine. But he was a great spirit and dedicated to the growth as persons of the students in his house. The simple idea that he imparted to me was that service was the key to a fulfilled life. He quoted on occasion that line from Mark in the New Testament: 'Whoever would be great among you must be your servant.' It was a very deep conviction with him and four years of his influence so shaped my own image of myself that I believed that, if one has a career in a university, the greatest opportunity one has with students is to pass on the tradition of serving. When my opportunity came to join the faculty of this university, where this is not in the structure, I ultimately found a way to start this work. In a way it has been a much greater challenge (and I think a more rewarding experience) to carry on this work here, somewhat without the encouragement of the culture, than it would have been had my teaching opportunity come in my old university or one like it. The simple answer to your question is that I am doing this work because I *have* to do it, for my own fulfillment as a person. My old mentor was fond of saying that the ultimate test of servanthood is that those being served, *by the way they are served*, ultimately become disposed themselves to be servants.

"We have heard from the veterans of the house," said Mr. Billings. "What have the newcomers to say? Martin," he said, responding to my raised hand.

I said that I didn't have a comment but I would like to hear discussed how the house decides what service it will undertake and what it wants to contribute to the university.

"Who wants to speak to that? Ron?"

"An interesting part of this house," said Ron, "is that we have no formal organization, we elect no officers, there are no procedures, we write no reports—except on our summer work after our junior year, the annual evaluation that each of us makes of our work in this house, and the one that Mr. Billings makes to the administration. We meet here a lot and we talk a lot and we are challenged by the many visitors who come. We speak of the house as having a program, but in the sense of writing down a list of things that make a program, we don't have one. We have an aim, which Jeff outlined earlier. The program is what we get together to do as a result of initiatives taken by individuals. These activities are focused by our aim, which is very clear to all of us. Because of the screening that we all passed through when Mr. Billings admitted us we are service-oriented people. We find our fulfillment in action that serves other people (including the university).

"We are not an 'encounter' or 'sensitivity' or other 'introspective' or 'human potential' group. You can be a very private person in this house. We interact a lot and there is some criticism of each other but it is all related to service, which is our common aim, our reason for being here. Our common bond is that we want to be effective servants and we want to learn how to grow in stature as servants through the work that we undertake together. By the time you are a senior you will learn from the many visitors who come here what a vast opportunity there is to serve in this society, how difficult much of it is to do, and how exacting the preparation to do it well is. This is by way of preface to an answer to your question about how we decide what we undertake because, as was mentioned earlier, we are not the collegiate equivalent of a community service club—we are undertaking what we do only partly for the value to others of the service rendered. Equal in importance to that is our continuous growth in our capacity to serve and to learn a conscious growth strategy, one that will carry us on through a long term of experience after we leave here. We are not thinking of what we do here as complete preparation. We are working to start a process that will stay with us over a life span. And we are not preparing for some idealistic future utopian society. We are learning to be effective as servants in whatever situation we find ourselves—beginning with this one right here in this university.

"When you get caught up in this kind of thinking, and with the stimulation of what goes on here, you will begin to get ideas of things you would like to do—in cooperation with some of us. This is not a place for loners. There is a lot of good work done here and elsewhere by loners. But here in this big university, and in the big world you will graduate into, the most effective servants are those who can persuade others to go with them and who have learned to work in teams."

"That's right," Jeff continued, "Jefferson House is a good place to learn this because everybody here gets ideas and tries to persuade others. Nobody is a pushover. The competition is keen. But it is important to learn to be a good follower as well as to be a leader—when that is right for you. So don't be surprised if, for a while at least, you find yourself going along with somebody else's idea. And some people here conclude, after four years, that they are effective as servants but that, for the most part, they do better at following than at leading. If that is the right judgment for a person, this is a good place to work it out. But not many of us reach that conclusion. At the end of four years most of us are effective leaders.

"Occasionally something gets started here that is a bell ringer. The mathematical game we have been building here is one of these. Year before last a senior mathematics major in this house was working with a new math project in the local elementary schools. He invented this game and persuaded some of us to help him make it and teach its use. It continues to be a major house project in which several of us are deeply involved.

"Within the university last year a group of us took on the food service. It is probably no better or no worse than the usual university food service, but a few of us began to study modern nutritional knowledge and concluded that the food offering could be vastly improved at no additional cost. At least, we felt, the option ought to be available for students who are sensitive to the importance of good nutrition.

"This project, again, was originated by one of our members who made a long, uphill, persuasive struggle to get enough of us with her to make this a feasible thing for us to undertake. Quite apart from the issue of good nutrition, we have learned more about bureaucratic inertia out of this one than any other project we have undertaken while I have been here. Pessimists should take notice that if we can put this over (and I think we will), anything is possible in this world.

"Part of the value of this house is that, with the exception of Mr.

Billings's role, we proceed without an overall formal structure. There are always several ad hoc structures that are carrying on the active projects. But the tenure of any one of these is not certain because it is always possible to displace one with a new one. Part of Mr. Billings's influence, you will find, is to check us from doing this too fast and thus diminish the potential learning in what we undertake. This house is really an open political system with a servant-leader who gives it continuity and works to optimize the learning for all of us. Its success (and it has been successful) rests largely on the depth and durability of the servant motivation that brought us here and our willingness as individuals to keep the learning aim always in mind—partly to make this a productive experience for all of us while we are here and partly to establish and clarify the learning motivation so that it will withstand the buffetings that we all know are in store for us in the future."

Another student interrupted at this point and asked, "Aren't you understating what some of us here do as individuals?"

There was a quick rejoinder by another who asserted, "But that is not the value of this house. We can all do things on our own, but some of us need to learn to work together in groups. That is hard for some of us to learn."

"If we have any distinction," Ron continued, "in how we go about doing things together, I believe that it is the acceptance of a good deal of silence in our deliberations. If we get in a jam when we are discussing something, by tradition we sit quietly for a while or we adjourn and take it up again. And we don't vote to decide things. Those who want to do something together just go and do it.

"One of the questions frequently asked of us is, 'How do you find the time to do all of this and still maintain the academic standing that most of you have?' The answer to that is simple: if you live in this house and survive, you have to learn to be good time managers and avoid being time wasters. And it becomes second nature to us to find the time to do what is important to us. Most of what goes on here is important. We have to make some hard choices."

"That was a great statement, Ron, and thank you for it," said Mr. Billings. "We are nearing the time that this session should close. Are there any other quick observations? Yes, Irene."

"I was struck by the cogency of Ron's statement and the others. There is one aspect of what he said that might be elaborated a bit. He said that we are not an 'encounter' or 'sensitivity' group. It should be noted for newcomers that there are a lot of these activities on this campus and elsewhere. We are not picking a quarrel with people who do this. They are seeking the same things we are: fulfillment, wholeness, a sense of belonging. We simply find these values in service to others and we have no need to try to apprehend them by means that are separated from the normal course of living and interacting with people as we do our work. We are trying to make life whole through the process of learning—in action, dealing with real things, by serving. And, in the course of this we hope to learn to be served by the present society—because *we need to be served*. We believe that if we learn to serve this university well, we will see more clearly how this society and others we may be involved with in the future can serve our legitimate needs, psychic and material. *Serve and be served by* is our motto.

"But before we close, some further mention should be made of the requirement that Ron alluded to, that is, the absolute condition that if one is to enter this house in one's senior year, the summer before must be spent on an approved (by Mr. Billings) assignment which is fully reported. As we go along you will be aware that one of the central concerns of this house is that if one is to serve effectively, especially if one is to be a servant-leader, one must understand and learn to deal with the issue of power. At the close of our junior year each of us is expected to spend the summer in a close relationship with someone who is wielding considerable power. Sometimes these are paid jobs. But sometimes the best opportunities cannot or will not pay a salary, and one of Mr. Billings's good works is to raise enough money so that stipends can be provided by the house in those cases where the student needs the income but the best opportunity is not a paid job. Another absolute requirement is that one send in a journal account at the end of each week during the summer assignment. In the course of the year each senior in the house will have an evening in which the experience of the summer is reviewed from that journal."

A freshman asked, "How many of these reports will we hear this year?"

"About fifteen," Irene answered. "And they will cover a wide range of experiences. There is a by-product from these summer internships in that a solid support for this house has evolved out of this work. There are now several people who wield considerable power who will take one of us on as a summer assistant. Some of these people pay a stipend, or contribute money to the fund to finance opportunities where stipends aren't paid, and they come here and spend an occasional evening with us discussing matters of mutual concern.

"For those of you who are new, this emphasis on the issue of power may sound strange in relation to the primary service motive of this house. But by the time you are seniors I believe that you will not only understand the place of power, its use and abuse, but you will begin to feel comfortable about dealing on equal terms with holders and wielders of power and venturing into a career will not seem as formidable as I know it does to many who have not shared our experience in this house. By the time you graduate from here you will have had the opportunity to listen to about sixty reports from the summer internships which each of us spends working closely with someone who holds and uses considerable power."

One of the seniors interrupted. "One of the people most interested in this house is the president of a large business in another part of the country. He takes on one of us juniors every summer to work as his personal assistant—and he later hires some of them permanently. He comes here at least once every year and spends an evening with us. And he contributes generously to the support of the house.

"I mention him because I believe I have learned more from him than from any other visitor—and we have a lot of good ones. He comes through as a tough, aggressive, high achiever and a successful person. What makes him effective here is that he really has sorted out the issue of power and he is very realistic about what is required to be a servant in this highly organized and very competitive society. Some people are put off by the word *servant*. It connotes soft dogooding to many and a lot of people who ought to be in this house are turned off by the word. But here, at the head of this large company, is a fellow as hard as nails who has thought it all through and can communicate what he believes a servant has to be if he is to be a constructive influence. By the time we have had three sessions with him in our junior year, half the group wants to spend the summer with him. If Mr. Billings would let him, he would hire all who want to come. But Mr. Billings says no (and I think he's right), only one can go.

"I mention this because I think it is important for newcomers to know that, to us, being a servant is real. It is real in several important dimensions that I want to note briefly. First, of course, servants, to us, are not fuzzy idealists. They are very practical and able people who carry out important leadership roles. They are doing imaginative things to make this a better world. And they are performing as we can learn to perform."

Irene spoke again. "Two further comments. You will learn by living here that dreams are important—both those that come in sleep and those that come in various states of reverie. There are very meaningful silences among us. And we learn to pause in our debates and discussions so that the creative processes that bring fresh insights can take over. We are not alone in this world with nothing but cold, hard logic. Part of the real nature of the servant role that evolves here is that it builds up the wholeness of the person. It is reassuring to believe, as many of us here do, that if one is willing to take the risk and venture, when the path ahead is not clear, that, in the heat of the situation, the imaginative insights that justify one's having taken the risk will be forthcoming.

"Finally, one important aspect of this house deserves mention. After three years here I am impressed that one of the notable differences between this house and the rest of the campus is the quality of the laughter. We have times of uproarious hilarity, but you can find that anywhere. Here we laugh at our mistakes (and we make plenty), and we laugh at our common predicaments (which are many), and we laugh when we comfort each other in pain. I do not know how this came to be in the tradition of this house or why we are so different in this regard, but we are. Laughter is a part of our way of life."

"Thank you, Irene, and the others who commented. I am glad for the feeling that we are off to another good start in Jefferson House. We get right into motion with our first guest tomorrow night. A prominent attorney, Mrs. Florence McLean, will be with us to discuss her experience in what has come to be called public interest law. Whether or not you have any aspirations for the law as a profession, I believe you will find what she has to share of considerable significance for our work here.

"One further comment before we close. Reference has been made to the requirement for the summer after the junior year in which, among other things, a journal is to be kept. I suggest that journal keeping has been an important part of the experience in Jefferson House for many people. It is easy for some and hard for others but important for all who do it. You might consider starting a journal on this evening's discussion. A great deal has been said that will be well for newcomers to ponder on. A good journal account of it while it is fresh in your minds may serve you well. Good night."

I Begin My Journal

I WILL ALWAYS BE GRATEFUL for the suggestion that a journal would be an important part of this experience because, on the way to my room after that first evening at Jefferson House, I resolved that I would immediately endeavor to record this first meeting. I worked on it far into the night and it enables me now, ten years later, to reconstruct this first evening, and the events that led up to it, as if all of it had just happened. I am grateful that in high school I studied shorthand, because, after that first evening, I have a near verbatim record.

As I review my journal and start to write this account, it does not seem ten years have passed because those early experiences are still so vivid. Yet what has transpired in those ten years—a pattern of life that started on that first memorable evening when the students themselves gave the down-to-earth image of what Jefferson House is about—has given me a solid base for a serving career that is the envy of my present associates.

I majored in political science as an undergraduate, and then I completed a master's program in administration. For six years now I have been making my way in a large business that is based in a major city. I have a happy marriage with a woman who is the light of my life, and we have two wonderful daughters.

I have given this much of an account of where I am now so that you will understand the perspective from which I view the events in my experience at Jefferson House that have set the course of my life so firmly. Beginning with the first night, I became a dedicated journal keeper, and in those four years it ran to many volumes. Much of it, in retrospect, is trivia. And it is not my intention now to write my autobiography from it. My reason for writing this now at age twenty-eight is that I still consider myself as contemporary with today's undergraduates, and yet I am also well into my career. What I want to do here is to reconstruct the main events of my four years at Jefferson House so that the reader will see how this helped to get me launched into my career. I want to do this in a way that will be useful to three groups of people.

1. There are those students now in colleges and universities who do not have access to programs like the one that Jefferson House offered. They may be able to construct something for themselves that will help guide them to a more confident future than many of them now foresee. From that first night at Jefferson House I never had any doubts about my being on my way. The ultimate destination was not clear; it isn't clear now. But, beginning with the first evening, the structure that Mr. Billings provided at Jefferson House gave me a needed security at age eighteen and I began to learn to be comfortable with moving into the unknown with confidence. Darkness does not scare me. I am hoping that, by what I write here, I can give some guidance to those who will have to make it more on their own.

2. I am confident that among the half million or so faculty members in American colleges and universities there are at least 500—one in a thousand who have a value system like Mr. Billings has but who did not have the benefit, in their formative years, of seeing a true servant-leader in action. I want to give enough of a view of how he looked at Jefferson House so that those in whom such a motivation can be awakened will feel the urge to get with it and serve students in these terribly important ways that Mr. Billings demonstrated. If 500 faculty members who are servants at heart could only know the wonderful life Mr. Billings leads as housemaster of Jefferson House, and the fulsome psychic rewards that are his, and if they would do as he does— with no resources given to him, with just his will and his spirit—the times of the next generation could flower into a golden age of leadership. I am not asking that self-serving people (of whom there are plenty) be turned into servants, or that scarce university resources be diverted into new programs. All that I am asking is that members of faculties who are disposed to be servants, who get their greatest joy out of serving, seize the opportunity and use some of their own time and money and, perhaps, sacrifice some academic achievement, as Mr. Billings did. The rewards, I assure you, are enormous.

3. I hope to reach with what I relate here those legions of people who are strategically placed, in our many institutions of business, church, government, and philanthropy, who will do as many do who cooperate with Jefferson House: find ways to help establish and support adjunct programs in colleges and universities for the service of young people whose undergraduate years may be profoundly influenced by an apprenticeship with a trusted servant-leader.

Working from my journal in which those memorable four years come vividly alive every time I turn my mind to them (which is often) I will endeavor to reconstruct just enough of the highlights of this experience so that my account will serve these three groups as well as any other reader who may be stimulated to use his or her opportunities to help in the education of the young—especially those who have the potential to serve and to lead.

A Life View Emerges

MY ACCOUNT WILL HAVE MORE COHERENCE if I first summarize a point of view about myself and my career that evolved during the four years in Jefferson House. I will follow this with a quite full account of the evening sessions with two guests of the house who, along with the key people in the company I now work for, and who are described later, were most influential in shaping my own perspective. Then I will summarize the reports of five students, including myself, who describe their internships the summer after their junior year.

As I have told you, I majored in political science and this gave me a better view of the contemporary world than most undergraduates had. And, with it all, I emerged with a perspective that, while far from finished, provides the basis for what I want to share now.

When I entered college I saw society as an entity—something "out there." It was an impersonal thing. I was detached from it and referred to it as "it." Now I see it as, what they call in mechanics, a resultant of the interacting thrusts and positions of every being on this earth. Most people band together in groups for certain purposes: nations, states, cities, neighborhoods, churches, businesses, schools, clubs, gangs—legions of them, large and small. But these too are merely the resultants, out in space, of the thrusts and positions of individuals. There are instruments called corporations, but they are merely pieces of paper locked in a safe. As Chief Justice John Marshall said of them in an early landmark case (1819): "A corporation is an artificial being, invisible, intangible, and existing only in contemplation of law."

It seems an elementary point, but it is very basic, and it took me nearly four years to arrive at it. I finally came to see that there is nothing in this world but beings like me, and it is the obligation of all who think of themselves as responsible to act so as to optimize their own constructive personal influences. And I came to see the problems of the world as not so much the result of the work of destructive and harmful people (granting there are plenty of them) as they are the consequences of the neglect of the so-called good people who are capable of exerting a constructive influence. Too many of the good people are not diligent in searching for opportunities to be effective, they do not prepare themselves to be of optimum service, and they do not persevere with spirit. Too much of the effort of the so-called good people goes into trying to reform someone else or into tilting at abstractions like "the system"; and not enough energy goes into positive actions and services that become part of the forces that help that abstract resultant called society to be as serving to all people as it can be.

Then I concluded that ours is an institution-bound country. Aside from artists, writers, craftspersons, and the like who still make their contributions through their dedicated aloneness, there are few legitimate roles for individuals who work alone. Most opportunities for constructive service are in and through institutions—businesses, governments, churches, schools, hospitals, social agencies. And I do not believe that society-nurturing institutions like churches, schools, and foundations have yet accepted this. They are still trying to help individuals to perform as lone workers and there is very little evidence of effort to prepare people to be effective in institutions. I resolved, on graduation, to try to do something about those in the society-nurturing institutions who are performing so poorly. They, of all the people who should be serving and leading, are failing us.

In our hero worship we have made a fetish of individualism— the lone person who stands against society. In truth, I believe, most could be held to a higher level of ethical aspiration through involvement in institutions than they are likely to achieve alone. There is a place for the lone idealists, but their servant-leadership will have much greater influence if they become institution builders and take their stand for ethical quality within those institutions where it will have the effect of supporting the performance of large numbers who otherwise might falter. I have cast my lot with institution building.

I saw myself on graduation, and continue to see myself, as an unfinished, seeking person. I don't ever expect to conclude that I have found it. The zest in life for me is in seeking and growing. Accomplishment is important, of course. But I know that sustained accomplishment will come only as seeking and growing are my prime concerns. This leads me to accept a very difficult idea: that in growth there is likely to be a measure of failure; not so much failure that life is a net loss and one is overcome by it, but enough that one knows what failure is, and has compassion for the failing persons one sees around oneself all the time. One must learn those lessons that are best learned in suffering from and overcoming the shock of failure. This I learned in Jefferson House because I was involved in projects that failed; I failed personally and suffered from it; and I watched Mr. Billings when he made the usual human mistakes and let us watch his suffering and his recovery.

II. Guest Speakers Add Perspective

IN THE COURSE OF MY FOUR YEARS at Jefferson House we must have had a hundred visitors from a wide range of experience. Most of them gave a talk and answered questions. In selecting two to present to you here, it was difficult to make a choice. These are two quite different themes, which give a good sample of the kinds of thinking we had the opportunity to share.

By the time I became a resident of Jefferson House its work was widely known and it had many dedicated supporters. All who came to speak and share came without fee and at their own expense. Some contributed money to support the house and some offered summer internships.

Mr. Billings was very open about it all. "I give my time and some money," he once said. "If others are interested in what we are doing, it is their opportunity to do the same. Most of those who come here as visitors feel quite rewarded. They feel as I do; it is a privilege to serve a group like this."

Mr. Billings's attitude stood in sharp contrast to the policy of the university, which brought occasional "big name" speakers at large fees. We at Jefferson House attended some of these lectures but rarely did they have the impact on us that the relatively unknown speakers had who came to us at their own expense and with no fee. Usually ours were not polished speakers. Sometimes we had difficulty connecting with them. But one thing we knew: there was a bond of common purpose over which a subliminal communication was apt to flow. The "big name" speakers who talked to large university audiences were seen by most of us as entertainment. The university seemed to have no purpose that related them to us.

Education and Maturity

DR. BRODERICK, a psychiatrist who came to speak to us, left some of us puzzled. Not until I transcribed my notes and read the record of the evening carefully did I feel that I understood him. His talk was substantial, but only one question was asked of him. His answer to that question revealed why Mr. Billings had invited him to come and talk to us. Here are my verbatim notes. (As I mentioned earlier, I am glad that I learned shorthand in high school because his talk was so condensed—every word was needed.)

* * *

Maturity has many meanings, especially when applied to people. But in my own association there is a strong link between the word *maturity* and the word *becoming*. Education, in particular a liberal education, can be a powerful maturing force. Depth of meaning about the process of maturing emerges only out of experience. This, briefly, is the framework within which I shall try to deal with the subject of education and maturity.

I do not have a how-to-do-it formula for achieving maturity to hand you. My sole aim is to encourage you to be thoughtful about your problem of finding the meaning of maturity in your own lives and the times you live in. Because we are all different, the problem will be different for each of us. The common ground I shall try to find is a way of thinking about the meaning of maturity.

The most important lesson I have learned about maturity is that the emergence, the full development, of what is uniquely *me* should be an important concern throughout my entire life. There are many other important concerns but this particular one must never be submerged, never be out of sight.

This I learned the hard way. There was a long "wilderness" period in which I sought resources outside myself. I looked for an "answer" to the normal frustrations of life (frustration used in the sense of the blocking of motives to which one cannot make a constructive response). Good years went by. No answers came. It took a long time for me to discover that the only real answer to frustration is to concern myself with the drawing forth of what is uniquely me. Only as what is uniquely me emerges do I experience moments of true creativity, moments which, when deeply felt, temper the pain of long periods of frustration that are the common lot of most of us and give us the impulse and the courage to act constructively in the outside world.

Every life, including the most normal of the normal, is a blend of experiences that build ego strength and those that tear it down. As one's responsibilities widen, these forces become more powerful. As good a definition as I know is that maturity is the capacity to withstand the ego-destroying experiences and not lose one's perspective in the ego-building experiences.

But this takes a special view of the self. The sustaining feeling of personal significance is important. It comes from the inside. I am not a piece of dust on the way to becoming another piece of dust. I am a unique instrument of creation, unlike any that has ever been or ever will be. So is each of you. No matter how badly you may be shaken, no matter how serious the failure or how ignominious the fall from grace, by accepting and learning you can be restored with greater strength. Don't lose this basic view of who you are.

A friend of mine once said of his four-year-old son, "His world is a six-foot sphere. He's in the center of it and moves it around with him wherever he goes."

The conventional view is that this is youthful egocentricity and that one grows out of it as one matures, as one becomes social and accepts responsibility. I would rather say that there is a transmutation as one matures. One is still at the center of one's world. (How could one be unique and be otherwise?) But with maturity one's world becomes the limitless sphere of people, ideas, and events that each of us influences by each thought, word, and deed; and each of us is in turn open to receive influence. The individual capacity of each of us to influence and be influenced and to absorb the shocks— this capacity is in proportion to the emergence of the sentient person, the drawing forth of what is uniquely us. This is an important idea to keep as your own private lamp when somebody undertakes to grind you down—as they surely will sometime, if you have not been aware of it already.

This, as I see it, is the central idea of maturity: to keep your private lamp lighted as you venture forth on your own to meet with triumph or disaster or just plain routine. And this is what a liberal education is about, because this is what life is about. If, in your college years, you learn nothing other than the importance of knowing who you are, that you have a private lamp, your stay here will have been amply justified.

The notion of uniqueness will bear some exploration. I will leave to the theologians the speculation as to whether part of what is uniquely a person is inherently evil. I prefer to say: whatever it is, draw it forth and face it; then make something creative and good out of it. Oscar Wilde has left for us the observation, "Every saint has a past, every sinner has a future."

We are all conditioned by the culture in which we have lived, more than we can ever know. So many of the conflicts of the world today may have had their origins in the sudden impact of modern travel and communication which bring these cultural differences face to face in sharp encounter. This makes it imperative that each of us understands the biases of our own culture which we bring to the confrontation.

Yet, acknowledging all of this, I believe that something of unconditioned uniqueness is prepared to show through in every person. It is the process of drawing it forth with which each of us needs to be concerned. It is a process which, at best, will be only dimly perceived; yet we must conjure with it. The remainder of this talk will deal with some ideas about the process that seem particularly important to me at this time.

I see four major issues that need to be faced and dealt with if this drawing forth is to proceed as an important life involvement. The relevance to your concern is this: in choosing a vocation you should have as your primary aim (there are other necessary aims, but this one should be primary) that of finding in the work in which you are engaged that which is uniquely you. No other achievement, no other end sought, will be worth the effort if through the work that occupies your best days and years you do not find a way to fan your own creative spark to a white heat—at least once in a while. So I want to talk about four of many issues, four that have emerged rather sharply out of my own experience, in the hope that something will resonate in your own experience, while you still have many choices before you.

First, the consequences of stress and responsibility. All work— whether in business, profession, government, home—both develops and limits. It stretches one out in some ways and narrows one in others; it both fans the flame and seeks to quench it. This has no doubt happened to some extent in the educational and other choices you have already made. It will happen more in work.

I see no exceptions: no completely whole persons, nor any chance of it. You must not look forward to an idealized achievement, no perfect or enduring adjustment to your life work. Whenever I think I have really achieved something, up come those powerful lines from Walt Whitman's *Song of the Open Road*—

> Now, understand me well—It is provided in the essence of things, that from any fruition of success, no matter what, shall come forth something to make a greater struggle necessary.

The greater struggle that will be necessary, as you learn to bear more stress and carry responsibility, comes because long exposure to these conditions tends to narrow the intellect unless a valiant effort is made to achieve an ever-expanding outlook. It is not enough just to try to keep up, to maintain the level of intellectual curiosity you have achieved in college. The intellectual life must expand. The great risk that the bearers of responsibility assume is that intellectual curiosity, the search for understanding, will atrophy and that only a calculating rationality will remain.

The test is in the heat of action. If one has a problem on which it is appropriate to act, and if one doesn't know what to do (which is the constant dilemma of all bearers of responsibility), one should turn to the search for greater depth of understanding about the problem.

If you are only going to remember one thing from this talk, I hope you will remember this: the main reason you will ever be aware of a problem is that your understanding of yourself, of the other people involved, and of the area in which the problem lies is limited. Therefore, the search for understanding—an intellectual pursuit—

is the most practical of ideas, even though the so-called practical people often spurn it. But it is a difficult idea to hold onto when one bears the weight of responsibility for action, especially if the need is urgent. It is difficult to seek to understand when the heat is on. If one is to be well served by a liberal education, one needs to use this period of relative isolation from real-life pressures to develop the firm habit of seeking to understand when the heat is not on. This is the best rationale I know of for concentrating such an important educational influence in your present age range. Learn how to seek to understand now, when the heat is not on; make it a firm habit, and try to be aware that this will only serve you well if the habit is firmly enough fixed so that you can manage it when the going is rough, when the stakes are real, and when the consequences of failing to understand may be overwhelming.

One of the important testing grounds in decision making is the meeting of personal conflicts, when ideas or interests differ. Please give some thought to Dr. Carl Rogers's wonderful formula for meeting conflict. It is this: try to state to the other person's satisfaction your understanding of his or her position; then identify and state as much of this position as you can agree with; then, and not until then, state your own point of view.

The risk in this procedure is that you might change. Opening oneself to understanding always entails this risk. This is bad advice for the brittle, the fearful, the dogmatic people. But then, our subject is maturity.

If change is too painful to contemplate, one had best adjust his or her blinders to shut out all peripheral understanding. But if one does this and winds up hating the world, one shouldn't blame the world for it.

There is a poignant line from *The King and I* when Anna is getting to the king with some new ideas and, in desperation, he pounds the table and shouts, "If you're going to be king, you've got to be king!" He seemed to me to be saying, "Don't mix me up with ideas when, at this point, the only thing I know how to do is to act!" This portrays dramatically the awful consequences of a life of action in which the intellectual lamp is not kept bright, in which the search for understanding is not a constant quest. And in this play the end, for the king, is tragic.

The second issue is the tension between the requirement to conform and the essential person.

Conformity has become a nasty word. It has almost become the battle cry of those of our generation who see their role as the modern version of the muckrakers of seventy years ago.

The attacks on conformity confuse the issue because in any organized society there must be a lot of conformity. Whenever two people undertake to work and live together, there must be some conformity. Even if one goes to some far-out community to live, one will conform. Either one will conform to the prevailing idea of what one is required to be in that community or one will not make it.

All organized effort, any concerted influence, requires, to some extent, that those who participate must think and act alike. Nothing important can be accomplished without a good deal of conformity. Only a hermit in his cave can completely eschew conformity and carry out his role. As our society becomes more complex, more highly integrated, it demands more conformity than was called for in simpler times.

The problem is to know conformity for what it is: a completely external adjustment to the group norm of behavior in the interest of group cohesiveness and effectiveness. Then, knowing conformity for what it is, always keep it in rational focus as a conscious adjustment in the interest of an effective society. Keep it external, never let it become a part *of you*. Hold it firmly on the outside. The great danger is that one will lose one's identity in the act of conforming, not knowing which is the essential person and which is the conforming act, and thereby forfeit one's right to be respected as an individual— by himself or herself or by anybody else.

When I was a boy one of the weapons of discipline held over little boys who used profane language was that their mothers would wash their mouths out with soap. My mother never did it to me, although there was ample provocation, but it was one of the things I heard about. I recall a story about a determined little character who did receive this punishment. He is alleged to have sputtered out through the soap suds, "You can soap my talk but you can't soap my think!"

Don't ever let anybody soap your think.

The third issue that needs to be dealt with, if the drawing forth of what is uniquely ourselves is to proceed, is the struggle for significance—the complications of status, property, and achievement.

One of the hazards of prolonged schooling is that one becomes accustomed to living in a system in which the ends of the system are to nurture significance for the individual. This is what a school is for.

Once in the world of work, the institution one is in—whether it is home, school, business, social service—uses people for other ends. All such institutions have other obligations and they commit people who do the work to these obligations. Most modern institutions are also concerned that the people who do the work find personal significance in their work. But this is a qualified obligation and one must not expect that any work will automatically provide the feeling of significance. A requirement of maturity is that one learns to find one's own significance, even under circumstances in which powerful forces may seem to operate to deny it.

But what is it that one is expected to find? I see it as something latent in the individual to be fulfilled. It is the seed of what is uniquely each person. Providing the conditions for its germination, emergence, and growth is the search.

A healthy adulthood requires that one find this seed of uniqueness, and find it among the available choices. History and literature are surfeited with examples of barren lives in which the search was thwarted because the searcher could not accept the choices available. If only some out-of-reach circumstances were present, the search might go on.

One fictional account that has meant a great deal to me is Nathaniel Hawthorne's *Great Stone Face*. This is a simple story that can be read in fifteen minutes and I commend it to you.

In this story we are in a small New England town nestled in the mountains with a view of a nearby mountain whose profile resembles a majestic face. The people in this town are living out a myth. Someday a noble person will come to them whose own profile resembles the great stone face. The presence of this person will bring into their lives the qualities of majesty that the great stone face symbolizes.

In the course of the story there comes a procession of people from the outside world, people of wealth and external status. The coming of each is heralded with great expectation, but always there is disappointment: the resemblance is not true.

Years go by. We see a generation live from youth to old age carrying this hope that the image of the great stone face will come and that their lives will be enriched by the presence of the one who bears this likeness. Finally, they recognize the resemblance to this image among them—one of their own people. This person has been there all the time, a living demonstration of those qualities which, in old age, came to resemble the profile on the mountain.

Viewed symbolically, this community is a person seeking from external sources latent qualities with the potential to emerge—if only they will be permitted to emerge. The people in this community did not realize that the external marks of character are the product of the way a life is lived. If they had been truly seekers they would not have been so preoccupied with the external marks. Rather, they would have attended more to the process, to what was going on in the lives they were examining. Had they been examining lives in process, lives around them to be seen, they would have found right before their eyes the demonstration of how to live nobly. And they would have found it when they were young enough for it to make a difference in the way their own lives were lived.

We see in this story the collective life of the community denied fulfillment because it is looking for a stereotype. Significance is more likely to come from holding an attitude of unqualified expectance, of openness and wonder.

So often, too, significance is blocked by compulsive drives for goals that do not provide fulfillment, something we pursue that we really don't want. When we achieve what we pursue, whether it is a tangible external thing or an internal state of mind, there is an emptiness. If we can name it and describe it precisely, the chances are we are seeking the wrong thing. I have seen so much of this among my contemporaries. If only they could lay aside the pursuit of overspecific and, therefore, meaningless goals and let their own uniqueness flower. The warning here is that our society holds up values that confuse the search: status, property, power, tangible achievement, even peace of mind—values that subvert the emergence of true uniqueness, the only real significance. These are elements of the society we live in at its current stage of development. We must make our peace with them and accept them as important, but we should not view them as basic or primary. Personal significance is primary.

Neither institutions nor aggregates of people have significance, except as it is given to them by living individuals who comprise them. Even traditions, powerful as they sometimes appear to be, are not viable unless contemporary people understand and believe in them and, by their thoughts, words, and deeds, give them current significance.

One of my favorite stories is about a prominent New York minister who was starting his career in the Depression of the 1930s in a very poor church. He had no car and he needed one for his parish work. But since neither he nor the church had any money this was a problem. Finally, he bought an battered old jalopy for $100. It wasn't much of a car, but it ran and served his needs. However, he was soon confronted by an objection from his parishioners. Poor as they all were, they didn't like the idea of their minister riding around in that kind of car, especially parking it in front of the church. Finally it came out at a meeting of the governing board when one of the members said that their minister should have a car that "added to his dignity." At this point the young minister rose and spoke one short sentence that disposed of the question about his car. "Ladies and gentlemen," he said, "no automobile adds dignity to a man, the man adds dignity to the automobile."

This is a point ever to keep sharply in mind. Dignity, significance, character are wholly the attributes of individual people. They have nothing to do with anything external to the person. The fourth major issue I see in facing the requirements for growth is accepting some process for drawing forth one's uniqueness.

I would like to see a word that has fallen into disuse restored to common usage. That word is *entheos,* from the same roots as enthusiasm, which means *possessed of the spirit.* These two words, *entheos* and *enthusiasm,* have had an interesting history in the English language, coming down side by side through separate channels of meaning from the sixteenth century. *Entheos* has always been the basic spiritual essence; enthusiasm, until recently, its perverter and imitator. *Entheos* is now defined as the power actuating one who is inspired, while enthusiasm is seen as its less profound, more surface aspect.

I want to use *entheos* as it is now defined, the power actuating one who is inspired, and, at the risk of laboring it, I want to build a concept of growth around this one word. For those who are concerned with maturity seen as becoming, it is important to see *entheos* as the lamp and to keep one's own private lamp lighted as one ventures forth into a confused, pressure-ridden world, but nevertheless a hopeful world for those who can maintain their contact with the power that actuates inspiration. From the little I know of history I cannot imagine a more interesting time to be alive than the times we live in—provided one can make it with *entheos*.

I see *entheos* as the essence that makes a constructive life possible; it is the sustaining force that holds one together under stress; it is the support for venturesome risk-taking action; it is the means whereby whatever religious beliefs one has are kept in contact with one's attitudes and actions in the world of practical affairs; it lifts people above the prosaic and gives them a sense of timelessness; it is the prod of conscience that keeps one open to knowledge, so that one can be both aware and sensitive, when the urge to be comfortable would keep the door closed. I like that line from William Blake:

> If the doors of perception were cleansed, everything will appear
> to man as it is, infinite.

Entheos does not come in response to external incentives. In fact, it may persist when incentives operate to destroy it. The individual cannot will it; it comes when *it* will and sometimes it goes when most needed. But it does grow.

All that can be willed is the search. There is no one pattern I know of. Each must find one's own pattern. One of the great challenges of maturity: find your own growth pattern in the search for *entheos*.

I can suggest some tests. If one has such tests in mind, these might help to plot the individual search. We are reaching, in the end, for *entheos*, the power actuating one who is inspired. First some misleading indicators—some events and conditions that might throw one off:

Status or material success. One's external achievement may be impressive and praiseworthy and yet, in the process of achieving, one may be destroying much that is really important.

Social success. The nongrowth people are sometimes more comfortable to be with.

Doing all that is expected of one. Who is doing the expecting, and what do they know about what I should be expecting of myself?

Family success can be a misleading indicator. Fine and desirable as it is, if it is an exclusive concern, it can be an egocentric, narrowing development. The family may be taking more out of the wider community than it is contributing.

Relative peace and quiet. This may simply mean that the doors of perception are closed.

Finally, *busyness—compulsive busyness.* Beneath the surface of much action there is the drive to avoid the implications of growth. "This is for monks in a monastery; I'm too busy," they seem to say. (Read the Mary–Martha story in the Bible and ask, what does it have to say on this point?)

These are six events and conditions that can be misleading as evidences of growth in *entheos.* These can all be positive and worthwhile, but they don't necessarily add up to growth of *entheos.*

Now, what I believe to be some valid indicators that there may be real growth of *entheos:*

First, two paradoxes *a concurrent satisfaction and dissatisfaction with the status quo.* One is not so unhappy with one's current level of achievement that one can't live with oneself. Neither is one so pleased with one's level of achievement that one has no incentive to break out of it. Then there is a concurrent *feeling of broadening responsibilities and centering down.* One is constantly reaching out for wider horizons—new levels of experience, and at the same time the idea of "This one thing will I do" is in the ascendancy.

There is *a growing sense of purpose in whatever one does.* The idea of purpose becomes important. Without being obsessive about it, the most penetrating and disturbing of all questions, "What am I trying to do?" becomes a constant query. One never loses sight of this question.

There are *changing patterns and depths of one's interests.* Old interests to which one was once attached drop away and newer and deeper ones take their place. Choices must be made.

As *entheos* becomes a more constant companion, one moves toward *the minimum of difference between the outside and inside images of the self;* one becomes more willing to be seen as one is. Living as we do in an unreal world, to some extent we all wear masks. Convenient as it is to let the mask do what only serenity can really do, I submit that all masks chafe; I never saw a well-fitting mask. It is a great relief to take them off. The power of *entheos* makes this possible; and the urge to remove the mask is one of the surest signs of its potency.

Then one becomes *conscious of the good use of time and unhappy with the waste of time.* As awareness opens, one of the measures one takes of the contemporary society is the number of elaborate and seductive devices lurking about that serve no other purpose than to waste time.

A further test is the growing sense of *achieving one's basic personal goals through one's work,* whatever it is—however menial, however poorly recognized. One of the popular illusions in our kind of culture is that one must reach a high-status position in order to achieve one's goals. In my observation there is really nothing in status but status, and the proportion of frustrated people is just as great in high places as in low places. I know it is an old truism, but the only place to achieve one's personal goals is where one is. Looking for a greener pasture for this purpose is almost certain to seal off the opportunity for achievement.

Going with some of these tests is the emergence of *a sense of unity,* a pulling together of all aspects of life. Job, family, recreation, church, community, all merge into one total pattern. While there remain obvious allocations of time to specific pursuits, the sense of leaving one and going to another diminishes. Peripheral, time-consuming activities that cannot be brought within this unified view are laid aside. None of us needs to accept all of the obligations that others would impose upon us and one way of making the separation between what to accept and what to reject is to test their compatibility with the core of unified activities. As *entheos* grows, one becomes more decisive and emphatic in saying "no!"

Finally, there is *a developing view of people.* All people are seen as beings to be trusted, believed in, and loved, and not as objects to be used, competed with, or judged. It is a shifting of the balance from use to esteem in all personal relationships. In an imperfect world one never achieves it fully, but there can be measurable progress. This is a critically important test. Unless this view of people becomes dominant, it is difficult for the inward view of one's own significant uniqueness to emerge. Love of oneself in the context of a pervasive love for one's fellows is a healthy attribute and necessary for the fulfillment of a life. Out of this context, love of oneself can be narrowing, introverting, and destructive.

The ultimate test of *entheos*, however, is *an intuitive feeling of oneness, of wholeness, of rightness*; but not necessarily comfort or ease.

These seem to me to be some valid indicators that give assurance that *entheos* is growing. If this kind of thinking doesn't strike a responsive chord with you today, please make note of it, tuck it away in the back of your journal, and look at it ten years—twenty years— from now.

In closing I want to return for a moment to work, vocation, and its relevance to growth, to the drawing out of the unique significance of the person.

When your full-time education is complete, don't just look for a job, even for an interesting and remunerative job. Think of yourself as a person with unique potentialities and see the purpose of life as bringing these into mature bloom.

Don't think of your career in terms of finding a nice fit for your skills and abilities. You will find some work more rewarding than other work, but the perfect job doesn't exist. Anyhow, neither the person nor the job stays put.

Since there are no perfect jobs, no ideal fields, take one that challenges you as a piece of work to be done. Make other requirements subsidiary to this one, because nothing else really matters if the job is not rewarding in this sense. Whatever your work is, make something out of it that enriches you. Work itself cannot be truly significant except as it is seen as the means whereby the people who do the work find themselves in it. Do your work well; keep your sense of obligation high; cultivate excellence in everything you do; but above all *use* your work, *use* it as a means for your own fulfillment as a person—your own becoming.

If you have goals, be sure to state them in terms of external achievement, not in terms of what you will become. You don't know what you can become, and no one can tell you.

This can be one of the great excitements of life—the surprise when you discover what you have become and realize that more is yet to come. Let your watchword be *becoming!*

* * *

The one question that was asked was: "Dr. Broderick, as I understand what psychiatrists do, mainly helping mentally ill or confused people, I don't see how you could draw this talk out of your experience. You seem to be talking about very sane people, the kind we here in Jefferson House hope we are. How can you explain that?"

"I can understand your question," he replied. "I was trained like most doctors are—to help heal the sick. There is precious little medical practice in any of its specialties that is devoted to keeping the healthy people healthy or to helping the healthy ones to realize their full potential for health. Part of the reason is economic; most people are willing to pay doctors only when they have symptoms of illness. They are not willing to pay for health, only for help in recovery from illness. Then part of it is that doctors are human, and most humans in all walks of life, if they can get away with it, settle for dealing with problems that are brought to them. Very few in any field take initiatives to deal with the conditions that create problems. You people in Jefferson House are an exception: that is one reason why I am willing to travel 700 miles and miss two days of work to be with you. You here are reaching out to identify places where you can initiate constructive action. That is what I chose to do about ten years ago.

"In the first ten years of my practice I did what most psychiatrists do; I sat in my office and waited for sick people to come to see me. I helped some people and I made a fair living out of it.

"Then I realized that this was a losing game. Most of these people needed my help because they were no longer able to cope, alone. This is a lonely world. We do not have the quality of life in community that everybody needs. Even churches, which, of all places, should be supportive, seldom are. So the burden of my talk this evening was to share what I can that will help you, all very sane people, to cope with the rough world—alone. I know that being in this university is no bed of roses. But you are young and your resilience is higher than it will be later on. And, as you know, some in this university cannot cope now and need help while they are here. But not many of those are likely to come here to Jefferson House. The hurdle that Mr. Billings puts up is too high. I gauged my talk knowing that. I assumed that I was talking to the more resilient, the more sane. And what I said was aimed to help you stay that way.

"Now, to return to the change I made ten years ago. I concluded, after ten years of conventional practice, to try to direct my major effort to the strong and healthy part of the population, with less of it going to the weak and the sick. The weak and the sick need help, but they are ones most medical practice is organized to serve. *My new aim is to try to help the strong be more effective as servants of society.* I want to serve and strengthen those who will work to build community wherever people are gathered so that the weak will be supported and the ill will be healed *there*, rather than in the doctor's office where it is not only terribly expensive to do, but where the effort to help them is not very effective. Since, as I said, there are not many among the strong and the sane who are willing to pay a doctor's fee for this kind of help, and since I am not endowed and need to be paid for what I do, I realized that I would have to reach out and educate some of these strong, sane people so that they would want— and pay for—the service I hoped to be able to render to them.

"So I began to talk and write to the needs of these strong, successful, sane people as a special audience. There were four years of consistent work in this before I got my first response, 'I want to learn to do what you are talking about; will you help me?' This was an exceptional person and it has been a rewarding relationship. Another year passed before the second one came. In the next five years I added a few more. Now I can say that I have a reasonable practice as psychiatrist to the strong and the sane. It is still small, but it is significant, and it is growing.

"There is nothing new, conceptually, in what I am doing. What one learns in being trained as a psychiatrist is that nearly all persons of good motives are ill in the sense of not living the quality of life of which they are capable—which includes not rendering the service to society which they are capable of. What I gradually became aware of is that, in our competitive society, it is the achievement of others that sets the level of aspiration of most people. If one places well in the competitive race, then one is okay.

"The two ten-year chapters of my career as a psychiatrist that I have described do not seem as different to me, sitting in the consultant's chair, as you might suppose. In the first phase of my career there were those whom society (or the individuals themselves) label 'sick.' In the second phase there came the successful and the powerful who are generally judged healthy—by both society and themselves. But from my vantage point both may be sick. The latter, in the quiet of my consulting room, reveal their neediness. They have been corrupted by power and they have worshiped false gods who, when they came to assess their lives, have betrayed them. To be sure, they have done conspicuous good works and they have received honors and decorations. But there is an emptiness: *they have not been servants*, not in the sense that you are learning about it here in Jefferson House.

"I am hopeful for the future, despite the dismal outlook on so many fronts. I have hope for the future because a few of the successful and the powerful have heard the signals that I began to give ten years ago and have come to my consulting room with the expectation that they can learn to be servants—*where they are, as successful, powerful people.*

"The strong, the successful, the powerful can best serve as they use their power to make serving institutions of those they influence or control—including building community and creating fulfilling opportunity within those institutions. In these ways the weak, the inept, the confused—or just the undistinguished—will be strengthened and supported in the useful roles they are able to carry. *Servanthood is ultimately tested wherever one is with one's power!* If one has power (and nearly everybody has some), the primary test of one's morality is not the good works one does with one's money or energy. *The primary moral test is what one does with one's power—in those places where one's power is greatest.*

"The hardest struggle I have with my powerful patients is to convince them that generosity and good works in other places are *not* currency with which one's neglect of one's primary opportunity to build a better society can be redeemed. The fact that I have been able to convince people of this in a few cases gives me great hope for the future. Then, I am hopeful because of Jefferson House where a few, at least, can learn to be servants while they are young and build their careers on it."

* * *

There was a long pause and most came forward to shake Dr. Broderick's hand, and thank him, without comment. And we went to our rooms to think about what we had heard.

Institution Building Is Sharply Defined

A VISITOR WHOSE MESSAGE stands out clearly in my memory came to Jefferson House early in my third year. He was Mr. Arthur Moore, a man in his sixties who had spent the first part of his career as a staff person dealing with the problems of organization in one of our largest industries. The latter part of his career was spent as a consultant on organization for businesses, universities, churches, and foundations around the world.

The premise that guided his work was that whereas we in the United States were once a nation of people on family farms with a small fringe of commerce and industry, we are now a nation of institutions—some of them very large. While the source of values and initiatives is still, as always, from individuals, the effect of their effort on the quality of the total society is now mediated mostly through institutions.

He challenged us. If we, the students, were to become the effective shapers of a new and better society (which nearly all of us in Jefferson House aspired to do) we would need to learn how to operate in and around these many discrete institutions, and we would need to know by what standards we would judge their adequacy as important segments of the larger society. Mr. Moore was very forceful on the point that, if a better society is to be built, it will come from reconstructing its constituent institutions, one at a time, with exceptional ones operating as pacesetters and exerting a pull on the rest. Pressure from government and from individuals and groups who are outside can compel attention to the need for reconstruction, but the response to that pressure, the actual work of reconstruction, must come from persons inside those institutions who have the motivation, the skills, and the leadership influence to get it done. And whether the compliance is judged good or bad, and whether the reconstruction proves to have a durable base, rests almost wholly on the quality and force of those persons inside who design and lead the reconstruction.

This was not a new idea to us because we in Jefferson House were well exposed to the world outside the university, and we were enough concerned with the functioning of our own university in which we were deeply involved, to be aware of its problems. But Mr. Moore gave this point of view much greater meaning when he presented his detailed estimate of how the society-building institution of the future might look—from the inside.

First he defined two levels of institutional performance:

Exceptional—It stands far enough ahead of the field it is in to put a competitive pull on those institutions which, in the absence of such a challenge, would settle for being *good*.

Good—The average of the better performers, those which use effectively the conventional wisdom.

Then he elaborated.

* * *

Those institutions that have sustained *exceptional* performance, as distinguished from those that are *good*, are not simply the better users of the conventional wisdom. There is a different quality of thinking, let us call it *unconventional wisdom*, among those who carry the top leadership of *exceptional institutions*. The term *top leadership* refers to those who are ultimately in control. In the voluntary (nongovernmental) institutions these are the members of the governing boards—trustees and directors. Particularly, this quality of unconventional wisdom is possessed by the chairperson, who leads the trustees.

I cannot overstress the importance of the quality of thinking by trustees and their chairs because we live in an age of belief in "gimmicks." This is an opprobrious term and I have used it advisedly in order to emphasize the difference between the exceptional institution, where the quality of thinking in the top group is determining, as distinguished from the good or the ordinary institution, where the governing board is nominal or honorary, and where there is a belief in the efficacy of gimmicks: procedures, formulas, programs that can be bought on the market and installed or operated by experts. Some of these are very well done and produce a measurable improvement on the performance of the institution. And reputable people advocate them.

But I have made it my business to look into institutions that seem to be exceptional from all observable criteria and most of them are conspicuously free of the popular gimmicks. Interested observers from comparable institutions are puzzled when they examine the exceptional ones because, when they look to see what accounts for the exceptionality, they don't find the popular nostrums or gimmicks. The different quality of thinking by the ultimate leadership is not easy to discover and its crucial importance is not recognized. We live so much in the age of gimmicks that it seems difficult for many intelligent observers to conceive of an institution beginning with a philosophy rather than a concern with procedures. Institutions sometimes resemble people who think of health as the state in which one has quick access to the right procedures for suppressing pain. I call it the aspirin effect. By taking successive aspirins something resembling health may be maintained. But this is not the way exceptional health is built, in either persons or institutions.

I have labored this point because it is fundamental—and difficult to accept for many who are in a position to give new conceptual leadership to major institutions. It is much easier for such persons to think in terms of imposing a procedure on someone else rather than to face what some seem to regard as the trauma of examining the assumptions by which they, the top leadership, carry their roles. In my experience with institutions of all sorts, and from my study of their histories, those who have given the guiding leadership to build exceptional institutions, in addition to being able, have simply made better assumptions than most about what they are trying to do. So, before getting into the details of the kind of top thinking that builds exceptional institutions, I want to state my basic position: the first step for one who would lead an institution to be exceptional is to examine one's own assumptions. *To refuse to examine these assumptions one lives by is immoral.* One must examine these assumptions in order to be able to choose the unconventional wisdom by which the leadership of exceptional institutions is guided. One may then choose to stay with conventional wisdom to some extent. All of us do some of that. But if one does not examine one's assumptions, one has no basis for making a choice and one is a slave to the conventional.

I want to give a brief summary of the unconventional wisdom that might emerge if an able top leadership of any kind of institution, large or small, carefully examines the assumptions and chooses those assumptions that seem to offer the best chance of lifting it above the level of merely being good. The first element of the unconventional wisdom needed to build the exceptional institution is that *the governing board—trustees and directors—is strong.*

The greatest strength of conceptual leadership of any institution should be in its governing board. Unusual conceptual strength may, of course, be found anywhere. But the institution that becomes exceptional will manage to get its best conceptual leaders into its board, and best of all, as its chair. This is in sharp contrast to the usual practice of assembling merely conservative, dependable high-status people for board membership. High-status people may give the institution the aura of respectability, and thereby their presence may elicit, for a time, an undeserved trust. But a board of trustees of merely high-status persons has little chance of leading the institution to be exceptional. Trustees should stand as the symbol of the primacy of the public good.

Unfortunately, we seem to have built our modern institutions on the assumption that internal administrators are the key to optimal performance. Of course, the contributions of all persons on the employed staff are important, and strong administrators are essential. But we have allowed a common institutional design to emerge in which governing boards are weak, and administrators try both to *manage* (what the laws of incorporation say the governing board should do) and *administer* (what the board should delegate to internal professionals). And it is not working well. So the first element of unconventional wisdom is that the governing board is strong enough to assert its management role in order that exceptionality becomes a possibility. An early result of the acquisition of strength in the board will be to organize the top administrative level so that it will function optimally in building an exceptional institution.

The second element of unconventional wisdom (not necessarily second in importance—who knows which is more important?) is constant awareness that we live in an era of low trust, and that a component of every decision should be a concern that the action taken should have a trust-building effect—even if some other important goal might suffer a bit. Trust is not usually built by actions or maneuvers designed explicitly to build trust. Such actions are usually transparent and, with discerning people, they have a negative effect. The important trust-building actions are those that have many effects. The institution that is trusted, and that contributes to building a trusting society, calculates *every* action to build trust. In other words, *every* action takes into account its effect on people; and it is designed to serve, and not to harm, every person who may be affected.

The third element is that the planning of every action takes into account its effect on both survival and creative development of the institution. Sustained and exclusive concentration on *survival* will result in ultimate demise. Exclusive concentration on *creative development* without regard to survival is likely to do the same. Therefore, it will reflect a balanced view of what is required for both survival and creative development. No matter how imminent or remote the threat to survival may seem when any given action is contemplated, both survival and creative development will be weighed in balance.

The fourth element of unconventional wisdom is acceptance that most important decisions have enough of an intuitive base that they cannot be fully explained in words. It is not that such decisions are irrational; the reasoning about them is simply not reducible to verbal concepts. In the unconventional wisdom there will be the attempt to carry verbal rationalization of decisions as far as it will take one, but, on some decisions, that may not be very far. And there is *always* the acknowledgment that what is expressed in words is only part of the explanation. Such a constant acknowledgment acts as a check on one's tendency toward intellectual arrogance. And, alas, far too many of the very bright people I have known are intellectually arrogant in that they are presumptuous about how much of what they know, or what needs to be understood, can be verbalized. And they fill the air with words when they would do better simply to point and say, "There it is. See for yourself."

Then there is the very difficult fifth element, that trustees and directors are expensive (or should be). To be sure, it is always possible to fill trustee chairs with very acceptable—but ineffective—people. And there are some able trustees who are willing to give dedicated service free. But they should be paid, and paid well—even in the eleemosynary institutions! Businesses usually pay, but not very much in comparison with executive salaries—even in the very large and profitable ones. Directors should be paid, based on the time they invest, more than the executives because their service is, or ought to be, more valuable.

There will be much complaining about this, but my experience suggests that this is a necessary condition if an institution wants maximum assurance that it can rise to the exceptional. Some of the reasons:

1. Ample compensation nails down the obligation in the mind of the trustee or director. The individual may not need the money or may not want to accept it. But one should accept it for one's own protection because it binds one to a higher sense of obligation than most trustees and directors assume. (The operating executives may not want trustees and directors to assume the kind of obligation I have in mind. But trustees should assume it anyway. And as long as any are paid money for their services, trustees should be the highest paid because, ultimately, theirs is the most valuable contribution.)

2. Nothing will establish as quickly or as firmly the role of the governing board, in the eyes of all constituencies, than to pay what ought to be paid for this service. And this new role of the governing board needs to be established, especially in the minds of internal administrators, because they will need to adapt to it and develop new roles for themselves that fit a new relationship.

3. Paying trustees and directors adequately will radically reduce the size of governing boards to the six or seven that are needed if the board is really to manage. (And *manage* is what they should do. The typical incorporation law says that the institution *shall be managed by* trustees or directors, usually not fewer than three.) There could be, and often is, a larger unpaid group (governors, members, overseers, etc.) that meets infrequently and takes some legal actions such as electing new members of the governing board. But these members of the larger group, which may represent constituencies and may be politically based, are not the well-paid trustees and directors that I believe are necessary to build the exceptional institution.

4. Paying governing board members well, and therefore reducing the size of boards and requiring acceptance of a firm managerial role for the board, will go far to make board membership attractive and challenging to board members and their chair, and will help to

bring into board positions the very best and strongest persons—persons who are not necessarily the best administrators. But they should be the very best trustees possible.

This brings me to the most difficult point of all: among the elements of unconventional wisdom is the resolve that people, *all people touched by the institution*, are to be served and not to be used or exploited.

Serve is a difficult and overused word. The unabridged dictionary I consulted gives two full pages to *serve* and related words, and *serve*, *service*, and *servant* among them have over sixty separate definitions. And many of the meanings and related words like *servile* have definitely negative connotations. Yet I can find no other word that is capable of carrying the meaning I would like to convey. And I do not want to define the word *serve* abstractly. I would rather use it in terms of the consequences of being served. I prefer to say that all of those persons who are touched by the institution are served and, *while being served*, they grow as persons; they become healthier, wiser, freer, more autonomous, more likely themselves to become servants. Furthermore, whatever the action, the least privileged in society will benefit, or, at least, not be further deprived. Serving and service are the attitudes and actions that produce such a result. (And it really doesn't matter how *serve* is defined, if that is the result.)

Sometimes serving is only an attitude, as in the concluding line of Milton's sonnet "On His Blindness"—"They also serve who only stand and wait." But, even there, action is implied. Presumably he or she who serves by only standing and waiting is *prepared* to serve—the discipline and practice have been done, but one has not been called. And sometimes one serves only with one's presence; there is no waving of arms, but the subliminal communication of an attitude can be a powerful service. The result is what counts. Serving and service, to me, are what produce the result in personal growth in those being served, which is *anyone* who is touched by the actions or influence of the institution. And the total ramifications of what that might be exceed the capacity of language to describe. The challenge to one who would assist in building a truly serving institution (and therefore exceptional in these times) is enormous, and the most dedicated, longest life of the ablest person cannot possibly exhaust it.

And, finally (and this list, too, could be inexhaustible) there is the element of unconventional wisdom that is probably implied in what has already been said, *there is a great idea,* an exciting goal that lifts the aspirations and spirit of everyone involved.

And it is a contemporary idea. This is the most difficult test for the many "good" institutions that once were exceptional. They lost their once great idea partly because they did not keep it contemporary. It *was* a great idea, and it supported exceptionality. But now the idea is not *great* in this sense. It no longer has *the power to stir men's blood,* to borrow Daniel Burnham's great phrase.

An exceptional institution will have a contemporary great idea, one that does have the power "to stir men's blood." The test of greatness in an idea is pragmatic. No amount of logic avails. *If it does not stir, it is not great.*

Here is where the trustees and directors are ultimately tested. The administrators and staffs of institutions, who operate with both the supports and constraints of professionalism, are not likely to think in this way. Administrators occasionally do this kind of thinking, but it is a chance event. The trustees of an institution that would be exceptional have, as their own personal task, the nurturing of the great idea for their institution. It is their obligation—and their opportunity. They will probably have the support of their own staff which is attuned to trustee support, not the support of administrators (a very different role).

These seven elements suggest the kind of unconventional wisdom that the ultimate leaders (trustees and directors) of exceptional institutions might have. There is nothing final or complete in this summary. I learn something new about it almost every day. What I have given you very briefly is simply a summary statement of my best thinking at this time, out of my own experience.

Remember, in listing these elements of unconventional wisdom, I am not making general recommendations for all institutions—only for those who want to be exceptional. I am too much of a realist to expect that many institutions, even those that profess high idealism, like universities and churches, will accept such a need for unconventional wisdom. Consequently, I am addressing only those institutions where there is enough ability, determination, tough-mindedness, and venturesomeness to move the place out ahead as a pacesetter in its field. I realize that those that are comfortable with just being "good" will probably stay where they are until competitive pressure shakes them out of it or they fall by the wayside.

* * *

There was a moment of silence. We were a little shaken. As I write this now from the copious notes in my journal, after an elapse of several years and some experience in a large business that is trying to be exceptional, Mr. Moore's summary does not seem so unconventional. Yet when I talk with those outside my company about why the business I am in is so successful, they shake their heads in disbelief. Nothing like that could possibly work. I sometimes think that they find the contemplation of it so threatening that they do not want even to consider it. They seem to say, "There must be some fluke that accounts for your success. It cannot possibly be the result of what you describe." Such people (and they are legion) are locked into conventional thinking. Although we in Jefferson House thought of ourselves as venturesome and idealistic, when we thought of ourselves as trying to make *these* ideas work, even in our university, we were—well, I already said it, we were shaken.

The first student to respond, a woman, was quite aggressive. "What you are advocating is elitist. And every bone in my body rejects elitism. I would not want any part of it!"

Mr. Moore smiled and said gently, "You yourself are elitist—every bone in your body. You are one of the privileged in this society. You made a major step into elitism when you entered this university; I know that it is quite selective. Then you were selected for Jefferson House, an elite group if I ever saw one. Now, I don't accept some kinds of elitism: for example, that which goes only with social status, race, the power of brute strength, or of money. But I do accept the notion that a good society is one in which the more able and the less able serve each other. Also I accept that every skill makes one an elite. The doctor who serves me, the woodsman who cuts the trees to thin my too-dense woods, are both elitist. There is a notion abroad that we are all alike, but we are far from it. Any person or institution that serves must be seen as elitist. And the institution that becomes a pacesetter in its field and exerts a competitive pull toward greater service *by the whole field* will be exceptionally elitist. Every society, from the most sophisticated to the most primitive, can function only because of the existence of elites. I believe I know what bothers you when you react so strongly to the elitist notion. But we must be able to distinguish between the serving elites, which we should embrace, and the parasitical or destructive elites, which we should reject. It is important to know the difference."

Then a student asked, "But where is the ethic? If I have learned anything about what makes a good society it is that it must have an adequate ethic."

"I am not an ethicist," replied Mr. Moore, "and I don't know what a scholar in that field would do with your question. But let me repeat what I said earlier. All people touched by the institution are to be served and not to be used or exploited. *While being served,* they grow as persons, they become healthier, wiser, freer, more autonomous, more likely themselves to be servants. Furthermore, whatever the action, the least privileged in society will benefit, or, at least, not be further deprived. I have given this as a goal or result for any institution: church, government, business, school, philanthropy. The ethic for any particular institution at any particular time will be more situational; it will be those guides to actions that are calculated to achieve the result, in terms of impact on people, that I have described. I would not know how to describe a set of norms for all situations. I am a results-oriented person. That is why I like the word *serve.* My ethic, for the moment, is what serves best as I have described the results of being served."

"I am bothered," said another, "that you concentrate on the few exceptional institutions and have nothing to say to the large number of mediocre ones—what you call good. This seems to me to be an awfully slow way to remedy the poor ones. I'm beginning to get impatient."

"Ours is a pretty mediocre society," conceded Mr. Moore, "when judged in terms of what is reasonable and possible with available resources, human and material. The trouble is that what I call society-building institutions—churches, schools, foundations—are functioning just as inadequately as are governments, businesses, and hospitals. How to get a handle on such a problem? I've spent a good share of my career wrestling with that question.

"We now have the occasional exceptional institution—in all fields. But we know very little about how they got that way. And none seems to stay that way very long. The occasional administrator will lead part or all of an institution to exceptional status. But such a development is not likely to survive that administrator's tenure. I see no dependable way to raise the quality of many institutions except that the general social view postulates that exceptional institutions are predictable and reasonably durable only when trustees accept the kind of role I have described and choose to be governed by the kind of unconventional thinking I have outlined. My premise is that if a few trustee bodies could be persuaded to take the lead, there would be a better model for others to emulate.

"We have so far to go in getting an acceptance of building health in institutions, just as we have the same problem in building health in individuals. All that any of us can do is to work on both problems where we have the opportunity."

"I find it a shocking idea that trustees should be paid," another said. "Do you not see any place for volunteer effort?"

"Yes, I see a great field for volunteers, but not as trustees or directors. We have to break out of the notion that governing boards are largely honorary and do little more than give legal shelter. First, these are becoming hazardous occupations in terms of being sued. People who are aggrieved by the performance of institutions have caught on to the fact that trustees and directors are legally responsible. But, mainly, trusteeship, as I conceive it, cannot be entrusted to volunteers—it is too important a function and really requires a level of dedication and time investment that none but the wealthy could afford to give (assuming they want to). A structure that limits trustee service to the wealthy *does* make an elite out of board service because there are many able people who could make excellent trustees—if they could afford to invest the time. But, mostly, I urge adequate payment for all trustees as the only way I know to bring that role to the stature and dimensions I believe it must have if we are to have exceptional institutions that really become persuasive models for others. We need to define the trustee role, draw the most capable (as trustees) into it, and discourage the dilettantes, the status seekers, the unqualified."

Then someone asked, "Isn't the era of great ideas in the past? I sense mostly cynicism and pragmatic thinking. Can you give me an example of a contemporary great idea?"

"I have difficulty with that question because what is great is usually what is durable, and the judgment of greatness needs the perspective of some history. But let me say that if *any* contemporary institution postulates its goal to serve in the way that I have defined it, it will be recognized as a great idea now and I believe it will stand the test of time. A sociologist friend of mine tells of attempting, a few years ago, to persuade a major church organization to accept the servant theme as central to its work—but they would not buy it. This supports your assertion: ours is a cynical age. But I am not talking to the cynical world this evening. I am addressing the students in Jefferson House who are the most hopeful bunch I know of. I am trying to undergird your hope with a strategy for changing the world—not tested and tried, but a basis for hope.

"The basis for hope is seldom in the tested and tried. It is not in the conventional wisdom. Hope rests in the imagination. Someone must, in his or her imagination, conceive of a better world before it can be built. Hope is not practical; it is visionary. Sometimes it is belief in the impossible. The seven elements of unconventional wisdom I have suggested are all visionary. Russell Baker, writing a few years back in the *New York Times*, said of our government in Washington: 'Almost everybody of importance, man and woman, has run out of imagination. Wits end seems not far off. We are in the hands of men who make no music and have no dreams.' This may or may not have been a fair appraisal, but it signifies a loss of hope.

"I have come, as I have said, to give you a realistic basis for hope. However, I am realistic enough to know that all I have done here is to plant a seed. You will have to guard it, nurture it, pray for it if it is to grow and flourish."

"I detect," another student said, "a bias in your position toward large institutions. Much that I dislike about this university is due to its being large. I believe that small institutions serve better."

"I reject that idea," answered Mr. Moore promptly. "In my

experience with institutions, which has been considerable, whether or not they serve has nothing to do with size. And I am not aware of an objective study that relates quality to size. There are advantages, different of course, to being both small and large. You would find life different in a small college, say 500 students. And you might like it better. But you certainly would not have the advantages you have in a large one like you have here. The differences, I believe, are a matter of personal preference, not of intrinsic quality.

"I have no quarrel with the person who feels that she or he will be more comfortable, perhaps serve better, in a small rather than a large place; there are plenty of small ones around and they can use good help. But I do challenge the idea that only small can serve well, and I strongly object to the advocacy that young people should shun big institutions. I say this because we have built a society that is too dependent on big ones. If you are going to serve this present society, and if you have the talent for it, I would urge you to use your creative efforts to make servants of big institutions. It is possible, if enough of us work at it. And, for some of you, it might be more satisfying to be creative in something big than in something small."

Then there was a final question that really nettled Mr. Moore. "But I don't like the present society. I want to prepare myself to help build one that is a lot better than this one. What can you say to me?"

"I can't say anything to you," Mr. Moore responded sharply, "unless you change your attitude. And, frankly, that is not a question I expected to get in this house. Although, I admit, it is rather common among your generation.

"I can only urge that you ponder those wonderful lines from Hermann Hesse (but I cannot tell you where they are in his writing): 'It is only important to love the world,' he said, ' . . . to regard the world and ourselves and all beings with love, admiration and respect.'

"Now, you may ask, how can I possibly love this lousy world and all of these despicable people? You may say that such an assertion is hopelessly unrealistic. And, viewed through the attitude that your question suggests, it would seem hopelessly unrealistic. But if you can bring yourself to see the good (no matter how much may be bad), and if you can believe that behind *all* of these unlovely exteriors there is a spark of spirit, however small, then you can accept Hermann Hesse's assertion—*it is only important to love the world.*

"But I cannot give you such an attitude of love. I can only suggest that you search for an experience that will teach it to you. And when you get it, *if* you get it, you may then see the opportunity to rebuild this society on nobler lines, by starting with the institution that is most amenable to becoming exceptional. And this will give you a basis for being hopeful about the future of this society. I have said that I see that my mission here is to plant a seed. You will have to guard it, nurture it, pray for it if it is to grow and flourish."

I went to my room and thought and thought. Did I have the hope and the courage to nurture that seed? Did I really understand the full implications of what was said? Now, ten years later as I write this I know that I did not understand it—not based on that one evening. But in the context of my next summer's experience and what happened in my senior year, I left the university with at least a faint glimmer of understanding of what Mr. Moore was saying to us.

III. A New Project Is Born

I FOUND MY ACADEMIC PROGRAM in my first two years both absorbing and demanding. There was plenty of work to do on continuing projects and new ones that were started by upperclass students, and I tried not to miss any of the house meetings and sessions with visitors. With all of this and some social life I found myself pleasantly busy, and with Mr. Billings's benign leadership I saw in the total activity a quite satisfying experience. I realized that the time would come when I became a junior that I should begin to take responsibility for initiating the work of the house; I was willing to wait for the right opportunity. There were subtle suggestions that one would spend one's last two years more profitably if the first two were spent in learning what was abundantly there to be learned about serving and leading and working in teams. I was faithful in keeping my journal, and the constant awareness during the day that a journal entry would be my bedtime task made me more alert and attentive than I might otherwise have been. I was active in the group discussions, I took controversial positions on issues that arose, and I frequently questioned our guests; but on the house projects, I followed the leadership of juniors and seniors. Above all I watched Mr. Billings because, fortunately, I was early alerted to the opportunity to study, in action, a man of unusual dedication, skill, and integrity. Even *if* I had left Jefferson House at the end of my sophomore year, Mr. Billings's example would have marked me for life. But my last two years are the ones that now stand high in my memory. And my appropriate role unfolded quite naturally.

In my junior year I worked as a reporter on the student newspaper. In the spring term I was given an assignment for an investigative report on the trustees. "What are they doing for the university?" the editorial board asked. This question was stirred by two parallel developments. First, there had arisen within the university some searching questions about governance. Some of these questions had harsh implications, such as, is the faculty giving too little attention to students and too much to their scholarly advancement and status striving? And, is the medieval model for the university, which evolved when only a small percentage of the population attended, an adequate concept for today in our country when 50 percent of the university-age young people are enrolled? Furthermore, who is really responsible for seeing that the university gives the best possible service to students?

Then, we were aware that there was a new questioning about the role of trustees in all sorts of institutions. We knew that the corporation law in our state stipulated: "The institution shall be managed by a board of trustees." And we wondered what our trustees were doing to "manage" our university. It seemed to us that it needed some managing.

These two parallel developments had prompted the editorial board to take a fresh look at the governance of our university, to assess the present state of our institutional health, and to report to our student readers. A large order. I undertook it with some enthusiasm, but without realizing where it might lead me.

My first step was to ask for an appointment with the president of the university. He was a hard man to get to see. When I finally saw him I realized that I was confronted with a troubled, harassed man. When I stated my mission, he literally exploded. "What are you trying to do, wreck this place?" he asked in a shrill, angry voice. "The last thing we need is students boring into the trustee function. We are having enough trouble providing you with a good education. Why don't you find something to do that will help the university rather than add to the confusion?" He went on and on in this vein until I just excused myself and left. He hardly seemed to notice my going. I found myself both feeling sorry for him and being furious at the rebuff. I did the only thing I could think of: I went to see Mr. Billings.

I found him working quietly in his office at Jefferson House. When I told him of my session with the president, he smiled and asked quietly the question that always came when we reported an experience. "Well," he said. "You had quite an experience. What did you learn from it?"

"I learned that the administration of this place is pretty shaky. I'm scared by what I heard. And I don't know what to do next."

"That's interesting," Mr. Billings replied. "What do you suppose is the root cause of what you experienced with the president? If you can just set aside your being disturbed by this encounter, you may see through to what to do next. I take it that you still want to continue with your assignment for the newspaper."

"I certainly do," was my quick response. "But what do you mean by root cause? I'm really shaken up by this man's inadequacy. He seems to be afraid of his shadow. How did he ever get into that job anyway?"

"That's what I mean by root cause," answered Mr. Billings. "How *did* he get into that job?"

"I guess he was appointed by the trustees."

"Then why does he stay there?" was the insistent question.

"I guess the trustees let him stay," was my answer.

"Then what is the solution?"

"They shouldn't have put him in that job and they should get him out of there fast."

"But is that really the answer?" Mr. Billings asked quietly. "Suppose they take your advice and sack this man promptly. What's to prevent them from putting another person equally impaired in that spot—perhaps one who would look even worse to you?"

That question really puzzled me. "You've pushed me into a corner," I said. "I don't know how to answer that."

"If you're going to write a credible article for your newspaper, you had better be able to answer that question," said Mr. Billings with a note of firmness in his voice that he usually did not use with us. "Why don't you think over that question? Talk to the staff of your newspaper about it. Perhaps you might discuss it with your housemates here. But it is a question you should answer—for yourself. Come back and talk to me after you have thought more about it."

That was like Mr. Billings. He always tried to get us to answer our own questions. He believed firmly that this was what we needed to learn to do. We knew that he believed that it was more important for us to learn to think a problem through than to be given a good answer. So I did what he advised. We talked about it at the editorial office and in Jefferson House. Our conclusion was that the trustees were not doing their jobs—and they probably did not know how.

And the editors wondered whether we were really up to doing the investigative reporting they had asked me to do. There clearly was a problem. The president, as we had long suspected, seemed an inadequate man. But the problem was deeper than his inadequacy and there was a note of warning in what he said: by a careless article in the newspaper we could make matters worse. We did not want to do that.

I reported our conclusions to Mr. Billings. "That's good thinking," he said. "I believe you are getting somewhere."

"It seems to me we are getting nowhere," I said. "We're at a dead end."

"You are never at a dead end," he said gently, "as long as your efforts are enlarging your understanding of a problem. You are on the trail of something. I have thought some about the inadequacies of our president and the consequences in the university which is not as good as it is reasonable and possible for it to be if it were well led. The president is really the fall guy because the trustees—good, earnest people, most of them—don't know how to do what only they can do. Theirs is the primary failure. The president's failure is secondary, as I see it.

"I have been aware of this for some time because the issue of trusteeship is being discussed in the educational journals. And I have talked to a couple of our trustees. They are aware of the problem, but they are busy people and they haven't taken the time to think through what they ought to do about it. And, what's worse, they seem not to know what their full responsibilities are. But from my spot on the faculty I should not take on the trustees even if I knew how to do it. I have made my major commitment, beyond my family and my teaching, to this house. But somebody ought to take it on. Since you are steamed up about it, why don't you take the lead now and make a Jefferson House project of it?"

I was stunned, and I literally sputtered, "Good Lord, how would I ever do that? What would I be taking on?"

"It is simple to define," was his prompt rejoinder, "but probably very difficult to do. What needs to be done is to help the trustees find their most effective role and then get with it and do what only they can do to make this a great university—a standard that is now missed by a wide margin. Your project would be to help the trustees do this."

"It seems impossible to me," I said. "But if you think we can do it, I am for trying."

Mr. Billings paused to reflect. "I do not know whether or not you will succeed. The worst you can do is fail. We fail at other things and we might fail on this. And, if we fail, we will learn something out of our failure. Also, if you go at this carefully—and fail—you won't do as much harm to the university as you would if you wrote the articles you planned for the newspaper. Most important, though, in view of the depth to which you have been stirred about governance and the trustees, if you go out of this university without having done something constructive about them, you will never be happy about your university experience. You've got too much of the servant in you."

"I will think it over and present it at the next house meeting," I said.

In the next few days I was preoccupied with the challenge and had many conversations with my housemates. At the next house meeting I took fifteen minutes to give the whole story beginning with my assignment for the *University Daily* and concluding with a brief summary of my talks with Mr. Billings. Then I said, "I am going to take on the trustees, alone if I have to, but I will welcome help."

There was a long silence. My good friend Adam, a senior who had not participated in the discussions I had had with housemates, broke the silence with, "Well I'll be damned! So that's what's wrong with this place. I've been stewing about it for almost four years, trying to get a handle on it. Now I'm about to graduate and a light dawns. I have never thought of the trustees. How could it have escaped me? Mr. Billings, why have you kept quiet about this all of this time? I would have loved to have about three years to work on those trustees. Now I will miss the opportunity. I'm a little mad about that."

"I'm sorry," said Mr. Billings. "But, you see, I learn slowly too. I've become aware of this only in the past few months. After all, I am not a student of sociology or political science where one would consider such things. I'm a physicist. And some of you should have spotted this problem before I did. But I do follow the educational journals and recently there has been a growing comment on the role of trustees. And, as Martin told you, I have registered my view with the trustees—but only a couple of months ago.

"This is a good example of how the urgency of a problem will bring knowledge about it to the fore. Only within the past few years has there been much complaint about the inadequacy of our institutions, including the universities. And, after a good deal of ferment, this has finally led us to examine the ultimate source of power in these institutions, their governing boards. It is strange that we have taken so long to trace the malaise of our institution-bound society to trustees. But, now that we see it, what are we going to do about it?"

I took over again and asked, "Tentatively, how many of you would like to work on a project to get the trustees of this university to do their jobs?"

There was not an immediate response. After all, we were accustomed to taking on discrete projects with some tangible element. First, Jane, a sophomore, demurred by saying that she was already overcommitted and that this looked pretty big and murky to her. Then Bill, a junior, questioned whether we were up to anything as difficult as this. He preferred more manageable things. After three or four such comments there was a long silence. I just waited. Finally, in a gruff voice Jane said, "What the hell. Why are we here if we don't want to take on something difficult? I want to do it," and up went her hand good and high. I waited while she held her hand up—maybe two full minutes. Then, slowly, other hands began to come up—twenty-five finally.

Wow, I said to myself, now what am I going to do? But Mr. Billings, bless him, came to my rescue with, "Well, Martin, it looks as if you have your work cut out for you. And you are in about the right place to take on the leadership of this, with your senior year ahead of you. But this is the kind of idea that I think you all ought to sleep on before you begin to make your plans about how you are going to tackle it. Just to save time I suggest that you, Martin, select a small planning committee to put some intensive work on this. It will help, I believe, with as large a group as you seem to have interested at this point."

I have seldom been as grateful for an intervention in my affairs as I was to Mr. Billings that night. A day or two later I had selected four to work with me on a planning committee and we met with Mr. Billings. He said then that he suggested this procedure because he felt that this was probably the most important project ever suggested for the house and we should have some advice that he was not able to give. He proposed that we confer with Professor Elsa Winters of the Sociology Department, a friend of his. He had already spoken to her, and she had shown a high interest in helping us.

We had a long conference with Professor Winters that resulted in her agreement to act as our consultant. The first step she advised was that our committee of five should ask for an appointment with one of the trustees who lived in the town and who she was sure would be interested in what we wanted to do. She felt that in this first conversation with this trustee we should just listen to what he had to say about the trustee role. We should be prepared with some questions, but she believed we would not need them because he would probably talk freely. This would be the first step of the inquiry into how our trustees view their role and what they believe they might do to help make of ours the best possible university. From our report on this first interview she would then help us design an interview plan that our group would follow in talking with each trustee.

At this point we met with the group that wanted to participate—all twenty-five of them—and got their approval on this procedure. It was agreed that after we had worked out the interview plan with Professor Winters she would meet with all of us and give us some guidance in conducting these interviews of the entire board of trustees—in which all of us would participate in teams of two or three. A careful report would be written on each interview.

I turned to Mr. Billings and said, "Some of these trustees live at a distance. There will be some travel expense and a few telephone calls. How about that?"

"I will find the money," was his prompt reply. Later I learned that, although it took a lot of his time to raise money for the house there were several dependable donors who could be counted on to pick up the tab on really important matters.

Mr. Billings did the right thing, procedurally, by sending a note to the president of the university telling him what was going on. But (he admitted later) he did it rather perfunctorily and the president missed the import of it. So there were complications—especially when the president finally learned what was going on. He jumped on Mr. Billings, who quietly responded, "If you want this stopped, just give me an order in writing and I will stop it." Well, that stopped the president. He did complain that he should have been informed. Mr. Billings's response was that he had sent the president a note but that he apparently did not read his mail. He said further that the president was welcome to visit Jefferson House at any time and then he would know what was going on. "We are not operating in secret you know," he said. "At the end of the year we comply with the only request you have ever made—to make a full report on what we have done during the year. Do you want to make this every month? Every week? Every day?"

The president hung up on him. Poor man. We heard no more from him. Mr. Billings did hear from a few trustees—some friendly, some critical. To all of them he replied, "As I understand the plan you will be fully informed. I am not aware of an intent to publish anything about this. Though, of course, it will be talked about."

It took a while, but we interviewed all of the trustees. With Professor Winters's help we coded the content of the interviews. From this we wrote a summary of how the trustees regarded their role. We sent this report—a document that revealed considerable confusion about their role—to each trustee, saying that we would like to visit her or him again and discuss it. Most of them wrote back saying that they were surprised by the range of opinions and they would like to talk some more.

When we discussed these replies with our group of twenty-five, Mr. Billings made some perceptive observations. "I have been watching with considerable interest. As you know, I am a physicist and I have not been involved in anything like this before. But I have been doing a lot of thinking. I have had a rather negative feeling about our trustees—about trustees in general. It is inconceivable to me that trustees could go on year after year and allow the university to function essentially without a goal other than to provide for some courses to be taught in a range of subjects. It seems so clear to me that the university ought to assume the obligation to prepare its students (those of them who want to learn) to serve and be served by the present society and to grow with their opportunities. That is what we try to do in this house. Why can't the trustees say that the university ought to do this for all students who want it or would profit by it? Out of 18,000 students there must be 5,000 who would elect it if it were officially a clear option.

"But as I read the reports on these interviews these trustees see no initiating role for themselves regarding education. They elect to provide legal cover and deal with some issues that are thrust upon them—and that's about all. I hear some rumblings among our group that we need new trustees. Do you think we would do any better with other trustees that might be selected at this time? These trustees are good people—as good as you are likely to get.

"As I see this project now, if, as a result of what you have started here, there is the expectation that the university will become a substantially better place—say 5,000 in programs like we have here, or even 500—these trustees, these very people, will need to define it and give the leadership that brings it about. It will never happen spontaneously within the faculty and administration. If I should be run over by a truck tomorrow, there is nobody on this faculty who would take my place. These trustees, these same twenty people you talked to, will need to bring it into the pattern of the university."

There were groans in the group.

"No way," someone said sadly.

"It will never happen—not with these trustees," another commented. This seemed the general view, including mine.

"O men and women of little faith!" exclaimed Mr. Billings. "What other way is there? Either you persuade them or you coerce them. Suppose you whipped up some kind of student rebellion and forced the trustees to do something. You might feel some of the short-run exhilaration of winning a battle, but what would the long-run consequences be?

"This is a large and fundamental question. But I have very strong feelings about it. And I am convinced that there is no other way to make this a great university than to persuade these trustees— these twenty people that you have talked with—that they should give the leadership to make it great. And I do not believe that there is any group that is better positioned to do the persuading than the group of twenty-five that is right here in this room.

"This may have to be a mission for Jefferson House as long as the youngest in this room is still around. I venture that it will take at least five years of unrelenting effort by the people who inhabit this house. And I promise you this: *if* those of you who want to participate will take this on as a sustained mission of study and persuasion, you will gain a maturity and a perspective on the world that will serve abundantly for the rest of your days. *Serve and be served by the present society and grow with your opportunities is a motto that I hope will become the governing slogan—not just of this house, but of this university.* And I believe you can make it come to pass if you give it your best sustained effort."

Mr. Billings sat back in his chair and folded his arms as if to say, "Well, I have passed my torch to you. What are you going to do with it?"

There was a long silence. I finally broke it with, *"I want to take on the persuasion of these trustees.* Who wants to go with me on it?" Slowly hands began to be raised. Finally, after quite a wait, there were twenty-five.

Professor Winters stayed with us as our consultant; she was fascinated by what we were doing. We revisited, in teams of two or three, all twenty trustees and had some exciting discussions in which we listened to their reactions to the summary of the first interviews. Most of them were puzzled and some seemed a little stunned when they saw reflected back to them how they collectively viewed their job. There was a little hostility and some indifference. But most of them, in one way or another, said, "I don't know what we ought to do, but we've got to do better than that. What do you think we ought to do?" We had anticipated that question and agreed among ourselves that we would not answer it. Rather we responded, "At this point we don't know what you ought to do; but we know that the university is failing in what we think ought to be its primary goal, to prepare its students to serve and be served by the present society and to grow with their opportunities. And, as we see it, the university misses this goal by a wide margin. But we are willing to work with you to help you find out what you can do about it, because, as we see it, you not only have the ultimate power, but you are in the best position to give the leadership that will bring the university to the acceptance of such a goal. And we do not believe that such a goal will ever be reached if you do not give this university a new kind of leadership. Those of us at Jefferson House would like to reflect on this second interview and come back to you again with some suggestions." Not all said that we would be welcomed back but we had enough encouragement to keep us going.

Our next step at Jefferson House was to organize a study to see what we could learn from the literature. And there wasn't much. The Association of Governing Boards in Washington sent us its publications and reports of conferences. Reading these convinced us that what we wanted in our trustees had not yet emerged—anywhere. This dismayed us. Who were we to invent a new role for trustees, and what chance did we have of getting it accepted in practice? So, as usual, we went to Mr. Billings.

He listened patiently as we explained our dilemma. "I thought you understood that in the beginning," he said. "This reminds me of a visitor we had once—a famous rabbi and scholar, Abraham Joshua Heschel of Jewish Theological Seminary in New York. He spoke to us about the Prophets; he had just written a book about them. And in the course of his talk he made reference to false prophets and true prophets. In the discussion after his talk a student asked him, 'Rabbi Heschel, you mentioned the false prophets and the true prophets. How does one tell the difference?' The good rabbi, in a voice that seemed to me to have the authenticity of an Old Testament Prophet, answered tersely in measured tones, 'There-is-no-way!'

"And he stood there looking sternly at his questioner for a long, awkward silence. Then his face broke into a beautiful smile and he said gently, 'My friend, if there were a way, if we had a gauge that we could slip over the head of a prophet and say with certainty that he is or is not a true prophet, there would be no human dilemma and life would have no meaning—it would not be worth living.' After a pause he returned to his prophetic stance, and said firmly, 'But it is terribly important that one know the difference!'

"I wish," said Mr. Billings, "that I could convey to you the full drama of that incident. It means so much to me as I ponder your dilemma where there seems to be no way. In the course of his talk Rabbi Heschel said some things about that great line from Isaiah 'and a little child shall lead them.' As he looked at the students who were absorbed by his story he said, 'You do not think of yourselves as little children and yet Isaiah, in this chapter, was giving a prophecy of hope—that those who are inexperienced, who have not yet learned all of the things that cannot be done, will lead us because they are possessed by hope.'

"I suspect that you in this room will lead some segment of society to a worthwhile goal because you have hope and you will trust your intuition. Your strength may be in the fact that you accept *that there is no way*. If there were a way, *it* would already have been done and it would not need your attention.

"But I have an idea for you. Why don't you go to the library and read the literature on trusteeship and prepare a digest of it? Then send this to the trustees with the suggestion that you will visit them again to discuss the implications of what they read for their own trustee roles. I suspect that then things will begin to happen. It may, in fact, provoke a crisis and whether that crisis is resolved for the good of the university or whether it leaves us worse off depends, I believe, on how determined you people are to see this through and how you play your roles. I wish you well if you decide to follow this course."

We quickly decided to reconvene as soon as we could do the library research and make the digest. When we did meet in a few days we decided to follow Mr. Billings's suggestion and send our digest to the trustees with the suggestion that we visit them again to discuss the implications for their role. But now it was spring and I was nearly ready to graduate. A new project chairman was selected to replace me, a junior who was majoring in sociology and was close to Professor Winters, who remained intensely interested in the project and continued to be very helpful.

Over the next four years I kept in touch with the trustee project, visiting the campus four or five times a year and participating in some meetings with the trustee board as a whole. Jefferson House kept this as its major project over that period and I am sure that most of the hundred or so students who participated in it will be institution builders all of their lives as a result.

Sure enough, Mr. Billings's prediction was right. During the year after I left there was a real upheaval in the governance of the university and the trustee chairman, four other trustees, and the president resigned. One side effect was to start talk of closing Jefferson House as a subversive influence. But Mr. Lord, the great business leader and staunch friend of Jefferson House in whose company I now work, came to the rescue and spent a couple of weeks on campus talking with the surviving trustees, faculty, administration, and student groups. He was a tower of strength and as order began to emerge out of the chaos it was clear that the university was moving into a new and much higher level of quality. An interim president was appointed because a majority of the trustees wanted to reflect on what was the best way to administer the university.

What we had done in the trustee project was to bring to the surface a number of thorny problems in the university that had been brewing for a long time. The challenge to the adequacy of the trustees forced them to confront these issues as well as their own way of operating. And the consequences of facing a number of serious problems all at once produced a tension that split the board of trustees and brought a crisis of confidence in the administration. It was quite an imbroglio and there were many bruises. But it had to come.

With the guidance of Mr. Billings's steady hand and cool head, the Jefferson House group continued to study and consult. Their service was widely sought by student and faculty groups and they kept their eye unswervingly on the simple goal that every student should know that the university was prepared to help them learn to serve and be served by the present society and to grow with their opportunities. What Mr. Billings had foreseen was how difficult it was to persuade faculty and trustees that that option should be offered to every student who wants it. Countless hours were spent by Jefferson House members in explaining and persuading that nothing in the established program of the university had to change, no new courses for credit had to be offered. All that was asked was that every student who wanted that opportunity to learn should know that the resources were there to provide that opportunity. It was one of those simple propositions that one would not expect would require so much persuasion. But it required the five years that Mr. Billings said it would.

The university at that point had a board of twenty dedicated trustees. They had a coach who monitored their work and advised them on the *process* of their deliberations—not their conclusions. They had a full-time paid chair, and the work of the trustees was supported by several staff persons and consultants who worked under the direction of the chair. What the influence of Jefferson House had accomplished was to produce trustees who wanted, and were qualified, to carry a role in the university that conformed closely to what was required to build ours into a truly great university.

Just five years after that night when, as a junior, I had proposed that we set up a project at Jefferson House to reconstruct the trustees, I was asked to become a trustee.

My compact with my fellow trustees is that I will concern myself with the goals, organizational structure, and performance evaluation of the university. The cooperation of my colleagues is assured and the president of the university has told me that he will welcome my concern in these areas. The new chair has publicly stated that the trustees are committed to take any action that is reasonable and possible to build a great university.

One of my early accomplishments as a trustee was to persuade my colleagues to promulgate a much more explicit policy on governance in the university than is usual in universities. After a wide discussion among all constituencies (but principally faculties), an explicit and detailed governance policy was established which included the following:

A clear separation was made between academic work (that taken toward a degree) and nonacademic work—such as athletics, Jefferson House, and other adjunct programs. Academic governance is still to be worked out with faculties.

Nonacademic programs, such as the experience in Jefferson House, which do not count toward an academic degree, are judged to be equally vital to the academic in the education of students. But the administration of these is under a deputy provost who is responsible only to the university administration and trustees, not to the faculty governance process. Faculty opinion is welcomed and valued on such matters—but on a par with the opinions of students, parents, and the wider community.

Both academic and nonacademic programs are to be responsive to the leadership of university administration and trustees. The trustees accept the obligation to install and support an administration that is capable of sustaining such leadership. They also adopted the policy that the students who wished to learn how better to serve and be served by the present society would be offered the opportunity in adjunct programs for that purpose. Mr. Billings was then made deputy provost in charge of extracurricular programs carried on within residence halls. This became a major part of the university's program. Several, but not all, were patterned after Jefferson House, and Mr. Billings personally conducted a summer institute for housemasters that was attended by faculty members from all over the country. Part of the distinction achieved by my university was that it became a center for the development of a new nonacademic pedagogy in which adjunct programs like Jefferson House took their place on a par with intellectual pursuits.

IV. Mr. Lord and His Company

LET ME RETURN NOW to that part of my experience at Jefferson House that was a major influence in shaping my career. One of the able friends of Jefferson House whom I learned about on my first night there is Mr. John Lord, president of the large company I now work for. And, because my involvement in that company is so deep, I will give you quite a full account of how it came to be what it is, and what goes on there.

Mr. Lord goes to Jefferson House for at least one session each year, he always takes a summer intern from the house to work as his personal assistant, and he is a regular contributor of financial support of the house. In that crisis over our project with trustees when the house was under attack, he spent two weeks on campus working to save the program, an effort that helped, ultimately, to expand our work greatly and to gain acceptance of it as a vital part of the university program. I will summarize what I learned about Mr. Lord and his company from the evenings he spent with us at the house, from my summer after my junior year working closely with him, and from six years of work with his company.

I would judge Mr. Lord, now forty-five years old, to be in the top 10 percent of the adult population in innate ability and personal charm. In other words, he is able, but there are ten million other adult Americans who are equally able. But in leadership, character, determination, administrative acumen, staying power, perspective on the world, and the quality of his value system, he is in the top one hundredth of one percent. Whatever intelligence and personality he has he attributes to inheritance. Any ability beyond that, he maintains, is due to the influence of the great man, now the chairman of the board of directors of our company, who has been Mr. Lord's mentor for over twenty years.

Mr. Stephens, the chairman, is approaching mandatory retirement at age fifty-five for his office. I suspect that Mr. Lord will succeed him and that, in ten to twenty years, there will be perhaps a hundred women and men in top leadership positions in American (and worldwide) institutions who have been developed to unusual leadership stature under the influence of these two men. I dream that

I might be one of them, or helping one of them. Either role would be as welcome as the other. I have learned from Mr. Lord that it is just as important, and rewarding, to help a great leader to function as it is to be one. Mr. Lord is quite successful in sharing the satisfaction of his leadership achievements with those who help him. This quality, which is so exemplary in both Mr. Stephens and Mr. Lord, is partly what makes this company so strong. The view that Mr. Lord gave of himself and his company in my first meeting with him at Jefferson House has survived ten years of my close scrutiny, six of them as an employee of the company.

First, he gave us a view of the imperfect society in which we live and his belief that it is the responsibility of all institutions to raise all of the people in them to a higher level of quality as persons and as workers than they would achieve on their own. This was an astounding view to me.

Then he took on the role of competition. Competitiveness was one of man's less noble drives, he maintained. But it was there. He hoped that by developing a teamwork relationship within his company, he could help build an institution that would compete successfully with other businesses in its field without the individuals in his company competing with each other.

He also felt that competition between firms was not a social good. Unfortunately, competition between firms is required by social policy and affirmed by law. Someday, he believes, a better way than competition will be found to encourage businesses to serve. But until that is accepted as social policy, he will have to settle for reducing the competitive incentive among individuals in the firm.

He was pressed by the students on his assumption that competing was one of man's less noble motives. But he stood his ground. He was not interested in competing with anybody or anything. His business had to compete to survive and prosper so that it could serve well all of those whom it had the opportunity to serve. But he did not like that aspect of business. In fact, he asserted, churches, schools, hospitals, even foundations also compete. He considers it a challenge to the business he helps to lead that it will compete successfully with other businesses in the marketplace without the people within his business competing with each other. He admitted that they had not reached perfection in this regard but that they were striving toward it as a goal and were constantly working to build a noncompeting team of the people in the business. Because it is as successful as it is in building teams, it was his judgment that, in addition to serving better the people in the business, his company was a stronger competitor with other businesses and in this way better served their customers and the communities where they operate. Thus it was a more responsible contributor to society at large.

"How did your company happen to choose such a course?" was a question always asked when he talked at Jefferson House. His answer was one of those gems that I recorded four times in my journal. I give it as if he were summarizing it today.

* * *

Ours is an old company. It has always been well regarded—good products, good earnings for its owners, a good place to work, and a good corporate citizen. But it was quite conventional in its policies, in its organizational structure, and in its way of doing business. It was one of a number of such good businesses. Both Mr. Stephens and I, who are ten years apart in age, entered directly from college and worked our ways up the ladder in the usual manner. A few years ago Mr. Stephens was president and I was one of his key vice presidents but I was not number two. There was an older executive vice president in that spot. Then Mr. Stephens, at age forty-three, had a very serious coronary. For a while it seemed he might not survive it. Then for a long time there was doubt that he would ever return to work. The executive vice president, who was two years from the mandatory retirement age of sixty-five, was made president with the expectation that Mr. Stephens would be made chairman when and if he returned. Mr. Stephens did return as chairman on the retirement of the old president, and I was made president at the time at age thirty-five.

Mr. Stephens was always an able and thoughtful man. As I said, it was a conventional company and he was a good but conventional executive. But he did not return as a conventional man after his two years of absence. During those two years, he went through a remarkable transformation. And, because I spent many hours with him during that period, I shared the transformation with him. He did the studying and thinking and he tutored me. When he returned as chairman and I was made president, he and I and the board of directors were in complete agreement that we would build a different kind of company—one that was a better servant of all who depended on it and that did not use up its executives as Mr. Stephens had been used. We were not sure what its exact design would be. But we were determined that it would be regarded as exceptional by every person it touched.

Let me digress to give credit where credit is due. Mr. Stephens was not suddenly struck by a vision like Paul on the road to Damascus. He was an action man, not given to philosophical thought, and left to himself on that hospital bed he would probably have been thinking about how he would go charging again, as he always had, when he got well. It was his great good fortune that he had a wife who had been his quiet, sustaining helper for over twenty years. Mrs. Stephens is warm, lovely, very bright and thoughtful, and a very good person. His lifestyle as the aggressive, successful builder of a large business was certainly not hers. And she did not share his office life: she had a life of her own as mother, civic servant, *and* student. She read widely; much of her reading was for her husband because she read in fields that were important to him. She was wise in the ways of the world because of the breadth of her interests.

Temperamentally the two are very different. Now he is much more like she has always been. The coronary is what did it—it brought him to his knees and humbled him so that he was willing to learn from her.

Mrs. Stephens has never given me a full consecutive story of what happened, but I will share with you a brief summary of how I believe the fundamental change in Mr. Stephens's outlook took place.

Mrs. Stephens knew even before they were married that her husband was on a collision course and that he did not have a lifestyle that was dependable for a whole career. But she also knew that he had to follow his own star as long as he was able to, and she was determined that she would follow her own quite different star. Somehow they would live happily together and she would help him as much as she could. She really never predicted that he would fail in such a calamitous way and nearly die. But she was sure, as I said, that his was not a durable lifestyle that would see him through to the end, and that sometime he would need her to set him on a sounder course.

So, somewhere in the long series of quiet talks in his hospital room before he was able to see anybody else, he told her that he believed that his illness was providential and that he did not want to get well to go back to the very materially successful life he had been leading, that he had always known that her dream was better than his, but he was trapped by an ego drive to succeed in a conventional way—a drive that would not let him go. Now he was humbled. He knew that he would never again have the stamina to follow that old star and he was ready to be coached by her on how to reconstruct his life.

Her reply to him was that there was nothing wrong with his ego drive, he had simply had bad advice, as Moses had. And he had organized himself poorly. He saw himself as realizing his goals (as Moses did) through being chief, whereas the greater satisfactions come from being servant. He had the advantage over Moses in that the rug was not pulled out from under Moses until he was an old man and there was nothing for him but to be left alone to die in the wilderness. Mr. Stephens was under forty-five—his most productive career was yet ahead of him. He *could* radically reconstruct his leadership style and he just might be more successful in a fundamental way than he had been before.

"But this is a great risk," he complained. "There are no models to draw on for doing this. I might fall flat on my face."

Mrs. Stephens smiled and said gently, "Darling, you *have* fallen flat on your face, about as flat as you can fall and survive. Now you have no choice but to invent a new nonconventional way that puts your company out ahead as a pacesetter.

"Every great advance," she continued, "is conceived in the imagination first, then some able person has the courage to try it and make it work. Of course, you may fall on your face again. But what are your alternatives? To take up shuffleboard?"

There were some long discussions after this interchange. And Mr. Stephens finally agreed with characteristic spirit that he would accept the challenge of building a new kind of company. "Fortunately," he said, "I have a board of directors that I believe will accept this challenge with me." And they did!

During those two years away from the company he read widely under his wife's guidance and he did succeed, I believe, in finding her star and in setting his course completely on it. They have continued their separate interests. He is as absorbed in the company as he ever was and she has no detailed interest in it. But they do read and study together. She has become his mentor on lifestyle. The result is wonderful to behold.

In the course of this, while Mr. Stephens was still convalescing, he started to reeducate me because he believed that I should become president when the incumbent retired and Mr. Stephens would come back as chairman in a new role.

Mr. Stephens made it clear to me that, in succeeding him as president, I would not step into the role as he had carried it, as the single chief at the top of the pyramid. In his long period of recovery, he had come to the view that it was the design of his office that had brought him down and that it was not good for either the person in that spot, or for the company, or for anybody else, for the job to be structured as he had held it. He knew that he was confronting one of the oldest organizational traditions; in the Western world that tradition comes down from Moses. But he was clear that, in the modern industrial world—something that Moses could not have envisioned—the pyramidal structure of organization had become obsolete. Furthermore, he felt strongly the obligation to carry on the experimental work to build a new organizational model and to demonstrate that everybody who depended on the company in any way—employees, customers, owners, suppliers, the communities where we operated, and the total economy—would be better served. And he convinced me that it would be the crowning achievement of my life to take the operating leadership in building such a company. He would undertake to lead a board of directors who would assume a new affirmative role and contribute what can best be contributed from the detached, yet involved, position that the board occupies. He expected as comprehensive a change in the role of the board of directors under his leadership as he expected me to accomplish with the operating organization. He told me that during his long recovery period his wife had provided him with reading that would help him reconstruct his role—on leadership, institution building, trusteeship, *and* being a servant. He had discovered that one of the pope's titles was *The Servant of the Servants of God*. He didn't propose to clothe his future role in theological terms but he had resolved to think of himself as servant and to use that term. He knew he would be criticized for explicitly espousing the servant concept. But he was prepared for anybody who challenged him on it. His response to such a challenge was to say, "George Washington signed his letters 'your most humble and obedient servant.' And if it was good enough for George Washington to think of himself as a servant, it ought to be good enough for you." He did not have to use that response very often before the word got around. Mr. Stephens was a tough-fibered man, and he taught me to be tough-fibered. There is nothing soft about our company. We hold tenaciously to our vision and our goals. We know that we operate in a rough, often unscrupulous, sometimes dangerous world, and that we have to be strong to survive. When Mr. Stephens returned as chairman he was very clear that our strongest possible posture was to see ourselves, and to be seen, as *servants*. It has not been easy. But it has been more fun, and life is more serene for everybody. And we are successful to an awesome degree—nobody in our industry is even close to us. If we wanted to (and we don't want to) and if there were no antitrust laws, we could gobble up the whole industry in short order.

What have we done to achieve this?

First, Mr. Stephens has organized a board of directors who are committed to functioning fully as trustees. I won't go into the details. We lost a few directors who didn't want to assume the new kind of responsibility or to work as hard as our directors now work. We now have a small board of entirely outside directors. I am not a member of the board. No internal officer is on the board. The long-range planning for the company is done by the board. They have a separate office across the city from the operating headquarters of the company where I am, and they have a small staff that does their work, plus some consultants. One of these consultants acts as mentor to the board, attends all board meetings, and comments and advises them on their way of working. This consultant is not involved in board decisions. The outside auditors report to the board. Every three months we have a two-day operating and financial review in which the entire board meets with about fifty top officers. Everything is shared in these meetings. At other monthly meetings of the board, which are usually one-day affairs, presentations are made to the board by their own staffs. Usually the ten members of the executive council of the operating management attend those meetings and we are free to raise questions and join the discussion. But in the latter part of the meeting the board is in executive session—alone. If there is anything to be communicated from those closed sessions to the executive council, Mr. Stephens does it with the ten of us together, rarely to one of us individually, or even to me; and all of this is quite different from the usual board procedure—in business or anywhere else.

The operating management follows the team structure. There is an executive council of ten principal officers. We are a council of equals—with the same salary scale. As president I am not chief executive officer. I am *primus inter pares*—first among equals. My job is to see that this group of ten functions as a team—and that the company functions as a team. In an emergency I am expected to act for the group. But my action is subject to review by the group—and I may be censured by them. Sometimes I am. The design of our individual responsibilities and relationships is made by the board after consultation with us as a group. The design of the rest of the operating organization is made by our group of ten, and we make operating decisions as a group. If we reach an impasse, as we have done—but rarely—we bring the matter to the board. On two occasions in the time I have been president, the board has replaced a member of the executive council because he seemed to be a person who could not learn to be a team member. There are some capable people who seem not to be able to operate in a team relationship. We really hurt when we have to separate these people. But that is the price we have to pay for the kind of strength we have. You may be interested in the liabilities these two persons presented.

One was a very able executive and most valuable to us for his great technical knowledge. But he was so competitive that he seemed not to have a sense of accomplishment unless he was putting somebody down. Accomplishment to him was solely winning. We searched hard for a place in the company where he could serve us and win as a person. But, having adopted the philosophy we have, we could not find such a place. Unfortunately, he was mystified. He knew he was a winner and he could not understand why we would not want him.

The second presented a very different problem. We discovered early that, to build a collegial group of the ten on the executive council, we had to learn to accept silences in our deliberations. Often the resolving insight when there is controversy does not emerge as long as there is constant debate. It comes out of the silence. There comes a time when debate has exhausted all of the ramifications of a subject, yet substantial differences remain. We know now that the most productive approach is to lapse into silence so that the creative impulses, the imaginative insights that will bring new ground for resolving the issue, can emerge. Unfortunately, this one member of our group just could not accept silence. He was willing to listen carefully to others. But when others were ready for silence he had what seemed like an uncontrollable urge to talk. And he would talk interminably. We struggled with this for a year after we recognized the problem. He, too, was mystified and could not understand why his impeccable logic was not acceptable.

Both of these men were mature and well set in their lifestyles. We finally concluded that, if we kept them in the group, we would have to give up the notion of functioning as a council of equals and return to the hierarchical arrangement with one of us as chief executive officer. And that was a price we were not willing to pay. The rich, creative insights that came to one or another of us as we sat in silence, and relatively free of the shadow of personal competitiveness, were too valuable to us. In sheer economic terms, the fruits of the imagination that were born in the silences far outweighed what these two able men could contribute.

In the process of resolving the issue of what to do about these two valuable men, we became much more fully aware of the elements of the process by which our deliberations as a group reached a level of quality of executive judgment that none of us had ever experienced before when we worked in the conventional hierarchical arrangement. When there is no "boss" in the group, only a leader who both sees himself and is seen by others as an equal, one of the noticeable changes that takes place in the deliberations is in the role of questioning. Questioning relates not only to the act of listening and the development of vision on the part of the servant, it is one of the most effective means by which the servant is able to relate to the consciousness and conscience of others. In an atmosphere that is free of personal competitiveness and the dominance of a boss, however benign, questioning becomes what I would call a high art form. And it is a great time-saver because it minimizes hang-ups and facilitates the resolution of differences. And it produces, in the person like myself, who is designated as leader but not chief, a wholly new style of relating to my colleagues. It is simply the most satisfying and efficient means of arriving at critical decisions that I have ever experienced.

There is another aspect of our executive council that may interest you. We are not only paid the same, but our salaries are about 10 percent below what most of us could command elsewhere. We are well paid, and, taxes being what they are, we would not take home much of that 10 percent. Furthermore, there is no incentive compensation, and no opportunity to buy company stock that is not available to every employee.

Why do we do this? We would rather that those who have to wring the last buck out of their jobs would work for somebody else. Then we believe that the serenity and the sense of accomplishment that go with working in our company is worth something. And we want the top executives who work for us to put a dollar figure on that opportunity. This policy applies only to the ten members of the executive council. Everybody else is paid a full, competitive salary, even though this brings some members of the subordinate executive family quite close to the pay in the executive council. The facts are, however, that in the years that I have been president, aside from the two able men who were removed by the board because they were not team players, we have not had any losses except for retirement. And I really believe that most of the rest of our executive family would accept a move into the executive council even if it meant a cut in salary.

At this point I should note that it is really the genius of Mr. Stephens that makes this system work. And I have come to believe that it is the chairman's role, as he has developed it, that is crucial to the success of the enterprise. Most businesses that I know about do not conceive of the job of chairman as we do, and they would be hard put to produce a man like Mr. Stephens even if they accepted the concept. The basic problem is that, in our culture, such organizational ideas are not accepted and consequently few people are produced who can carry the chairman's role as we have it. There is a dogmatic theory of organization that postulates a different kind of chairman and a different board role than we have. We are challenging that prevailing theory.

In our arrangement, I carry the active day-to-day role of leading the executive council; but it is Mr. Stephens's comprehension of collegiality and noncompetitiveness, and his alert and objective watching of the operation of the executive council, that maintains the quality of relationship and decision making that we have achieved. I, as the designated leader but not the chief, could not maintain this quality by myself. In answer to the question, "But is not Mr. Stephens then really the chief?" my answer is, "No." The board of directors is the boss and Mr. Stephens speaks as the boss only when he speaks for the board. My reason for saying that he is not chief is that he never injects himself into the decision making deliberations of the executive council. There is the safeguard that I mentioned: the board will step in if the council reaches an impasse and cannot agree. But that is rare.

There is an interesting consequence of all of this on the organization as a whole. It is Mr. Stephens's belief that if we in the executive council can achieve this noncompetitive collegiality, our model will dominate the spirit of the whole organization; and we believe this is the case. We have little problem with maintaining a team spirit in the whole company. We don't talk about it: we don't have slogans or songs or creeds; we don't have conferences where we exhort people to be team players. The executive council simply dominates the company by its example. And everybody in the company knows what Mr. Stephens stands for and how he carries out his role.

The secret of the success of our company is not in our quite different organizational structure (though, at the moment, I can't think of a better one). The secret is that we have in Mr. Stephens a person who understands collegiality, and who believes firmly that it is the best basis for our kind of organized endeavor. He works constantly to maintain it at an optimum level in the executive council, he knows when it is there and when it is not there, and he has the toughness to remove any member who consistently violates it and seems not to want to change his or her ways. We feel lonely as a business because the principle of the hierarchy with a single chief is so firmly embedded in our culture and is so stoutly reinforced by our schools of administration. But we have an esprit de corps that none of us would trade for the assurance that orthodoxy gives most people.

Collegiality has a special meaning for Mr. Stephens. Administration by a group of equals who are led by a *primus inter pares* accomplishes two important things for our company.

First, administration of any large and complex institution requires several talents to an exceptional degree. No one person is capable of developing them all, and superior performance would limit each person to only one. After extensive study, our board of directors settled on ten of these talents as being indispensable in the top executive group of our company. This is how we happen to have ten in our executive council. For each of these talents to be developed to the full, the ten of us need to be equals. If we were subordinate to a chief, the chief's limited talents would color the whole administration.

Mr. Stephens's role as chairman, acting for the board, is to see to it that each of these ten special talents makes its optimal contribution to the whole. The individual does not have to wage a competitive fight with his or her peers to make a contribution. Quite the opposite: competitive striving with one's colleagues will be penalized. Mr. Stephens, working partly through me, undertakes to assure that each talent is drawn out to its fullest possible flowering, both in its individual contribution to the company and as a part of the group process in making broad operating decisions.

The second accomplishment of collegiality is that it favors the growth of the individuals in the group as persons, as people whose full human potential is worked toward. People are not used up by the struggle; they do not "burn out" after a few years. Mr. Stephens holds that the most destructive aspect of executive life is a preoccupation with "What's next, where is this taking me?" Part of his strategy of leadership is to make every position in the company significant. Achievement in the job one has is the primary means for personal fulfillment.

My colleagues on the executive council accept that the chairman's job, when Mr. Stephens leaves it, will go to that person who, in the judgment of the directors, is best prepared to give the quality of oversight that the chairman's role, as it is now conceived, requires. It may be one of us. It may be someone not now in the company. All ten of us accept that we are healthier and happier that this is not our preoccupation. And we also know that any deviant urges that are the normal lot of most of us had best be sublimated because, under Mr. Stephens's watchful and practiced eye, the slightest indication of an aspiration for the chairman's job will disqualify that person. I believe we are all more effective than most executives because we are healthier.

Underlying our whole way of operating is a policy on the use of power that may be summarized as follows:

1. In an imperfect world, there needs to be an ultimate source of power in any institution that has some autonomy. In our case that power (between annual meetings of shareholders) is vested in our board of directors.

2. The right to use that power, either in the top administration of the company or in its major divisions, is delegated only to collegial groups, never to an individual.

3. The board of our company, like most other boards, reserves certain decisions to itself. But beyond these, the board does not make operating decisions, except in rare emergencies when collegiality breaks down. The principal use of the board's power is to make sure that collegiality works in the operating administration. Board power is not used to second-guess administration.

This policy on the use of power makes the governance of our company quite different from any other large organization I know about.

Then we are distinct from many companies in our attitude

toward work. *We believe work exists as much for the enrichment of the life of the person who does it as for the service of the person who receives the benefit of it or the reward to the investors who put up the money to do it.* This attitude leads us to make a great effort to organize all of our work so that teams of individuals can have discrete parts of it. We are not so concerned to design the scope of work which individuals do as we are to give work groups as much autonomy as possible and encourage them to develop a communal bond that will enable the group to take responsibility for a segment of the work. We would prefer that individual tasks be worked out within the group. And we provide ample staff counsel to help them do it.

We place a management representative in each group as work leader and we have arranged with the union to have a steward in each work group. The work leader is not the foreman in the usual sense. He is given extensive training in leading by team building. We pay for the time of union stewards that is spent in the union's training program that the union conducts for its people. At the top level of the union and the company we try to stay in close contact so that the influence of each of these two leaders in the groups, the work leader and the steward, will operate in a way that does not interfere with the other's function and so that the net effect is a community that not only gets the work done well but provides the climate in which there is a strong supporting psychic reward in the relationship. It doesn't work evenly and we have to inject more outside direction than we would like in some situations. Also, as we have found in the executive council, there are some workers who seem not to be able to work in teams. Fortunately, at this level, we do not have to fire people as we do with top executives. We have enough tasks that are best done by individuals so that we can accommodate those who don't fit in work groups. But the psychic rewards in group identification, especially when a strong sense of community evolves, are so great that the percentage of failures is less than it has been in the executive council.

We have issues with the union. We have had some strikes. But we have been quite successful in keeping the differences that arise between the top leadership of the two bodies from disturbing the relationships in the work groups. We clearly recognize in the executive council that we may not use our influence in the work group to defeat the union on an issue. And we believe that the union accepts the same restraint.

There are some large businesses with attitudes like ours that do not have unions. But the older ones among them developed their character before unions became common. We rebuilt this company after the union was well established. There are times when the dream of life without a union seems quite attractive. But when Mr. Stephens and I worked out the philosophy that would guide us in reconstructing the company, we knew ourselves to be imperfect enough that we acknowledge need of the union as a check upon us, uncomfortable as it might be at times. We have so completely evolved a design for our company that includes a strong union that something valuable would go if we ever lost the union.

Another characteristic that separates us from the usual company is that we have much more staff—people who think, plan, advise, help, but who have no formal authority; and we have many fewer people in middle management than do most companies that are comparable to us. All major divisions of the company function under the leadership of executive teams with a *primus inter pares*, and they have ample staff resources. But there are very few links in the "chains of command." We operate on the theory that the work group is the basic element of the business. We try to give the work groups as much autonomy as they can handle along with the access to all the staff help they want. We really administer the business through the way we prepare the staff to give their help and advice. Many of our best administrators are in the staff and we lavish attention on their growth and skill. We try to follow the ancient advice of Lao-Tzu, "When the leader leads well, the people will say, 'We did it ourselves.'" We judge the effectiveness of staff persons on how well they can serve the organization in producing this belief—that *they*, the large numbers of people who get the work done, are doing it themselves—on their own responsibility. And, of course they are. There is no deception in our strategy. We are simply trying to get the bosses and the experts to make their contributions in a way that raises the sense of autonomy and responsibility of those who actually do the work. And we have been successful enough at it that we believe that we have raised the quality of the organization—and the actual service it delivers—far above the usual accomplishment.

One of the problems that has vexed us and on which we have not made so much progress is in what has been called "white collar crime"—particularly in the area of bribes, kickbacks, and payoffs. The nature of our business exposes us to the temptation for a great deal of this and it is a common practice in our industry. We have never had a policy of condoning it, but in times past we were not so vigilant to check it because it was so much "the way business is done." But beginning with Mr. Stephens's return we have toughened our stand against those practices, and we set up procedures that reduce the pressure on our people to give in to this temptation. We spend a great deal of time and money to watch this and to lift the penalty our people sometimes bear when they lose business to a competitor who does practice these things. Sometimes I believe that we spend much more to prevent payoffs and kickbacks than these practices would cost us if we were lax about it. The pain in it is that we lose a lot of business. But the benefit is that we maintain a good moral tone in our company that prevents many kinds of fraudulent things and we have an esprit de corps that is exceptional. And it reinforces other aspects of the business that give us a much greater capacity to serve than any of our competitors have. In truth, we are able to maintain our level of ethical practice, imperfect as we admit it is, only because our productivity is the highest in our industry and we are able to make up in some areas what we lose in others because we refuse to pay off.

Out of all of this we think we have learned (or, in the minds of some, we may have confirmed) something about human nature that may be useful to others who will be making assumptions that guide their decisions about organization.

The usual assumption is that most men and women are naturally competitive, and that they will only perform well under the spur of competition—for fear that someone will surpass them. We don't know about that. But, from our experience we would say that, when an administrative team is designed, and closely monitored, to be noncompetitive between members of the team, there are plenty of able people around who want to work under such an arrangement and their team effort will be superior—in competition—with other administrative groups where there is more interpersonal competition between members of the group. We don't know, but we suggest the possibility that we would have a better society if there were less competition between institutions that render a similar service. It seems to us, from our limited view of the world, that those institutions that presume to have the good of the whole society at heart (churches, universities, foundations) might be more careful in making assumptions about what makes a good society. Our culture so thoroughly reinforces the competitive urge, from infancy to old age, that it is difficult to think rationally about it. I concede that competition is a powerful motivating force, given the climate that nearly everybody supports. But it is a low-grade and debasing motivation. The times we live in are enough out of joint that we had better take some risks and gamble on the assumption that humankind will respond to a higher motivation than we generally ascribe to it. The experience of our company suggests that it is a valid assumption.

When I take this position publicly, as I sometimes do, I am usually asked, "But would you let monopoly and exploitation run rampant? What would you put in place of the antitrust laws?"

My answer to these questions is that I do not know what to do with the person who amasses power and uses it to hurt or exploit rather than to serve. But I do not believe that the antitrust laws are a good solution because I hold competition to be a low-grade motivation. My guiding principle is: *one of the first steps toward finding a good solution to any problem is to take the mask of sanctity off accepted poor solutions.* The antitrust laws were not brought down off the mountain chiseled in stone! They are a crude man-made attempt to deal with a difficult problem. Maybe they are the best we can do. But I refuse to accept them as a good solution.

However, when the question is asked, "What is the long-term outlook, how does what we do and how we think affect the general level of business practice?" I have to say that we can operate as we do in the present climate only so long as our people do more for us than other companies' people do for them. If we ever lose the competitive advantage this gives us, we would have difficulty maintaining the ethical standard we now enjoy. This worries us and we don't know what to do about it other than to talk freely with all of our people on these issues. Since it is a moral question, we try to get everybody to accept it as their problem—and I mean everybody, all 50,000 of us.

On the second part of the question, how does what we do affect the rest of our industry, or other companies generally? I can only say that we have not noticed any effect. Many come to visit us and to examine what we do. We have no secrets, aside from technical work that might lead to patents. But I sense no discernible movement for others to try to operate as we do. It seems as if those who lead most companies would prefer to fail completely doing the conventional things rather than risk the innovations that would build the kind of company we have that is demonstrably so successful. The trouble is, I believe, that most people think of improving their position by the introduction of what I would call "gimmicks." I could give you a long list of popular ones on which a lot of money is spent, but I don't want to denigrate other people's work because they are doing the best for themselves as they see it.

What troubles us most about the loneliness of our position is that the business community as a whole feels so defensive about the lack of esteem in which they are held and the constant encroachment on the autonomy of the voluntary sector by government. And they waste a lot of valuable breath in defending the ideology of privatism on the ground that our system is the most productive of goods and services the world has ever known. When they do this they are defending something that nearly everybody who knows the facts concedes. My quarrel with the voluntary sector is that the autonomy these institutions have, all of them—churches, schools, hospitals, businesses, foundations—is not used to serve society at anywhere near the level of which they are capable. With businesses in particular, there is the question about the quality of life people enjoy who work for them, the impact of questionable business ethics on the moral tone of our whole society, needless waste of natural resources, fouling the environment, flagrant violation of sensibilities in advertising. The case against business on all of these scores is impressive and business performance cannot be defended on the ground that, as a nation, we have more automobiles and bathtubs per capita. However, in my judgment, businesses do as well with their obligations as do churches, schools, governments, hospitals, philanthropies. None of our institutions does very well with its opportunities.

In our company we work hard at being productive, in a material sense, *while* we try to serve all who are touched by what we do. And, on both scores, I believe that we do much better than most. But, despite the clear edge we have in performance, there is little interest by other businesses in the basic thinking that underlies how we operate. It is our basic thinking about purpose and structure that makes us different.

We are different because of the fundamental rethinking of the concept of the business which Mr. Stephens did during the two years of his illness and the intensive education which I received because I spent so much time with him during that period. As a consequence we, first, have a different sense of our mission. As an institution we are here to serve; *that is our only franchise—to serve.* And we are here to serve, in balance, everybody who sees himself or herself as in any way dependent on, being affected by, or having an interest in our business. The list is long. We always start with employees, because they have the greatest stake in the business. Then there are customers, shareowners and other investors, government at all levels, the communities where we operate, suppliers and others who serve us, those who breathe the air and drink the water that we may pollute and listen to some of the discordant sounds we make, and, last but not least, those society-building institutions that are in a position to judge our performance as citizens: churches, schools, foundations, social agencies. Part of the elaborate staff structure we maintain that I mentioned earlier is made up of groups of competent people who watch our performance *as judged by every one of the constituencies I have just named.* It isn't just what *we* think we are doing to serve that counts. We try to find out how all of these groups judge us. It is a big job and very expensive, but it pays off because it enables us to act in a balanced way regarding all of these groups. The staffs that do this evaluating report to me.

This gives us quite a different organizational structure and way of operating than you will find elsewhere. And these fundamental differences are what make it so difficult for others to learn anything from us. When they visit us they seem to be looking for gimmicks

that they can graft onto their existing structures and ways of thinking—and they don't find any. The structure and the concept of our
company are so different, beginning with the role of our board of
directors and our chairman, that they present too great a challenge.
One of the things that puzzles me about our society-building institutions (churches, universities, foundations, social agencies) is why
they fail to come forward with the concept of the serving institution.
Why is it left to Mr. Stephens, in the loneliness of his hospital bed,
to think this through? Even after he has demonstrated that it works,
these people who presume to have the good of society at heart seem
not to be interested.

Without burdening you with too much detail, let me summarize how we are different. I have mentioned four ways that we are
different from most companies.

1. Our chairman is a full-time employee, but he is not chief
executive officer (we don't have one of those). The board of directors has six members in addition to the chairman. Each one of the
six is limited to seven years as a director. None of them is an officer of the company. The chairman and directors have their own
small staff and have the following major functions:

A. They define the business we are in, they set its goals,
and, as a group, they are the long-range planning committee.

B. They appoint the members of the executive council,
they specify the duties of each member, and they watch
closely how we function.

C. They assess the performance of the company and its
major parts —the certified public accountants report to
them.

D. They take appropriate actions based on what they find
on the above assessment. In short, they *manage* the company (as the law of incorporation under which we operate says they should).

2. *Administration* of the company in its day-to-day affairs is delegated to the executive council. As I mentioned, there is no chief
executive officer; the group of ten of us reports to the board and

meets with them. I am *primus inter pares*. The staff groups that
watch our service to the various constituencies named above all
report to me. The information that comes to me from these staffs
is the basis for my leadership of the team.

3. I mentioned that we try to organize the work we do so that
groups take responsibility for a segment of the work, under the
leadership of a team leader.

4. And I mentioned that we have much more advisory staff than
most companies and many fewer line administrators between the
executive council and the work groups. We guide the efforts of the
work groups more through the advice of staff than through direc-
tives coming down through a chain of command. We have a skele-
ton chain of command so that, in an emergency, we can operate
swiftly. But the principle that guides us is that the chain of command is used as little as possible. The credo of line administrators
is to be as inconspicuous and as unobtrusive as they can manage.
Let information and good judgment (which is what the staff is for)
direct the operation—not people.

5. The final major distinction between our company and others—and it is a big difference—is that one member of the executive council is in charge of personnel. And we mean, *in charge*.
Everybody below the level of divisional administrator (which is
almost everybody) reports to that person. There is a network of
personnel administrators—who report directly to the chief personnel officer—at all major locations, and they are *in charge* of all
the people. People are assigned to work leaders and other super-
visory people but they *belong* to the personnel department. The
personnel department hires all the people, trains them, assigns
them, and can remove them if they feel they are not being well
used. Any problem of any employee is the province of the personnel department.

6. Occasionally (but it is getting to be rare), we have to fire
somebody. But that act can only be taken by the personnel department—and that decision must be approved personally by the top
personnel officer. A work leader or other supervisor may find an
employee unacceptable. But all she or he can do is to return that
employee to the personnel department.

7. All communication between the company and the individual worker is handled by a representative of the personnel department. Twice a year every employee is invited to a one-day meeting in small groups with a representative of the personnel department just to talk about the company—or anything that may be on the employee's mind, other than grievances that are handled in the usual way with the union. However, this too is a direct responsibility of the personnel department.

Beyond these seven differences we are quite conventional. But the total effect of these seven major differences is to make us quite unconventional.

I have noted that Mr. Stephens will retire soon at age fifty-five. This is the retirement age for about thirty of the top executives. For the remainder it is the usual retirement age of sixty-five. The reasons for the lower retirement age for the top group are several.

First, we want to keep the top leadership young, and we want the stimulation of opportunity to grow in the organization which this principle enforces.

Second, a few of this group, after they retire, will serve a few years as consultants or directors of our company.

And, third, we try to prepare our top officers for public service careers when they retire and their level of compensation and pensions makes possible retirement at fifty-five with no economic strain. The prospect of this kind of two-stage career gives an excitement to executive service with our company that is quite unusual. We believe it is a very healthy thing to do—both for the company and for the individuals. We wish there were a way to do this on a selective basis for more of our people and someday we may work this out.

* * *

For six years, as an insider, I have looked closely at the operation of this large business. I see it as far from perfect, although there is constant improvement. It is conspicuously successful in both human and material terms, and it seems to have a bright future. But there is much yet to do.

I have given this detailed description of my company a central place in this account for two reasons. First, I want to explain why one like me who entered the university without the aim of becoming a businessman, and who was exposed, in Jefferson House, to four intensive years of preparation for service, would choose a profit-making business as a career. I think it is clear, from my account, why I made this choice. Then, I believe this company is unique in its goals and structure; therefore, it warrants close study by any who are concerned for the present state of our many institutions and are searching for ways to rebuild them from the ordinary to exceptional as servant.

I do not offer my company as a model in any of its procedures. It is instructive for others in one particular only: such a rebuilding from the ordinary to exceptional as servant begins with a new conception in the mind of the top leader in the institution. The problem of ordinariness is seen by the top leader as *in here,* in the thinking of the top leader, not *out there* in the structure of the institution. The top leader then accepts the role of *servant* as a well-understood personal commitment. The appropriate structure for the institution flows naturally from that understanding acceptance. If, by that acceptance, a hard-driving competitive business can be transformed from the ordinary to exceptional as servant, it can be done anywhere!

✝ ✝ ✝

V. I Visit Mr. Lord's Company

MY DECISION TO JOIN Mr. Lord's company, and their decision to offer me a job, might not have come about had it not been for the requirement that each student who wanted to return to the house in his or her senior year *must* spend the summer after the junior year working in close association with an experienced wielder of power. These jobs were all approved by Mr. Billings and most of them were arranged by him. A weekly journal on this experience was required to be sent in. Each senior had an evening in the course of the school year to review the summer's experience—from the journal. All of these discussions were directed by Mr. Billings to examine how power was used. Thus, in four years all of us had the chance to participate in about sixty reviews. It was a rich experience.

This focus on the use and abuse of power had an interesting consequence within Jefferson House. No one who spent four years in that house will ever lose awareness of power. We all knew that power was inescapable, that we would all use it ourselves, and that we would be subject to the use of power. If nothing else emerged from the experience, the establishment of this awareness as a durable thing was well worth the investment. But most of us got much more than awareness. We acquired some skill in the good use of power and some toughness to ward off its improper use upon us.

I have already given a summary of Mr. Lord's several talks on his company. What follows is my report to Jefferson House on my summer internship with Mr. Lord.

I worked that summer as his personal assistant. I sat at a desk near his. There are no private offices in this company and the members of the executive council share one large pleasant office with their secretaries. There are a few extra desks for persons like me who were working with them. There are several conference rooms nearby for special needs; the desks are spaced out, shielded by file cabinets, so there is really plenty of privacy. Typewriters are of the "noiseless" variety and telephone bells are muted. With an acoustic ceiling and a carpet on the floor it is a quiet, attractive place.

All of Mr. Lord's mail, except a few highly confidential things, came across my desk. I traveled with him and attended most of his conferences. We ate many meals together and had private conversations at other times. He was a man who seldom seemed hurried, yet he accomplished a great deal.

The key to this company's success, I believe, is that the executive group is dedicated to carrying out the long-range goals and plans formulated by the board of directors. The executive group is consulted on goals, but the directors set the goals. There are problems, of course, and things go wrong from time to time. But the common ground on which issues are resolved is provided by the board. The executive council has a very clear mission.

Mr. Lord usually presides at meetings of the executive council and he gives strong leadership to this group that always acts by consensus. In an emergency or when this process takes too long, Mr. Lord, or whoever is acting for him in his absence, is empowered to move on his own but is accountable after the fact to the whole group. And I observed some interesting sessions when this happened. Although I knew that it did happen, occasionally, nothing had to go to the board to be resolved while I was there; but when a unilateral action was taken, Mr. Stephens was always notified so that the board would be prepared to act in the event that the executive council got into a jam. It was interesting to watch the group process among ten very able, experienced, and strong-minded persons. Each realized that there was the obligation both to stand for one's views and to help find a consensus.

In this process Mr. Lord wielded a lot of power, which came from the fact that his personal staff, a large one, had a section headed by an able specialist for each of the eight constituencies of the company (named in the summary of Mr. Lord's statements). Mr. Lord's special function on the executive council is to monitor services of the company; he wields power through the information that is necessary to keep the company's work balanced in the service of all constituencies. This, plus the goals and plans formulated by the directors, is his basis for working for consensus when issues arise.

His power stems in part from his consistent position that it is not his personal view that counts but what the plans of the directors and the findings of his staff require. When an issue became critical, Mr. Lord's staff and staff from the operating units of the business are sometimes called in to debate the issue before the executive council. It is a fascinating process to watch. Nobody strong-arms anybody. But the contest in the area of ideas is spirited.

The greatest power, however, is not Mr. Lord's; it is the group's power. Ultimate authority resides in the directors (I did not have the opportunity to observe their executive sessions). But the power of influence on the operations of the company is in the executive council because its manner of operating is well known throughout the company. And it is understood that its power rests on consensus. Unilateral decisions in emergencies are recognized as exceptions and all accept that too many of them will destroy the power of the group. During that summer I did not have the opportunity to watch the group process operate at the headquarters of operating divisions of the company. But I understand that the procedure is much the same.

I must not close this brief report on my summer's work without telling of the chance I had to get to know Mrs. Stephens, the wife of the chairman of the company, who was the prime influence in giving Mr. Stephens the new vision for this company over ten years ago. I said early in the summer that I wanted to meet her and I had dinner once with the family and had several discussions with her alone. She is a person with great interest in people and their problems and aspirations. And she was deeply interested in me. We talked long about our mutual interest in organization—how things get done. And she wanted to know how the servant and team ideas were working out in practice in the company as I saw them.

* * *

During my four years at Jefferson House I often wondered how Mr. Billings, a physicist, could be so wise in so many things. Now I understand this. He kept saying that he was learning to be a servant-leader from us. What he was really doing was listening carefully to what we students were bringing back as we ventured into the inner circles of a wide range of institutions. The rest of us also learned much from those reports. But we were not as accomplished listeners as Mr. Billings was. Part of his great productivity as a person came,

I believe, from the intentness of his listening. He was taking in more than anybody realized and he was digesting it and filing it away for future use. High on the long list of things I learned from Mr. Billings was the crucial role that listening plays in being a servant.

I don't think it would be fruitful to try to summarize those sixty reports on summer experiences that I listened to during my four years at Jefferson House. But four of them that were in quite different settings from my own will suggest the dimensions of our contacts with persons holding power.

A Church

ONE OF THE REPORTS that stands out vividly in my memory was from a student in our house who spent the summer with the minister of an unusual church in a large city. From her account of it, *extraordinary* is a better adjective to describe this church. Her account, in her own words as I recorded it in my journal, is one of the most moving reports in that long document.

* * *

I was puzzled as to why Mr. Billings was so insistent that I spend the summer at the Church of the Redeemer. I am not a religious person in a doctrinal sense. I don't know the Bible very well, and while I have occasionally attended church services, I am not what you would call a churchgoer. The minister of this church had been a guest at Jefferson House some years back, before my time, but I had no knowledge of him or the church except what Mr. Billings told me, which wasn't much; he just insisted that I go. And I had an experience that will influence the rest of my life.

I knew this was quite a doctrinal church and I went with the resolve not to get converted—and I didn't, not to any creedal statements. But I certainly was converted to the servant quality of that place and to the servant-leadership that is so admirably demonstrated there. And I have a profound respect for those people because they really believe something and they live what they believe. They are a great, loving, serving community. I found myself wishing that I could believe what they believe so that I could be like them. Yet I did not emerge from this experience feeling that their particular beliefs were a necessary condition. But I am sure that there needs to be a unity of belief if a group is to become what they are, and if they are to accomplish what they do in the Church of the Redeemer. I will have to think long and hard about this because I am not ready to accept as my own what these people believe, and yet I want very much to be as they are, to be a part of a loving community such as they have, and to serve as they do. I know that I cannot communicate to you in this brief period the depth of feeling I have about this. But I will do the best I can.

The Church of the Redeemer is a small church, about 150 members. It is located in an old mansion in the heart of a city of one million. The church is about thirty years old and was started by a small group of ten dedicated people, including the man who is the present pastor. These were all solid church people who had become convinced that existing churches were inadequate for them and that they would build a new church for a new world.

Four things distinguish this church group from the common pattern.

1. They are mission oriented. They exist to serve the poor of their city. They organize others to work with them, and what they do in the widely varying missions they carry on in their city is done largely with their own money and their own hands.
2. A three-year course of training, mostly in the evening, is required before an application for full membership is considered.
3. Members are required to tithe, both in the giving of money and the giving of time to the missions of the church.
4. Each member reviews his commitment to the church each year and discusses it with others. As a result of this review, there may be a move from full membership to associate status.

Their church building is more a center for their extensive programs than a conventional church. There is a chapel in which regular Sunday services are held but most of the building is offices and conference rooms and the place is as busy as a beehive at all hours of every day. The people who make up this church seem to have but three concerns: their families, their jobs, and the church. Membership in this church is a total commitment.

This church is as thoroughly a servant institution as anything is ever likely to be. A few of their many missions have a paid person to give them continuity. But most of the work is done by volunteers from the church and its friends. A scheduled service from a volunteer, and most of them are middle-class people with jobs, is regarded as an obligation that is as firm as one's regular paid job. The pastor appears regularly as a worker in several of these missions.

The missions to the poor include services to children, the elderly, housing, a coffee house, literacy, counseling. There are some missions that are not directly focused on the poor, including the creative arts, international students, retreats, the moral tone of government. On the last list I saw there were eighteen distinct mission groups. Each has its own organization and budget. Some of their funding is raised inside the membership, some comes from outside. All function under the wing of the church council, the basic governing group.

The church is the fulfillment of the dream of the present pastor, who is now about sixty years old. Many now share that dream and have helped to enlarge and refine it so it is no longer a one-man idea. The pastor is a good preacher, but others share the pulpit. He is also a good pastor to the group, but others share that role too. *But the thing that makes this church extraordinary is that he is an extraordinary leader.* There are others who lead well but, in my judgment, it is his consistent quality of leadership over the thirty years that has built it to be the institution it is. It is not only well led; it is well managed. Prudent management has gone hand in hand with a gifted leadership. With all of the diversity, there is also good order.

The work of this church is well recorded at this time. The assistant pastor, a woman and a gifted writer, has written of its history, its theological and psychological roots, and its program and structure. Those who want to lead a vital, serving church in this troubled era have no excuse for their not knowing how. If they don't do it, it is because they either don't want to or don't have the heart or courage to try.

So much for a description of what this church is. Now, what was it like to spend a summer there? In the course of the summer I had a brief spell working in ten different missions, a great learning experience. But my primary task was to study the use of power by the pastor. There is no question that he is a powerful man—persuasive in the pulpit and in conversation and clearly at the center of everything, especially new missions that are finding their way or ones that are in difficulty. He is constantly watching and listening and is always available for counsel when it is sought. Older missions that are well established and running well don't get much of his attention.

The heart of this church is its missions, its openness to proposals for new ones, the way it supports them until they gain an autonomy of their own, and its willingness to acknowledge failure (and some do fail) and to close them down. Anyone—inside or outside—can propose a mission. In my brief stay I proposed one. And the resulting process fascinated me. First, there was a meeting scheduled to discuss it. In the course of that meeting several said they thought it was a good idea and they would like to participate. These people met several times during my stay there—mostly with the pastor present. His role seemed to be to assure that there was full and careful exploration of the idea. Its ultimate destiny, if anything is to come of it, is a formal proposal to the church council, which would make the decision. What actually happened was that my proposal got merged with another related proposal and a new mission was finally launched.

The pastor's leadership in this process was not to judge, not to push, not to hinder, but to gently raise the questions, usually after much discussion in which he was quiet, in order to assure that a thoughtful discussion was pursued. And when a consensus was reached he usually restated it a couple of times to make sure that it was understood. If he had strong feelings on an issue, he stated them clearly but not in such a way as to prejudge the outcome. He was open to persuasion. The best possible group judgment seemed to be his aim.

In meetings of the church council his role was to state and restate the goals of the church or to raise the question as to whether the goal should be restated. His role was brought up from time to time for discussion and he stated his views about how it might be changed in order that his own personal sense of mission would be fulfilled. (Members readily accepted that only if his role was right for him would it be right for them.) And he was clear that unless it was right with them it would not be right for him. These were heartwarming discussions and I could see that the kinds of tensions that are generated between pastor and flock in so many churches would never happen here.

I attended one meeting between the pastor and several key

members of one of the missions in which there was some tension resulting from an aggrieved member who felt that he was not being fairly dealt with in the group. The pastor opened the discussion by asking that person to state fully how the situation looked to him. This person took a half hour to tell his side of the story, while the rest listened intently. When he finished, there was no issue remaining. He had resolved it for himself. The next Sunday the pastor, without identifying the persons or the situation, recounted the incident as I had witnessed it. Everybody learned from it. The pastor's initiative in talking about the problems of the church and its people, within the context of his ever-manifested love for these people, and the acceptance by members of his openness, placed the pastor in a position of unusual power within the church—the power to serve. He was an effective leader because he was powerful, and he was powerful because he was effective—as servant. And it was all possible because he used no other kind of power, only the power of servant.

I mentioned that I was not converted to the theological positions of this church. The whole atmosphere was one of belief and prayer. The missions were explicitly carried within this theological framework. They did not require it of me, and I was accepted for what I was and shown the same love they show each other. I left there, as I stated at the outset, with a problem of my own to work out.

As I reflect on this experience I have wondered whether the pastor's extraordinary leadership is understood in this church. It is so natural it seems taken for granted. I have wondered whether they will be able to replace him when he goes. Also I have some questions about whether what they have written about this church adequately portrays the element of leadership that makes it all possible. I believe that many could learn to lead as servant, as he does. But is what he does well enough understood so that others can learn from it? I would not have known about it had I not watched closely for ten weeks—and I watched from the vantage point of a relatively detached observer. Is this a possible project we can take on at Jefferson House? Could we learn what servant-leaders are actually like in real-life situations and bring what we learn into teachable form, with an appropriate pedagogy, for that teaching? Somebody ought to do it if our institutions of the future become what we say they ought to become—true servants of society. And I don't see anybody else around wanting to do that. We've taken on some other large assignments. I believe we could handle that one. But I am a senior and will soon be leaving. I give it to the rest of you.

* * *

Usually there are immediate questions and sometimes a spirited discussion after these reports on summer assignments. But when Sue concluded there was a long silence. I was also graduating that year and the trustee project was in full swing.

"How could we ever do that?" someone asked.

"Well," said Sue, "I spent ten weeks there and learned a lot. Maybe somebody else ought to go next summer and learn some more. Mr. Billings talked me into going this summer. I would hope that my report would encourage somebody else to go without so much persuasion. I would hope, though, that it would be somebody like me who has some resistance to the theology of that church. Without that reserve I do not believe that I could have been as attentive to the process, the servant-leadership that I believe makes the place so remarkable."

Mr. Billings entered the discussion at that point. "After your report, Sue, I don't believe we will have any trouble finding the right person to go there next summer. I would like to think that we could make the kind of contribution you suggest and bring the servant-leadership art that you saw practiced there into the realm of substantive knowledge so that persons with the right motivation can be helped to be servant-leaders. I recall an observation you made early in your presentation to the effect that the model is there for anybody to see who wants to see it. Perhaps in the course of your summer there you found the answer to why just the model of what they do is not influential. You stayed there long enough and you were objective enough that you got what may be a very profound insight about it.

"Many people from other churches visit there, but very few try to do likewise. What they see when they visit is the impressive program of missions, and they don't see how their church could ever do that. They do not see the servant-leadership in action as you saw it.

And that may be the fundamental key, the really revolutionary part of that church. Effective servant-leaders can be so subtle about it that all that anybody is likely to see is the result. They don't see the cause. And it seems to me that you saw the cause. It is not just that the titular pastor is the cause. He has trained a churchful of servant-leader-pastors or they couldn't manage all of those missions. The many servant-leaders are the cause of what goes on there.

"I would not be so fearful that the church won't go on, at least for another generation, after this pastor leaves. He has seen to it that it will. But if the generation that succeeds him does not train servant-leaders as he has, then I would wonder about its long-run future. I would agree that they do not provide too good a model for other churches to learn from them because the underlying servant-leader qualities are not evident. It will be a real challenge to see if we here at Jefferson House can contribute to that. In a way, this is what I hope we are doing here—helping those who are natural servants to be effective servant-leaders. It will be to our interest in our work here to learn more about it.

"Let me confess something to you. I have never visited that church, but the pastor spent an evening with us here one time. And I have wondered why more churches didn't try to emulate them. Your report, Sue, gives the best explanation I have heard. The main reason I was so eager for you to spend a summer there was that I felt there was something useful to be discovered, something that would be useful to our work here, and that you were the best one I knew of to discover it. And I think you have discovered something. Thank you for your wonderful report.

"I would suggest that we think about Sue's question to us. The least we can do is hope that someone will go to that church again next summer. But perhaps we can do more than that. Perhaps we can make a project of refining knowledge about servant-leadership so that it is possible to teach something about it—to natural servants. It would be a great achievement for this house if we could pull it off."

A School for Leadership

FOR EIGHT WEEKS each summer a school for leadership is held on the campus of one of our prestigious universities. It has only fifteen students, selected from as many institutions or agencies. These students are midcareer persons who occupy substantial administrative positions and whose next move, if they make it, is into a top leadership role in a major institution. Its purpose is to help prepare them for this important step, *and* to make a judgment about what they need to do to be ready for it. Jerry, one of the strong leader types in Jefferson House, and there were several, had the opportunity to observe a full eight-week session. Here is what he reported on it.

* * *

Fifteen students, all about forty years old, plus or minus a year or two, assembled at the home of the dean of the faculty on a bright Sunday afternoon in June for a cocktail party that preceded the opening the next morning of an eight-week course that they (and the institution or agency that sponsored them) hoped would accelerate their growth as leaders. It was not a school of management or administration. These fifteen men had already won their spurs in those dimensions. It was a school for leadership, for the nurturing of those qualities that would favor their holding the top position in some large undertaking in which leadership ability, including statesmanship, is the prime requirement. Their salary, tuition, and expenses were paid by the organization where they are now based. They had already done extensive reading in preparation for this summer session and each came with a project, a critical problem of his institution that he had selected in consultation with his superiors. During the eight weeks each would ponder this problem and discuss it with colleagues, the faculty, visiting resource people, and others in the university who might be available. Upon return to his institution in the fall, each would, over the next six months, while carrying his regular job, bring the study of this problem to a conclusion and recommendation.

These students were all strangers to one another. In addition to the fifteen at this party, there were the director (who was dean of the faculty), the three faculty members who would teach the courses, and me. It was obvious that the participants brought mixed feelings. On the one hand there was some excitement about the prospect of an intellectually stimulating summer. On the other hand there was some apprehension about the workload, which they knew would be quite heavy with much reading, analysis, group projects, and writing, and, perhaps for most, there was concern about the fact that the faculty would make a judgment about each participant which would be reported to the participant *and* to the head of the institution where he worked. These three tensions—the intellectual challenge, the load of unfamiliar work, and the concern about the reporting—would continue for the eight weeks. I did all of the reading, writing, and analytical work (or tried to) for the eight weeks. But, during their class sessions, I sat in the corner as an observer along with the director and the two faculty members who were not teaching. It was the custom for the whole staff of four to be present at all sessions.

Two of the three courses were taught by members of the university faculty. One, a professor of philosophy, taught a course in *Logical Analysis* in which, after a few concentrated sessions on college logic, the writing of contemporary and near contemporary shapers of modern thought were analyzed. These included: Sigmund Freud, Karl Marx, William James, Pope John XXIII, Reinhold Niebuhr, Gerald L. K. Smith, and Max Weber.

The second academic course, taught by a professor of English literature, had the intriguing title *The Language and Literature of Decision*. I will say more about that later. The third course was taught by a senior staff member from one of the institutions involved in the program. His course was entitled *Leadership and Goal Setting* and consisted of lectures, case studies on goal setting, readings from the literature of leadership, and writing projects.

In this report I will deal only with the course *The Language and Literature of Decision* because this was the most different from anything I had heard about, and I believe it had the greatest impact in two critical areas: the value systems of participants, and stimulating their imaginative and creative faculties. In addition, their oral and written expression received rigorous criticism. Very few escaped without bruises on both scores.

But, first, let me report on the opening session at eight o'clock Monday morning (the classes ran from 8:00 A.M. to 1 P.M. with a half hour coffee break). The first session was taken by the faculty member who taught the Leadership and Goal Setting course and who was not a member of the university faculty. Knowing that there was apprehension about the workload and the reporting, he took these matters head on. "This is like any other important administrative assignment," he said. "There is always too much to do. And the task of all who have a leadership spot is to sort out the less important from the more important from the urgent—and do the more important. More work is assigned here than the ablest and fastest of you can do. Part of your problem will be to do what you do every day on your jobs—choose to do the more important. Systematic neglect is one element of the leadership art, and this is a place where it will be consciously faced, and, we hope, there will be some new learning about it.

"On the matter of reporting, to you and to the head of your agency, here is our procedure: we do not grade anything or keep any records. At the conclusion of the program the director and the faculty will meet alone for a couple of days and spend about an hour talking about each participant. We try to summarize what we have learned about each of you that might be helpful to you. And we make a separate summary of what we feel would be useful for the head of your institution in guiding your future work. There may be some overlap between these two summaries, but they may also be quite different. I make longhand notes on these discussions (nobody else does). I will be glad to discuss the summary with each of you, if you want it. But sometime this fall I will visit the heads of the fifteen institutions represented here. After those visits I will destroy my notes. Are there any questions?"

There was a quick one. "What criteria do you use in making your judgments?"

"There are no criteria," was the answer. "What we discuss at the end depends on what happens here—and we do not know what that will be. Each member of the faculty has his or her own standards of quality and we talk about these—written and oral expression, analytical ability, and so on. We will have watched your work quite closely, and, insofar as there are criteria, they will be implicit in the assignments that are made. But if what you are asking is, do we have a rating scale, the answer is that we do not have one."

Another quick question was, "Will anything go into the records of my institution about my work here?"

"If the head of your institution or agency wants to put it there, it will. Almost all heads of large institutions have their own 'little black book' in which they keep notes on people concerning whom they may need to make decisions. But, as I said, there will be only an oral report by me. And I will keep no notes after that is done."

Then came a really sharp one. "Could something be reported from here that will adversely affect my future career?"

"Certainly," was the firm reply. "But it could also favor it. As I said, what is done here is a piece of work. And it will be judged like any other piece of work. You can have this assurance, however: whereas, in the usual organizational relationships, capricious judgments are sometimes made by single individuals about a person's work, and often they are based on fragmentary information, here, four people see the whole task and only a consensus judgment is to be reported."

Quickly came another sharp one. "Is it fair to make a judgment, one that may affect a person's career, based on how he looked to professors in a school?"

"I don't know," was the frank answer. "The fact is that the heads of institutions and agencies whose subordinates attend schools like this want to know, 'How did my person do? What did you learn that would be useful to me?' And they ask these questions even though there is a policy *not* to make such judgments—and they usually get an answer. We accept this as a fact of life and we prefer to meet these questions in what we regard as a responsible way. Now, most heads of institutions to whom such reports are made are ambivalent in that, on the one hand, they tend to dismiss an academic judgment as irrelevant. On the other hand, many accept these as unique judgments and that, regarding what is at issue here, the capacity to give top leadership to a large institution, what is learned about individuals in a setting like this may be critically important in decisions made about them. On this faculty we believe that when the decision is made to place a person in the position of ultimate leadership of a large institution, all data that would help prepare a person for that role, or that would help make a sound decision when the choice is made, is important. And we think we get some of that information in these eight weeks. We acknowledge that the fact we use this program this way adds an element of tension to it—for all of us, participants and faculty alike. But that tension is in every piece of work you do, every decision you make. And the existence of it here takes this program a bit out of the ivory tower and makes it more like the 'real' world you live in all of the time."

There was a silence and the teacher observed, "If there are no more questions, let us proceed with our course on Leadership and Goal Setting." During the ensuing eight weeks, there was no further reference to the issues raised by these questions, although evidence of the tension persisted to the end.

I have said that I would report on only one of the three courses, the one entitled *The Language and Literature of Decision.* The other two courses were interesting, provocative, and instructive, but they did not stand out as unique as did this one taught by Professor Gabrial of the English Department of the university.

The general aim of the course was to bring to bear the training, experience, and insights of a teacher of language and literature upon the problem of leadership. It had a double concern: (1) the study, both theoretical and practical, of language, semantics, rhetoric, and composition, and (2) the study of certain great works of literature, ancient and modern, with the practical view of discovering in them that which is immediately useful and valuable to the potential leader. These concerns were pervasive, and the two kinds of study were pursued concurrently throughout the course.

In *The Study of Language*, the first exercise was a close analysis of samples of writings of practicing leaders in the institutions and agencies represented in the course (not ghost written)—letters, memoranda, policy statements, public notices. This analysis yielded disturbing results. The writing was revealed to be often blurred and confused, wordy and flaccid. The rhetoric was cliché-ridden and evasive; the metaphors were weary and repetitive; the style was generally lacking in persuasive energy. As the course progressed, the writing of participants themselves (they were required to write constantly) served as further material for analysis. Under the pressure of this scrutiny, the writing improved. The discussions were penetrating on word usage; denotation and connotation; meanings and grammar; sentence and paragraph structure; precision, directness, and force; and rhetoric.

In *The Study of Literature*, the course proceeded from this basic premise: great literature is great not only because of formal excellence or style, but because its authors have a rare knowledge of and insight into human beings. Great literature is great because the authors know us so deeply and can impart their knowledge to us. Thus it is not impertinent to ask what Shakespeare can tell us about leadership or the setting of goals. Homer and Sophocles understood many of the central aspects of the corporate undertaking. It is not heretical to say that leaders in the world of affairs can teach literary individuals things about *Hamlet* and *Richard II*, or that professors of literature can teach businessmen things about running a corporation.

The central core of this course was the study of Shakespeare's Henriad tetralogy, *Richard II*, First and Second parts of *Henry IV,* and *Henry V.* In these plays participants found profound and searching studies of a large gallery of leaders, the weak and vacillating, the determined and ruthless, the drab and the charismatic, the successes and the failures. Nothing in them was irrelevant to the concerns of the participants. They discovered for themselves patterns and problems they had already encountered in their careers, newly illumined by Shakespeare's wisdom. The great literature of wisdom of the past shed light on the predicaments of decision making today.

The most dramatic single incident in this course occurred one day when discussion was centering on the buffoon character Falstaff, who was a roistering companion of young Hal when he was prince, but who proved not to be a suitable intimate when Hal became King. So Hal rejected him.

In the course of the discussion Professor Gabrial observed, "You have all climbed quite a way up the ladder in your organizations. None of you is yet king, but you might be. Did any of you have a Falstaff in your younger days, and did you find later that it was expedient to avoid him as you took on greater responsibility?"

I watched closely as he went around the big table, beginning with the student on his immediate right. Fourteen in a row shook their heads and said "no." None of them had had a Falstaff for an intimate whom they later avoided. Then he came to number fifteen, who was on his immediate left. Professor Gabrial was a reflective pipe smoker and I believe he started on his right knowing who would be number fifteen: a big, raw-boned, six-foot-four ex-Marine captain—and a wonderful person. Lou did not answer immediately. He leaned out on his elbows and looked slowly, and coldly, from one to another of the fourteen students who had said "no." Then, in his best Marine captain's manner he said, biting every word, "Every damn one of you has had your Falstaff and you ditched him for the same reasons that Hal did. Now own up to it!" And he began by pointing at number one and then he went slowly around the table pointing at each one as he got his grudging admission, "yes," each had had a Falstaff and each had done just that. Professor Gabrial sat there looking like the cat that had just caught the canary. Nothing like this had ever happened before in his teaching of Shakespeare. And nobody in that room that day will ever forget the incident.

The course went on to Melville's *Moby Dick*, which was analyzed as a novel about a business—the business of whaling and the leadership of Captain Ahab. And it concluded with the reading of some modern novels and plays in which the language of leaders was studied—as it related to success and failure. By carrying the study of language in parallel with the reading of great literature, there was a constant supply of ready examples in the literature of things being studied, examples that were useful in the language component. Throughout these explorations, the motto of the course was, "Our style betrays us." An individual leader or an institution will be judged by its language. "The concerns of language are finally moral concerns," argued Professor Gabrial, "a fact hinted at by the old fashioned term 'a man of his word,' and underlined by the morally uncomfortable phenomenon of the 'ghost writer.' If our modern institutions find themselves in a crisis of confidence (as many of them do), witnessed by their scornful rejection on the part of many young people, a contributing reason may lie in their language. Perhaps a new rhetoric, cleaner and more honest, more precise and more eloquent, is actually a pressing and practical need in all modern institutions. It has been the intent of this course at least to raise the possibility and consider it."

I came away from this course with an enormous respect for the servant stature of Professor Gabrial. I watched these fifteen students grow in moral stature under his influence. As Mr. Billings has defined the servant for us, and in a way that I fully accept, Professor Gabrial is a true servant. In terms of the emphasis on the study of the use of power in our summer internship, I would say that Professor Gabrial was a powerful teacher, morally powerful. And the fifteen men who worked so hard for those eight weeks (plus me) left with an understanding of power and a respect for the academic mind that they would not be likely to get any other way.

Part of my reason for describing the course *The Language and Literature of Decision* is that I believe that undergraduates who have an interest in leadership would profit from this course, perhaps more than the forty-year-old administrators whose class I observed. It would require a morally powerful servant-teacher like Professor Gabrial. Would that we had more of his kind!

A Foundation-Supported Aid Program in Africa

MELISSA TOOK ON perhaps the most demanding summer assignment. She worked with an aid program in one of the newly independent African nations, a program financed by a large American foundation. She reported on it vividly.

* * *

I had long wanted to get to Africa because I had read several of Laurens van der Post's books. These were on the southern part of the continent and I would be farther north. But it would be Africa and I would get a chance to visit one or two of the great wild animal parks. But I was mostly interested in getting a close (if brief) look at one of the newly independent nations to see what a place was like that was so recently a traditional village culture and that was now entering world society as a nation-state.

I went to the foundation office in New York for a three-day briefing. This was not very much preparation for entering as strange a world as I would go to, but I learned much in three days. And I realized that some people took on assignments to work for this foundation on programs in developing nations with no briefing at all, except what they read. Then I took a direct flight from New York to the capital city where I would be based and where this foundation maintained an office with two Americans and several local staff.

I received another briefing when I got to Africa. This consisted of some talks with the staff and about three days to read the files on the foundation's activity there. This was very illuminating because the foundation was involved in a wide range of work: agriculture, family planning, education, national planning, archaeological digs, health service, and training for administration. Most of the service of the foundation consisted of identifying areas, in collaboration with African institutions, where technical assistance from outside would be helpful. Then the foundation would undertake to locate the person, usually from the United States, who would come for a short stay of two months, as I did, or for a longer one of two years. The two-year stint was common because most of the technical assistants were university faculty people and two years was the usual limit of a leave of absence from their regular posts. I would be working as an aide for one month to two such faculty people. One was a professor from a U.S. school of public administration who was helping establish a new school of administration, and one was an economist who was advising the national planning office. I took the latter assignment first and, after about three days in the country, I found myself with a desk in a government office beside the American economist. Fortunately for me, the language spoken in the government offices was my own.

One would think that this would be a bewildering experience, but it was not. My economist boss had been there about a year and was thoroughly at home and well accepted by the Africans, whom I quickly found to be a gentle, intelligent, fun-loving people. But they were not naive. There was much that they did not know about the tasks before them. But they were very shrewd and careful in taking advice.

By chance, at a desk near mine sat a man who was in charge of receiving foreign aid and my boss thought that it would be a good introduction for me to get acquainted with him. He was very open and affable and interested in sharing with me. I quickly learned that receiving foreign aid was a problem because so many nations, some as poor as his own, were offering aid—together with a few private organizations, like my foundation. Receiving aid was a problem because aid was so much used, by the foreign aid giver, as a lever to build influence for the aid giver, and this country had to be wary to avoid being subverted. The head representative of my foundation had been there for some time before independence and was trusted by the government in ways that other aid-giving agencies, mostly governments, were not. In the course of our several conversations my African colleague made this statement: "You know, most of these aid givers are really not interested in us. They are primarily interested in building influence and status symbols for themselves. For instance, a community may have all the school houses it needs, but somebody will build you another one because it offers another place for one of those little brass plates, 'gift in friendship of the people of so and so.' But this community may desperately need a new jail."

Then with a horizontal gesture of his downturned hands he said in a husky voice, "Nobody will build you a new jail!" I went with this man on some visits he made to aid projects financed by different countries. He was looking carefully to see that they were doing what the aid agreement said they would do. We visited the family planning office and looked particularly into a room where ten Americans were sitting at desks seeming to do nothing. He just made a quick count and left. As we walked away I asked him what this was all about.

"Well," he said thoughtfully, "the last time we negotiated an aid agreement with your country your people got tough and insisted that they would give us no more aid unless we did more about family planning. We asked them what they wanted us to do (thinking that this was really our business). They said, 'We want you to accept ten American family planning experts to help you.' We said, 'okay.'" And then, behind his hand, he said in a hoarse whisper, "but we didn't say what we would let them do."

"So," he said, "here they are—and we don't let them do anything but shuffle papers in that office! Ridiculous? Of course, but in the realm of politics, especially in international politics, and most especially in aid-giving politics, there is a lot that is ridiculous. That is what part, but not all, of my job consists of—dealing with the ridiculous, and what you saw in that room is the most ridiculous of all."

"And it is my country," I moaned.

"Never mind," he said sweetly. "I will show you something to cheer you up." And he did. A lot of good work was being done by American aid.

The month I spent with the American economist in the National Planning Office was totally disillusioning. My boss was a kindly, thoughtful man, very intelligent and knowledgeable about economic planning and deeply interested in Africa. But I quickly learned from the Africans in the office, who were eager to tell me, that he was what I would call a nonfinisher. He had some sort of psychological block that prevented him from bringing closure on a piece of work. He was the consummate dilettante, he loved to play with ideas, and he did it very artfully, but he shrank back from facing the implications of making a decision and moving on. And he was standing in the way of the very work he was brought there to further. It was all very frustrating to the Africans because this was a man with impeccable academic credentials, no doubt an adequate scholar and teacher, who was brought to them by an organization they respected. And it was very embarrassing to me, his aide for one month. Finally I got up my courage to talk with the foundation representative about it. He was aware of the problem, but not to the depth I described it because the Africans had fully unburdened themselves to me. But there seemed to be nothing to do about it but let the man finish his contract. The problem, the representative told me, was that academics and retired people were about the only ones available for this sort of assignment, and that the persons who engaged them in the United States were virtually just recruiters and would not likely be sensitive to the kind of personal flaw that this economist presented, if, indeed, it would be possible to discover it short of putting the man in the assignment. The real shock came to me when the representative told me that this man had taken a similar assignment for the same foundation in another developing country several years before and with the same unfortunate result, but he (the representative where I was) had not discovered it until after the economist had revealed this flaw on his present assignment.

"How did you find out about the earlier experience?" I asked.

"I talked with the man who was our foundation's representative in the other country at that time," was his reply.

"And he had not reported it to New York?"

"No."

"And do you intend to report it?" I asked.

"Probably not," was his reply.

I was too stunned to comment further. And I slept little that night. What a tragedy, I thought. Here are two struggling developing nations who have asked for help and they have been handed a penalty. What is worse, it may happen again because this is a very attractive man of good repute as an academic. He likes this kind of assignment and finds it all very stimulating. And it probably is good for his academic career. But what of the terrible cost to these wonderful Africans whom I have come to love!

The professor of government who was helping to set up the new school of administration, and with whom I spent my second month, was, in sharp contrast, a hard-driving "getter doner," quite the opposite of the economist, but, alas, he was equally flawed. His notion of service to the Africans was to help them (practically force them) to set up a school of administration on an American model so that it could readily be staffed by American professors who would come for two-year stints until Africans were trained to carry on in this model. Unfortunately (as I saw it), this pleased the Africans. In the course of my conversations with them I learned that many of the Africans in these new nations that wanted quickly to become "modern" had come to denigrate the work of Albert Schweitzer in Lambarene, for which he was world famous, because he practiced what he called "jungle medicine," a form that he felt appropriate to the situation in which he worked. I met an English missionary doctor, whose specialty was plastic surgery, who told of his visit to Schweitzer's hospital at a time when a seriously injured African was brought in who desperately needed plastic surgery. Dr. Schweitzer asked the English specialist to perform the operation. But they did not have any surgical instruments suitable to the need. The best my acquaintance could do was to produce six new safety razor blades. These were sterilized and the operation was successfully performed. This kind of story affronted the new African spirit. They thought they were being patronized by not being offered the best. And the best, in their judgment, for the training of African administrators, was a close copy of an American model. It may have been the best. How was I, a college junior, to know? But I was deeply troubled that no one would examine the assumptions on which this decision was made—neither the Africans, the visiting professor, nor the foundation that brought (and paid for) the professor.

Before I left I heard a story, probably apocryphal, about two nuns who had been dispatched to Africa from a religious order in Europe with the intent of Christianizing the "heathen." Five years went by and no reports of conversions were received in Europe. A superior was sent to investigate and, on asking the two nuns why no conversions, the reply was, "We are still trying to understand these people; we have attempted no conversions!" From which I draw the simple conclusion that one does not try to convert a person whom one is trying to understand.

When I arrived back in New York I went to the foundation office for a debriefing. There was a pleasant twenty-minute conversation with a busy staff member and when I received the usual cue that the conversation should end, I said, "I have something to report that I can say only to the president of the foundation. Can you arrange for me to see him?"

There was a startled response. "The president? You want to see the president? That is quite impossible. I have worked here ten years and I have only seen the president in big meetings. This is a large organization and hundreds like you come through here. That is quite impossible. I am sorry."

So I said firmly, "I have something to say to the president that only he should hear. It is important that he hear it. And I intend to stay right here until I see him!" She narrowed her eyes in anger. "Well," she said, "I have never been up against anything like this before. Most people who come through are at least gracious. Here you are a college junior—well!"

She took a deep breath and arose and walked to another office. In a few minutes she returned and said coldly, "President Nathanson will see you. Come with me." We took an elevator to another floor where, without further word to me, she said to a receptionist, "This girl to see President Nathanson," and walked away. I waited for a few minutes and was ushered into an office where I was introduced to the president, a gentle, amiable, but very strong looking man who greeted me with a warm smile and said, "What can I do for you?"

"I will be brief," I said. "I have just returned from two months in Africa with your program there. The only two parts that I saw of the extensive work there have troubled me deeply—" I paused because just then I noticed a large framed bit of text on the wall behind his desk. "I just noticed this," I said. "Do you mind if I take a moment to read it?"

"Go right ahead," he said. "I put it there to be read and I hope everybody does. Not all read it, and some who do either fail to, or don't want to, understand. So I am grateful for your interest. Perhaps it relates to what you say troubles you about our program in Africa. I want to hear about that later."

The nicely lettered paragraph read as follows:

Giving is a potentially immoral act. Its danger lies in the assumption of virtue by the agent, of the virtue of agentry, with an accompanying train of other unvirtuous assumptions. The relatively innocent desire to help is so thinly distinguished from wanting to be the helper. But the latter is capable of all sorts of distortions: wanting to be widely known as the helper, wanting to make some decisions for the helpee, wanting to dictate, to paternalize, to manipulate. It is not likely that a foundation, any more than a person, will escape these faults by thoughtlessness or accident. Only by being conscious of the danger is there a chance to escape. In other words, a foundation must believe in the potential immorality of giving.

MERRIMON CUNINGGIM,
President of The Danforth Foundation

I paused after reading and said, "This disturbs me even more than what I saw in Africa. What is the meaning of this and why did you put it there?"

"Its meaning to me," replied Mr. Nathanson, "is that it states succinctly the moral dilemma we in the foundation field are in, of having no work of our own, just money to give away. There is more to it than what is on the wall, but that is as much as I feel people who walk in here like you did are likely to read. A lot of people come in here and don't notice it. Or, if they do read it, it doesn't stop them as it did you."

I was still struggling. "I have never known that there was a particular moral dilemma in giving away money. Since as early as I can remember I was taught that it is more blessed to give than to receive. Are you questioning that?"

"Yes, indeed I am," he replied. "But before I expand on the meaning of that statement and its implications for the giving-receiving relationship, let me give a quick answer to the second part of the question you asked, why did I put it there? I put it there as a constant reminder, to myself and others of the staff of this foundation, that we in this business are in a precarious moral position. I don't know yet what troubled you about our work in Africa but I will guess that you picked up some of the consequences of our peculiar moral dilemma. You may not know it but many able, honest, influential people, perhaps without fully realizing why, do not believe that foundations such as ours ought to exist. A good deal of this sentiment came out when the Congress took a close look at foundations in 1969. I happen to believe that the foundation instrument could be a very valuable social force. But I also believe that we are in a race against time to demonstrate, before our right to exist at all is terminated or greatly curtailed, that we can perform a valuable and legitimate service. Now, before going further into the meaning of the quotation (and, by the way, Dr. Cuninggim who wrote that was a theologian before he became a foundation executive) I would like to know what disturbed you in Africa. That may give us a better basis for establishing the meaning of Dr. Cuninggim's statement."

Very quickly I told Mr. Nathanson what I have told you. He sighed and said, "That really hurts. We should do much better than you report on both of those projects. But I am not surprised either. I hear enough reports to know that what you describe are not isolated instances. And I know, also, that one of our best field representatives is stationed where you were in Africa.

"First, let me say that none of our major institutions is doing well. If you take a close look at the best of universities, hospitals, businesses, governments, churches, other foundations, you will find much more than you should of the kind of performance you report. Despite much that is good, and sometimes heroic, the institutions that make up our society are mediocre—all of them. But, tell me, you are unusually perceptive about these matters for a person of your age. What kind of preparation have you had to do this?"

I gave a brief report on the work of Jefferson House and how Mr. Billings cares for it with no encouragement or help from the university. The university merely tolerates it.

"There you have it," he said. "Yours is rated as one of the better universities and yet the kind of opportunity to grow that should be offered to all students as one of the first priorities is merely tolerated, and with no support or encouragement from the university. You could not give me a better example of an institutional flaw—just like the kind you discovered in Africa.

"Since you are interested, let me tell you something about

foundations and why they are particularly vulnerable to the kind of flaws you uncovered.

"Foundations as we know them are a relatively new thing in the world—less than a century old. And they are a peculiarly American institution, a product of our affluence—and the tax system. They are the only kind of institution on which there is no market test. All other institutions have to satisfy some constituencies in order to exist. Foundations have only to obey the law. I have thought at length about why foundations are held in low esteem when their potential for doing good is so great. And I would like to share some of the fruits of my thinking.

"The widely held view that the best of our institutions are mediocre has emerged within your lifetime. It has come about, I believe, because of a rather sudden rise in expectations of large numbers of people. And this is accounted for, some hold, because, since World War II, we have raised the percentage of college age young people actually in college from fifteen to fifty. The majority of these students have found their college experience quite unsatisfactory. Educators have blithely assumed that the medieval concept of the university, which still dominates, and that may have been satisfactory a century ago when only one percent went to college, is good for everybody. And it has not proved to be so. Careful analysts have confirmed that not more than 15 percent of the population will prosper under any kind of academic education. So, we first stirred a massive disaffection with the university concept which was fertile soil for the disruptions of the late 1960s, and, once aroused, it turned to an examination of all institutions and found them all seriously flawed. Furthermore, foundations were judged flawed to the extent that some would abolish them entirely. Why are foundations judged to be the most seriously flawed of all?

"First, I believe foundations are the most vulnerable of all to the arrogance of power. In a foundation staff the greatest prestige tends to go to those who give away the most money. Anyone who has money to give away is in a position of unusual power partly because the normal corrective influences, the communication feedback from the environment, that tell people how they are viewed by their contemporaries and that help to keep most people and institutions on an acceptable course are either absent or muted regarding foundations. The combination of power to give money away and the absence of corrective feedback breeds an all too evident arrogance—and the kinds of liabilities that Dr. Cuninggim mentions in his quotation on the wall behind me.

"Then, if all that one does is give money, one is not likely to grow in stature in foundation staff work. Consequently, I have the uneasy feeling that foundation staff work does not attract the very best people. We have good people, but not the very best—and we need our share of the very best.

"And, finally, and I want to keep this brief, I believe that the kind of philanthropy we do raises a question about the biblical judgment that it is more blessed to give than to receive. The scripture writers may not have foreseen our conditions. There is a fundamental flaw in the approach of all our aid giving to the developing nations, both from governments and foundations. These people you saw in Africa have as much to give us as we have to give them. Different things, perhaps, but just as much. Yet, because we have the surplus funds to facilitate giving, we give but we do not receive. It is a conspicuous flaw in this foundation which does so much in the developing nations. And it is pure unadulterated arrogance that we regard the Africans as people who can profitably learn from us, but we do not intend to learn from them. This is one of the realizations of what Dr. Cuninggim warned us against, the potential immorality in giving.

"Now, you may ask, if you know these things, why do you not correct them? After all, you are the president!

"I try, but I do not succeed. I have not yet been able to persuade my trustees that these should be our concern and that they, the trustees, should state a policy regarding the basic nature of our work. I am an administrator, not the policymaker. And when I mention these things to my staff, they get so jittery that I have to back off. I could move the staff (although I would have to cope with a rebellion) if I had the trustees solidly with me; but so far I have not a single trustee on my side on this issue. They are horrified with the suggestion that we have something to learn from the third world, and the suggestion that ours is an immoral policy really leaves them cold. I keep working at it and I make a little progress, but so much more is needed.

"The choice I face in this job every day, and it is a painful one, is: shall I stay here and do the best I can with these trustees and this staff, and maybe make a little progress, but not nearly enough? Or shall I quit this post and join those on the outside who denounce the institution in the hope that someone else will emerge inside who will do better than I do? I don't need this job. Two or three times a year I am offered one just as good or better—heading another kind of institution that would pose problems of a different sort.

"This has been quite a speech, but this is the kind of explanation I give whenever some informed and considerate person like you really challenges me. What do you think of my position?"

I thought a minute and said, "I hope you stay right where you are and keep trying. Will you visit Jefferson House sometime? We are trying too!"

"I will come at the earliest opportunity," was his prompt reply.

An Independent Secondary School

LORRAINE'S SUMMER WITH an independent secondary school gave us one of our best insights into the possibilities for initiatives by individuals and small groups in our wonderfully plural society. There was a tendency among us at Jefferson House to be drawn toward idealistic solutions for global problems. Lorraine had a close look at one of those small molecular forces that William James talked about and pulled us back to an appreciation of the opportunity for small voluntary effort to blaze trails in a way that large established institutions are not likely to do. Let her tell you.

* * *

I went with some misgivings to spend my summer with a small independent secondary school near a big city. Mr. Billings had told me that something unusual was going on there, but I was not at all prepared for what I got into.

Mountlands is a private, coeducational school for 200, mostly boarding students, located about twenty-five miles from a deeply troubled inner city. This school, like most of its kind, had served an elite and, up to three years ago, its main service was to give a cloistered education to the children of parents who were ambitious for their children, who wanted to protect them from the vagaries of large public high schools, give them good study habits, and favor their admission to the "better" colleges. But it had failed, financially, three years ago, and was closed for a year.

Then a remarkable group of twelve men and women from the city took over the defunct plant and, largely with their own money, reopened it with a radically different purpose. They now admit sixty fourteen-year-olds each fall. About fifteen of them are bright ghetto kids on full scholarship. These are selected as having potential for leadership and seem to have values that will dispose them to return to serve others rather than use their education to escalate themselves into the more privileged segment of society. The other forty-five come from more affluent homes; these parents pay the full tuition for their own children plus enough more to cover the tuition of the disadvantaged students. The paying parents accept the idea that their children will get a better preparation for life, in the context of an adequate secondary education, by being associated with a program that has elements that are designed especially for the disadvantaged youth. I would not have guessed that there would be enough of a response among the affluent to make such a plan go. But I was surprised, and it raised my hope for the future. In fact, I would not have believed that such a civilized environment as I found in this school would exist anywhere. It is a great testimony to the power of an idea even in these times of low trust.

On my first day at Mountlands I attended a regular meeting of the trustees. This was an eye-opener. Had I not seen it, I would not have believed that such a group existed, anywhere. I have said that they were a remarkable group. As individuals, they were just ordinary good people. But, as a group, they were an inspiring lot because, I believe, they were putting power behind a great idea and they had a most exceptional leader—a woman of sixty.

Mrs. Margolis, the chair, is a large, motherly type; she is able and deft and full of humor and good spirit and she has her eye on a goal that is clear as crystal: *the disadvantaged must raise themselves; they must sharpen their demands to be better served by the larger society; and they must move in a disciplined way for a better life under the leadership of their own members.* The purpose of the program at Mountlands is to pioneer a new design on a small scale that other institutions can emulate on a larger scale. Two results are sought: (1) Search for and bring into the schools—all schools—young potential leaders, help them clarify their values, help them to find their leadership skills, and return them to lead others. (2) Carry on this training in the context of a normal secondary school program that will be ample preparation for those who want to go to college. An important peripheral benefit of it will be to prepare the children of the affluent to live in a society, and accommodate to the inevitable changes, in which the poor are determined to raise the quality of their own lives by their own efforts.

The ratio of one disadvantaged child to three privileged ones is based on a practical financial consideration that this produces a cost per paying pupil that the affluent are willing to bear. The school asks for no subsidies from government or foundations. The trustees, all of whom are active recruiters of students, rely entirely on their ability to persuade the affluent that it is in the best interests of their children to attend such a school and that they should bear the cost—and they do!

Now, what went on for the six weeks I spent there last summer? This is a special program for the sixty new students who will enter in the fall. Its primary purpose is that all of the group will learn to live and work together. The assumption is that the children of the affluent and those who are disadvantaged both have a great deal (if some different things) to learn, but that they will learn it in the same program. Those who need special help (and several in both groups did) are given it individually and privately.

It was a fun summer; there was plenty of challenge of physical exertion in games and swimming, and a relaxed social life. But it was also a disciplined and fast-paced program—seven days a week, and we all went to bed tired every night.

The design of the program was inspired by the work of the Danish Folk High Schools of a century ago—a work that had the effect of lifting the spirit of the dispirited Danish youth of that day and setting them on a course in which they would both master their individual lives and remake the Danish culture. The summer program I attended also presented some of the physical challenge of the contemporary Outward Bound Program. The combination was an intensive maturing experience. I deeply regretted that I had not had that opportunity when I was fourteen. I am sure that my high school experience would have been quite different.

There was a concentrated course in world history in which the group was brought, by the end of the six weeks, to a sharp realization of the character of the civilization they face as emerging adults. There was a well presented summary of moral history, including a view of the contemporary human dilemma. Many of us here in Jefferson IIouse would view this as straitlaced and dogmatic. But it was honestly and candidly done by excellent people. The import of it was to bring one to awareness of the kind of disciplined behavior that is required if one is to make the most of one's life. It was clear that the individual is free to take it or leave it, but one would disregard it at one's peril. The implications were that if one deviated very far from it, one's tenure at Mountlands would be short.

There was an introduction to poetry, music, art, crafts, in which talent was awakened, recognized, and stimulated. At the end of the summer this group had achieved a common cultural base that the specialized professional would regard as superficial, but it far exceeded what we have in common at Jefferson House.

It was an intense summer. At the end of the first week I was sure there would be some casualties. But there weren't any. It was done in good spirit and it was fun—but exhausting.

The summer program concluded one month before the opening of the regular school term. I regret not being able to continue with these students, but I plan to stay in touch with them, and with Mountlands. The curriculum of the regular school year is not too different from that of the usual secondary school, except that there is a sustained effort to maintain the development started that first summer. There is a member of the faculty who keeps a continuous relationship with the students and works to build their interest in leadership. They take frequent trips to see work on problems of the inner city. Then, and perhaps most important, there is a voluntary seminar on leadership for each of the four classes—to which all students in that class are welcome. This consists of talks and discussions with visiting resource people, some discussions of prepared cases, and a few readings and analyses of current happenings. I am told that soon most of the students are regular readers of daily newspapers and that the exercises in which they are asked to forecast events and invent solutions to current problems are exciting. For those who choose to take part in this leadership seminar (and almost all do) the program at Mountlands is both absorbing and demanding.

I suppose that what makes Mountlands different, beyond the first summer, is not just the presence of the disadvantaged students but the fact that their interest and concern is maintained by the presence on the faculty of a person who comes from a similar background who is deeply interested in leadership development, who has charisma and the spark of leadership himself, and who makes an explicit effort to keep the students identified with their roots. I suppose they will lose some of the very able ones to the enticements of the affluent world—but I suspect that those Mountlands students will have a special care for their home communities.

My principal learning for the summer was the powerful example of the leadership of Mrs. Margolis as the trustee chair. I learned that her husband has a lucrative medical practice to which he devotes only half his time. For many years the other half has been contributed to a community clinic. Mrs. Margolis, who was originally a nurse, has, since her children were old enough, worked with her husband in the clinic—and still does despite her great time investment in Mountlands.

"The inner-city clinic has been the great experience of my life," she told me, "because I learn so much from the people there, and I admire their great strength to cope with their conditions. I have come to realize the social solidity of the inner-city neighborhoods and what potential for leadership among them is lost because all of the signals they get from the other side of the tracks tell them that their only hope, as individuals, is to get an education so that they can make their way among the rich. I got the idea for this school because I believe it is important to give another kind of signal.

"I am not trying to discourage those who have a more self-serving motive if they want to make a try in the affluent world. All I want to do is to reach those who would rather stay in their home community and serve their neighbors; I want to tell them, 'There is a way—and we will help you.' Part of the basis of my confidence in the achievability of the goals of Mountlands is that I know and respect the inner-city people and they trust me. I find most of the students who come here from the inner city and I found Joe Blanford, the member of the faculty from the inner city. I also find a good share of the full-tuition students—among the families of my husband's fee-paying patients. And they trust me because they believe I know what I am doing even though they may only dimly understand it and have some apprehensions."

"How did you come by the idea to start Mountlands?" I asked.

"Joe Blanford gave it to me," was her prompt reply. "I got acquainted with him when he brought one of his children to the clinic and I recognized his extraordinary leadership qualities. So we talked. I wanted to learn from this very wise and able young man.

One day he said to me, 'I want to help my people. I want to help some of the young ones I know who want to help our people. We have a tremendous power to help ourselves if we only knew how to get ourselves together.'

"This started my thinking. My husband and I talked about it and we had some conversations with inner-city leaders. We finally asked them, 'If we started this kind of school, would you support it?' They thought about this a while and came back with the basic design of the school. 'We will support it if *you* head it, if there is no control of big money in it, if one of us is there to help our own kids, and if the rich kids are there because they want to know us and want us to know them.' That simple statement gave us the basic design for this place. And, do you know something, this design only dimly gets through to the wealthy families, but they buy it. Somehow, although they do not know the inner city as I do, they sense the total wisdom in this judgment and they know that their children will be better able to make their way in the future if they have this experience. Furthermore, they accept the obligation to pay the full freight, and they do not want us to seek big money sources to finance it. I suppose you would say that we exist by virtue of enlightened self interest."

I mulled this conversation over and the word *trust* kept coming through. Of course they would trust Mrs. Margolis. But it took nearly sixty years of living and great dedication to the inner city for her to earn that trust. This sobered me. I would like to be trusted right now to do something like this. And a faint voice of humility came through to tell me, "You too have to earn this kind of trust. It isn't automatically bestowed upon you because you are idealistic and able. You had better apprentice yourself to a leader who has already earned it and work with her or him until it is clear that you too have earned it!"

As I reflect on it, the difference between Mountlands and most schools is probably that it is following a course that is charted by its trustees, all of whom are deeply committed laypersons. The faculty persons are newly recruited professional teachers. Aside from the initial summer and the not-for-credit work of the inner-city faculty member, both of which are closely controlled by the trustees, the normal faculty governance procedures set the pattern for the school.

I believe that the accrediting agencies will find the academic program of the school quite conventional and of good quality. But the spirit and moral tone and level of maturity of the place are poles apart from the usual, and from anything I have ever seen anywhere. Mountlands, in my judgment, stands as a challenge to all independent schools, not just to uphold a standard of excellence which their small size and freedom from bureaucratic control make possible, but to venture, in creative ways, as servants of society with innovative solutions for its critical problems.

* * *

These five accounts of reports on the summer after the junior year—a business, a church, a school of leadership, a foundation, and an independent school—give, I believe, a fair account of the experience that is possible at this critical point in a student's career, and what it means to an undergraduate to listen to about sixty of these reports in the course of the four years. The students who spend four years at Jefferson House receive all of this as a bonus in addition to the other activities there and their regular university program. We were a normally social lot; we had great fun living and working together. We had some riotous times, and we had to learn early how to manage our time so as to participate fully in Jefferson House, lead an adequate social life, and take full advantage of the academic program. Some things we had to miss. We couldn't be on the football squad or in the school band, for example. But otherwise we led quite fully rounded lives and benefited from the total university experience to a greater degree, I believe, than if we had not been in the house. As a group, we were in the top cut academically. I am told that no resident of the house has ever been dropped for poor academic performance. Perhaps Mr. Billings saw to that when he selected us, or, more likely, the potential failures selected themselves out in the first place. The screen put up by that notice I read on the bulletin board would repel the casual, the indifferent, and the poorly disciplined. But those who passed through that screen made awfully good company.

The central idea in the summer internship was to give us the opportunity to study, at first hand, *power*, its use and abuse. The purpose of this was to give us a perspective that would enable us to design roles for ourselves as effective *and* benign users of power, and to prepare us to protect ourselves from the unhealthy use of power on us.

By the time we finished our junior year at Jefferson House, almost no one was interested in studying the use of coercive power. We saw enough of that around us in the university and in life in general. The literature we studied was full of it. What consumed our interest, after watching Mr. Billings work as our leader, was, how does a person *with a servant nature* wield power in other kinds of institutions? We wanted to study leadership rather than authority, and persuasion rather than coercion. The five examples given here, my own and four others, plus, of course, the remarkable work of Mr. Billings—making six in all—give, in my judgment, a fair representation of the best of the sixty reports on summer experiences by those who were in Jefferson House during my four years there.

Out of all of this, the overshadowing conclusion is the importance of a clear statement of goals. What is the institution trying to do and for whom? Jefferson House became a most important adjunct of the university, I believe, because it kept refining and clarifying its own goals. All of us in the house came to realize the impact of Mr. Billings's strategy on the opening evening each fall: he gave us, the students, practice in stating the goals. And, after four of those sessions, we knew how to do it. If an institution is to serve, its goals must be crystal clear, and *everybody* in the place should be able to state them.

VI. My Training in Administration

IT WAS CLEAR WHEN I made my decision to join Mr. Lord's company that I should have more formal training. I had not majored in business as an undergraduate, for which I will be eternally grateful—my major in political science was a much better one for me. So I considered attending a graduate school of business in the usual two-year program leading to the MBA degree. But Mr. Lord suggested that I consider the alternative of coming immediately to his company and studying part-time for a master's degree in administration. That is what I decided to do.

One of the early conclusions reached by Mr. Stephens and Mr. Lord was that if institutions are to be better, there is need for better ways to prepare people for administrative careers in them. These two men were far from satisfied with the influence that conventional schools of administration have. So they decided to start, with company funds, a new school of administration. This was feasible for them because the company headquarters is located in a large city with two major universities.

What they established was a school that is now chartered to give the master of administration degree but which has no campus and no faculty of its own. Its facilities are a few offices and conference rooms and a small reference library. It has a full-time president and a dean. But its faculty are all part-time—from other faculties and other callings. The assumption is that its students, with or without university degrees, will be employed in some local institution—including government. They will be given an assignment (or a series of them) by their employer that provides an immediate exposure to the administrative problems of that institution. This is the basis on which I went to work for Mr. Lord's company after my graduation from the university.

In consultation with the staff of the School of Administration a three-year program is laid out for each student which includes some course work at a local university if it is needed. It is a rigorous schedule for these three years because students are expected to carry a legitimate full-time job. There needs to be some bending of the requirements of the job, but it is essentially full-time. Also the program at the School of Administration is for eleven months of the year.

The faculty analyzes the involvement of each student in his or her work and then arranges its students into groups having similar assignments in different institutions. These groups meet frequently on a conference basis to discuss their work. The program of the school, in addition to the course work arranged elsewhere, is to design an analytical approach to the work of each student in his or her job and to develop the capacity to intuit the gap between what data and analytical thought produce and what a good decision requires.

A major facet of the program is training to work in teams on the analysis and solution of problems. When two or more students identify the same or similar problems in their jobs or in their institution, they may organize a team study of that problem in the several institutions. This is a rich source of learning when the several institutions may include a business, a hospital, and a unit of government. Team reports are prepared on all such studies and discussed in seminars.

The training in analysis and written reports is comprehensive. And the critiques of these reports by both faculty and students are penetrating. At the conclusion of three years the student is thoroughly trained in staff work. The emphasis is on staff work first, because Mr. Lord and Mr. Stephens believed this to be the most important need. They see staff work as good basic preparation for line administration, and as more amenable to training in a school. Furthermore, in my company, staff work is the more critical need. Able line administrators, valuable as they are, are easier to identify, and are more available than able staff persons.

The primary asset in this kind of program is that there are no prepared cases or simulations. Everything that is dealt with is real. At the conclusion of my three years in this program I was well established in a key staff position in my company. I expect to have a line administration post soon.

One interesting finding of my experience with this program was what it did for the universities that cooperated with it. The dean of the graduate business school where I took courses in computer science and financial analysis was outspoken in his endorsement of the advantage in a program like mine that operated independently of the university. He approved the trend toward this kind of training in administration because it would relieve the university from the need to be "practical" and free it to concentrate on what can best be done in the classroom, which is "theoretical" although it was admitted that this is an oversimplification of the distinction. The university, as he saw it, has probably suffered in recent years from trying to be too many things. The prospect that the university might soon be able to return to the areas of its strengths was widely endorsed by those faculty members who knew about my kind of program.

I conclude from my work in the School of Administration that the university can no longer imperiously preempt those vital years from eighteen to twenty-five. All of life cannot be brought into the classroom and the best of simulations are artificial. Students should not be isolated from what full involvement with the affairs of the world might teach them in that vital period. I found in my postgraduate education a new kind of unity between theory and practice, because in that period I was deeply involved in my long-term career.

VII. What I Learned

AS I REFLECT on my undergraduate experience I am impressed by the profound implications of the work at Jefferson House, and how much the reach into the world of affairs benefited all of us. It was done without any interference with our academic programs or our participation in the life of the university. We learned to make intelligent choices and we grew up *fast*. As I see him now, in the perspective of wider experience, Mr. Billings stands tall in his lonely role of provider of the highest priority need of young people: *to develop their common sense and to learn to live in community*. Not much else matters if one does not achieve these.

Mr. Billings had secret hopes that I would become a professor. I think he saw me as a future housemaster like himself, and I did carefully weigh that possibility and regretted that I could not choose it. By the time I became a senior I understood myself quite well and I knew what was required to carry out Mr. Billings's role. And I concluded that those were not my talents. I will be eternally grateful for the years at Jefferson House because they enabled me to sort out my life and to choose a course that made the best of my particular talents. Now that I have been made a trustee of my university, I believe that I can do more to extend opportunities like Jefferson House offered than if I had chosen an academic career.

I chose to enter the business I am in, and to undertake the training in the School of Administration, because I believed that this would give me the most satisfying and useful career. I came out of my work at Jefferson House with a good understanding of what service means. I believe that *serving* and *being served by* are reciprocal and that one cannot really be had without the other.

The lesson I learned from Melissa's visit to the foundation and its work in Africa was the importance of receiving. If one has power, it may be very difficult for one to receive—from the one being served. *Humbly receiving is the best protection against the arrogance of Power.* In striving to become true servants, as we in Jefferson House tried to be, we were aware that it was not some future or utopian society where this reciprocal serving action would take place. It was *this* society, the one we were in while we were in our university and in

Jefferson House and the one that we would graduate into when we left there. We believed firmly that only by learning to serve and be served by *this present society*, with all of its inadequacies and imperfections, would we be able to help build the future better society—which we all intended to do.

I realize that at age twenty-eight I do not have the *kind* of maturity that I will have at forty-eight or sixty-eight. But I believe that I now have a maturity with some assets that my older colleagues do not have. I have had not only the advantage of four years in Jefferson House, which none of them has had, but, because I am young and still identify with the young, I have a perspective on the world that I do not find among my elders, even in Mr. Lord and Mr. Stephens, for whom I have great admiration. And, to their credit, they respect what I have and they know that they do not have it. To those who question that a person at twenty-eight can have the maturity and perspective that I confidently believe are mine, I would say: do not make that judgment *if* you have not had an experience like mine from age eighteen to twenty-eight. I am more sharply aware of my inadequacies as well as my strengths, because of this unique experience, than I would be had I spent these past ten years the way most people in my generation have spent them. And I am grateful, more than I can ever express, for the influence of Mr. Billings and Mr. Lord.

Let me tell you briefly how I see my life unfolding from this point.

I will try with whatever influence I have to make my company a distinguished institution in the service of all who have a claim on it (and that is many people). After my description of it earlier one might ask, "How can you expect more of it? What is there left to do? There is nothing close to it in the business world. Perhaps no other institution, no matter how idealistic its pretensions, is close to it in quality." I like to think that this latter assertion is true, and it may be. But this company still is not very good, as I see it now, from the inside. It is operating in a very different world from the one that Mr. Stephens envisioned when he had his great insights just a few years ago. What I hope to do is help keep the thinking of the administration of the company sharply contemporary, as well as to raise the standard of what is reasonable and possible and to keep pushing the performance of this company closer and closer to that standard. I see so much to do that one lifetime will not be enough to get it all done. But I am hopeful that, as I gain more experience and stature in the company, I will be able to persuade others to join me.

Then, as a trustee of my university, I will try, with whatever influence I have, to make the university a distinguished institution in the service of all who depend on it. It is so far from that accomplishment now that I can spend the next few years doing easy things. As I told you, I have the concurrence of the chairman, the president, and the other trustees that I will concern myself with the goals of the university, its organizational structure, and the evaluation of its performance as a total institution. I have a good sense of the reasonable and the possible and I believe that I have developed some skill in working with the inevitable ambiguities in all kinds of institutions. But I am firmly resolved that if I find myself blocked for too long from making reasonable progress with this university, I will resign. I will not be a nominal or caretaker trustee. I have not threatened my trustee colleagues with this, and I do not intend to. But they know me well enough and I have made my expectations clear enough that they are aware of my feelings.

Finally, I have my obligation to my family. I intend not only to provide for them financially, but I will invest the time and thought to be a good husband and father. Furthermore, my wife is a fulfilled woman and I intend that she will have ample opportunity to grow as an autonomous person with a career of her own if she wants it. She is not expected to be a corporation wife. My career is not hers except that we are pledged mutually to support one another. If there comes a conflict between her career and mine, we will resolve it on the basis of what is best for our family and for society.

I fully accept these three claims on me and my time: my job, my one trusteeship, and my family. I believe that I can manage these three well; but I will accept no other claims on my time that interfere with my service to these three.

When I state this position, I am sometimes asked, "Will you accept no other directorships or trusteeships or the many civic chores that will be pressed on a person like you? How can you get away with this?"

My answer is that I will get away with it because I have carefully thought through what my priorities are, and because I believe that I can convince any who press other claims on me that, by operating this way, I will be rendering my best possible service to society. This does not mean that I will refuse all other service. It simply means that, if I take on something else, I will inform those concerned that I regard their claim on me as a secondary obligation and that I will drop it or slight it on a moment's notice if it interferes in a noticeable degree with any of my primary obligations. I realize that I cannot pursue a wholly idealistic course in this regard and that there will be inevitable conflicts and pressures where prudence will counsel that I compromise. But, thanks to the clarity of the example that Mr. Billings set by limiting the claims on his time to his family, his teaching and research, and Jefferson House, I have full confidence in the course I have chosen.

The trustee project that I started while in the university and have followed closely since has taught me a great deal. It was clear to me that many of the inadequacies of the university were directly traceable to the failure of the trustees to measure up to their opportunities. And part of their failure was a low-level concept of their obligations, which seemed forced upon them because they were overcommitted to so many other things.

In the course of this project, a trustee wrote me, "Most of the trustees I know are conspicuously capable and public-spirited people; but they have many pressing obligations besides this one trusteeship. It is almost impossible for them to educate themselves adequately and to perform the leadership functions that they are best equipped to carry out. I hope that I am more pessimistic about this than I need be."

I responded, "As far as the older trustees are concerned, those whose lifestyles are well set, you may not be more pessimistic than is warranted. Most, but not necessarily all, of these older trustees are probably going to ride it out as they are, and, as a consequence, they are likely to be judged failures by the younger generation that will replace them. But I am not pessimistic about the younger ones who are more likely to take seriously the essay *Trustees as Servants*, which profoundly influenced me. These younger trustees are more likely to accept (1) that trustee boards do not need to be as large as most of them are, (2) that there are large numbers of potentially able trustees who are outside the 'establishment' group from which trustees are usually selected when needed, (3) and that there are enough potentially able trustees available to supply all trustee boards with persons who accept only one, or at most two, trusteeships and who, if they are motivated to do a good job, will find the time to educate themselves adequately to perform the leadership functions that they are best equipped to carry out!"

By way of a postscript, as I look back, I realize that one of the major influences of my experience at Jefferson House was to learn that obstacles and problems are difficult to define, and that defining the problems that need to be solved and giving them an order of priority is one of the highest and most difficult of arts. Further, there are usually no simple and easy solutions; life presents a challenge of learning and understanding throughout one's years. I have much yet to learn.

Mr. Billings had consummate skill in confronting us with the hard facts that required us to accept this point of view by the time we graduated. He never talked down to us. He simply pressed us on to learn and to grow and to establish a pattern for growth that would carry us forward. And he stood there as a consistent model of what he was urging us to do. Yet he never even implied, "Be like me." Be yourself, *be your most effective self,* was clearly his guiding principle.

My Final Night in Jefferson House

NEAR THE CLOSE OF my fourth year in the university the fifteen seniors in Jefferson House met to consider what we wanted for our last evening there. We concluded that we would like Mr. Billings to respond to a few questions that we would give to him in advance. So we spent some time framing our questions, and we came up with nine that all agreed upon. Mr. Billings seemed delighted with the opportunity and a long evening was spent in listening to and discussing his responses. I will summarize Mr. Billings's comments.

* * *

These are nine very interesting questions and I am glad that you gave them to me in advance so that I could reflect on them. But let me say that most of what I will give in answer to these questions I have learned right in this room. How can I ever compress my answers to them into one evening? I will try.

First, how do I manage my life so that I can put so much time into Jefferson House and carry out my role as professor of physics and be a good husband and father? I am not sure that I know the full answer to that. My academic colleagues and my wife accept that I work at a relaxed pace. Neither complains that I neglect them in order to do my work at Jefferson House. My colleagues have other complaints that I will mention, and they do not understand how I manage it all—but my family does. There is an old Quaker term, *centering down*; I believe that we as a family—and individually—have managed that. In my life, as I have told you, there are just three things: my family, my teaching and related research and writing, and Jefferson House.

First, my family. I have the good fortune to have a wife who has a career of her own. She is a writer and editor and does her work at home. Without the income she produces we would not have been able to contribute what we do to the work of this house. I say "we" because *we*, our whole family, share everything. Our mealtime conversation has always been about what we are doing. What we are all doing impinges on the world in many ways, so we are not introverted. But we are all centered on action, on work, and we love the people we are involved with in our work. You know my wife very little because she seldom comes here. But she knows intimately what goes on here. If any wisdom shows in what I do, credit part of it to her. Ours is a rich, relaxed, loving family life. But work, the work of each of us, is at the center of it, and we all try to help each other.

My academic colleagues are less understanding. As I said, there is no complaint that Jefferson House interferes with my teaching or scholarly work. There is one curious complaint that will interest you. It is held against me by my colleagues that I am *too much interested in students*. Part of this may stem from my involvement with Jefferson House, but most of it stems from the time I spend with students outside of class. I say it is a curious complaint because there is a strange element in the academic culture that is averse to interest in students. Some of this is justified because the occasional professor is too social or develops dependency relationships to serve his or her own psychological needs. But that is not the complaint against me because I am quite reserved and all business with my students. I am not their "father confessor"; the university has other resources for that. The problem is, I believe, that, in the long period of expansion of higher education after World War II, faculty persons were in a seller's market and they took advantage of this to bargain down their obligations to teaching. Academic posts tended to become bases from which one "does one's own thing." This is not every professor, but that attitude became a large factor in the academic culture. My attitude collides with that. Teaching my students is the center of my work. I would not make a great research physicist if I tried, but I do enough research to keep myself intellectually alive and to enrich my teaching. The same for writing; I contribute an occasional scientific paper to enrich my teaching. And I leave the running of the university to the administration. I avoid committees like a plague. I accept that there is a legitimate faculty concern for the running of the university and that our elaborate committee structure may be necessary. I also accept that it may be the best role for some faculty members to be actively concerned with the larger affairs of the institution, to serve on a multitude of committees, or to spend every available minute on research and writing. And I respect those who make choices other than mine. I am glad that some of them do, because it permits me to make the choices that I feel I should make. My stance does not make me popular with my colleagues, but it does permit me to live my life the way I want to live it.

Related to all of this is my attitude toward time. I believe that I succeed fairly well in leading a relaxed, unhurried life. But I am ever watchful for the seductive enticements to waste time. Time is my most precious asset. By limiting the claims on my time to the three I have mentioned, I have managed to make of my life a manageable whole. The greatness of the university tradition, despite some limitations, is that it gives a few people like me the opportunity to work out a coherent lifestyle and to center down on what one sees as most important.

One can best use one's life well if one leads a disciplined existence. That is why I have emphasized that Jefferson House is a disciplined undertaking. And I have tried to help all of you to learn to lead disciplined lives. I know that this is now seen as an old-fashioned notion, but that is the way I see my opportunity.

Second, how did the concept of Jefferson House, as it now stands, evolve and what do I mean when I say I want to learn from you? You believe that I do want to learn from you, but you would like me to talk about it.

I have told most of you that I attended an undergraduate college where much of student living was organized on the "house" plan with professors in residence. And I had the good fortune to spend four years under the tutelage of a great servant who was a classics scholar. It was a different age and a quite different kind of university. And my housemaster did not conceive of anything like we have here. I doubt that he thought of himself as learning from us because his was a more intellectual leadership. He was serving us by sharing his scholarship and his human interest. And he hoped that he would set an example so that those of us who went into university teaching would do as he did. It was a great experience, but it was not a model for what we are doing here. However, I doubt that I would have taken an initiative of this kind in this university if I had not had his example.

I suppose that my learning from students was a matter of necessity. When this house first opened twenty-four years ago it was simply offered as a dormitory where a faculty member would spend time with students. There are many lost people among those who come to this university, so there was no problem with filling the house. But from my first meeting with those students it was clear that this was not going to be, for those who lived here, what I had experienced as a student. For one thing, drawing almost wholly on my scientific training, I did not have too much to share. Then, so many of the students were emotionally needy people and I was not prepared to serve them; I do not have a social worker temperament. Too many of them should have had professional counseling. But here we were together so I did the best I could; I tried to understand them. I did a lot of listening—and this in itself was therapeutic; and I learned some things. But by the end of the year I was certain that if I was to give my best service I would need to be selective, so that we would get a group of students for whom living here with me as their housemaster would be a rewarding experience—for both of us. I knew that I needed to be rewarded too, and being a therapeutic counselor was not my cup of tea.

The next year I took the first step, with an announcement that this was a house for those who were seeking a creative relationship together and that a contribution to building that relationship was required. We did a little better. In the course of listening intently that year I got the idea of service projects as a means for building that relationship. So, the next year that was included in the announcement. It was hard to get the first projects going but we did something.

I would say that there were about five years of this kind of experimentation before the concept of a house such as we now have began to evolve. Then slowly I realized that the success of this house really depended on my ability to select a group of students with greater than average maturity who are ready for a more demanding experience than the usual student is prepared for. I realized that I should not try to select a group of people who were alike, but they needed to be ready for about the same depth of experience. Another five years were spent in gradually learning—by listening to students—how to do this.

It was a student who suggested that the statement about the house that was given to prospective members be quite explicit on the *servant* emphasis. This student felt that the servant theme would both attract those who should be in the house and repel those who should not be here. I was quite slow to accept that I had an obligation to those who would profit most from being in this house: to try to keep out those who should not be here. We are not interested in reforming people or converting nonservants to servants. Perhaps the university should offer a resource for this, but we do not see it as our mission. We grew greatly in strength when we thought of the house as being here to help those students who bring a firmly set servant motive with them. Our task is to help as many as possible of the true servants to become servant-leaders. We have drawn a lot of flak for doing this, but it has served us well.

I have had a rich experience through listening to and learning from students who are quite mature and whose major interests are different from mine. Even if I had had unlimited time to take courses in this university, I doubt that I could have gathered the perspective on the world that I have gotten from twenty-four years of the kind of listening to and learning from students that I have had.

All has not been easy in following this course. One of the complaints from the faculty that you may not have heard from students, one that I have had to contend with all along—and it persists—is the charge that we are fostering elitism. Of course, the university itself is elitist. The athletic teams are elitist; Phi Beta Kappa is elitist. But ours is elitism of a different sort—our kind generates power within the university; and I am accused of wielding, through you, an unwarranted influence.

This is a difficult charge to refute—especially after this year when some of you set out to reform the trustees. I believe, though, that the principal reason for the criticism is that I have learned to select the more mature students. One can be a football hero or a summa cum laude scholar and *not* be mature. I think of maturity as simply *the ability to ride life's bucky little horse—and stay on!* There are quite a few members of our faculty who are not mature. They get thrown off once in a while. And we here in Jefferson House really threaten them. This is a tension that I have learned to live with, but it isn't easy.

Also, by listening to and learning from the students in this house, I have a knowledge of this university that few people have. This is partly because you are so disproportionately represented in the activities of the university, and partly because we spend so much time examining and discussing the university. Many of you share my perspective, and it is hard, in this position, to avoid being seen as big brother.

I mention these negative aspects because they represent an important part of the concept of the house that has evolved through the years. They are important to you because, as servants of society, you must learn to live with hostility. Although I did not consciously design it that way, I now accept that part of the concept of this house is that it generates hostility as a means of learning for students (including me).

In your third question you ask what is the basis for my optimism? You say that you feel I have an unwarranted optimism for the future. This surprises me. If we take one of the dictionary definitions, optimism is the belief that the good of life overbalances the pain and evil of it, and pessimism is the opposite. In this sense I do not think of myself as either optimistic or pessimistic for the future.

I believe I am a realist; I try to be aware of both the society-building and society-destroying forces that are evident around us now. But I have no settled view as to which will prevail in the future. I know that, in the past, civilizations, nations, institutions have risen and fallen, and I suspect that this will continue.

What then do I believe in now? I feel that I am supported by a sustaining spirit? I try to live fully in the present moment as a point on a continuum from past to future. My life motif is one that I have consistently maintained with you, to serve and be served by the *present* society. You may think of me as optimistic for the future because you may see me as cheerful and confident in the present. If you do, that is an unwarranted assumption. I believe that I do my best to assure the future when I do my best in the present moment. Practically, as I see it, there is no other alternative. I cannot remake the past, and I can only shape the future by what I do now. If the future turns out to be a disaster, according to our present values, I will continue to strive, with good spirit, to serve and be served by *that* society.

I not only accept the idea of impermanence in all things, as proclaimed by the Buddha 2,500 years ago, but I regard such acceptance as essential for the flowering of the human spirit.

I will try to anticipate future conditions and prepare for them. But my hope for the future is that, no matter what the conditions, as an individual person I will be effective as servant. In this sense, I am hopeful for the future, as far as my place—and yours—in it is concerned, but I am neither an optimist nor a pessimist. I will take it as it comes.

Now for your fourth question: How did the summer internship at the end of the junior year evolve, and how did you come to direct that work to the study of power?

Early on I invited guests for evening sessions. At first they were just interesting people with knowledge to share. Then I discovered a high student interest in spending time with people who represent some tangible accomplishment in the world. The latter became interested in the students, and some of our guests who could arrange summer jobs took the first initiative. This suggested that I try to extend these opportunities. Then one evening our visitor was an old dean from one of our prestigious business schools. He made the remark, "There is nothing that will help an undergraduate settle his or her own lifestyle more quickly and surely than the right summer job in which the student can relate to a successful servant-leader." That remark settled it for me.

Then I learned about an interesting organization that arranges a two-year program of a series of internships for university graduates. We borrowed from them the idea of journal keeping and seminar reporting on the experience. Making the admission to the house in the senior year dependent on an approved summer internship with regular journal reporting was added to put a formal disciplined element into our work, and it helps to bring together a group in which all members are mature enough to accomplish important work together.

Now, why the focus on power?

I am surprised, after your last summer's experience and all of the reports you have listened to, that you ask that question. But, then, I take it that you just want my personal views on it. After thinking about it I doubt that I can add anything to what you have learned in the course of your own experience. But I will try.

Part of the reason for emphasizing the study of the use and abuse of power is that I hope that you will look closely at the consequences of concentrating executive power in one person, a practice that has been deeply embedded in our culture from the time of Moses. In my view, such use of power is no longer acceptable. It always seems to have a destructive aspect. In the end, much more is lost than is gained.

The opportunity for those who still hold such power is to use it, while they still have it, to take the necessary steps to transfer that power to a collegial group under the leadership of a *primus inter pares*, a first among equals.

Then, if I have any pedagogical theory to guide what I do as housemaster here, it is this: In our work we differ from most of the rest of the university in one major particular. The formal program of the university upon which the degree is based is intellectual. In the academic program we don't assume that everything has been learned and that we will teach it to you; as a student you also partic-ipate in discovery. But it is intellectual development and you are learning to think in abstract ways. Reading, analysis, synthesis, artic-ulation, laboratory experimentation are the principal means. In a course of study of this kind you may learn something *about* power.

What I have learned about it has not come that way. What I know about power has been learned by using it, having it used on me, and watching its use by and on others and calculating the effect. In all of this I have concluded that power is a very central issue in life and that an element of maturity is to be able to pursue one's lifestyle and both use power well and respond in a healthy way to power (serve and be served by).

Power is *benign* when, in the course of using it, both the user and the subject grow as persons, when they become healthier, wiser, freer, more autonomous, more likely themselves to become ser-vants—as a result of power's being used. Power is a malignant force when people are coerced by it. No one grows when coerced. The best that can be hoped for is that they will conform—not a very happy state.

My value system calls for the benign use of power—and you know what I mean by that. It is *always* used to serve and not to hurt. This is what has brought me to the use of the term *servant-leader* as the central focus of the influence of this house. I believe that if one is to become an effective servant-leader, one must learn from one's own experience how to serve and be served by power. You won't learn all there is to learn about this in your four years here—I haven't at age fifty-six. But I think it is terribly important that you be alerted, experientially, while you are here, and that the process of learning from experience be firmly established before you leave here. I have not found that an academic understanding of power contributes much to this. The only way you will really learn about power is to be very close to its use. To *really* know, one must use power and have it used on oneself.

How do you see this university evolving? you ask in your fifth question. *The university seems to have a great need for change, and it doesn't have an adequate mechanism for change.*

I would feel more comfortable about living out my tenure here if I had an answer to that question. The shape of the immediate future was put succinctly recently by the governor of one of our large states that has an extensive tax-supported university system. "My goal regarding the state university system is to starve it into reform." When asked by a representative of the faculties what kind of reform he had in mind, he answered simply, "I don't know."

I believe this states clearly the challenge before higher education—both tax-supported and non-tax-supported. (Note that I have not used the terms *public* and *private*. They are all public, and the ones that have been thinking of themselves as private had better start thinking of themselves as public.) They are all going to be starved by a combination of three factors: a drop in the number of students, inflation, and a deliberate withholding of financial support—such as the governor announced. Each of these factors is a call for reform. And it is up to the universities themselves to design the reforms. The governor was wise in not specifying the reforms because he probably really doesn't know what they ought to be and because, by refusing to specify the reforms, he leaves himself in a position to judge whether they are adequate when they are proposed. I suspect that, in the coming years, colleges and universities—including the strongest and best of them—will be dealt with harshly. I will suffer along with the rest because teachers in my academic specialty are now in surplus.

You are right in your judgment that the university seems to need a lot of change and does not have an adequate mechanism for it. The dilemma, as I see it, is that our university has allowed itself to bring a medieval model into the modern world relatively unchanged. The medieval model is a status quo design. To be contemporary, one needs an adequate mechanism for change. As Cardinal Newman once put it concerning individuals, "To live is to change; to live well is to have changed often." Universities have done a great deal of tinkering with the fringes, but the core, the medieval tradition, has hardly been touched. Universities need more servant-leaders in them to bring about that change through benign, noncoercive means.

How do I see the university evolving? If university education is to be continuously sought at the level we have become accustomed to, with 50 percent of the population partaking, most of the existing institutions will need to become radically different places. Let me speculate on what our university may be like, five to ten years from now.

We will shift part of our admissions procedure to a search for potential maturity—regardless of academic aptitude—and many students will be admitted when they meet a benchmark standard of maturity. This may be as early as age fourteen or fifteen. Thus the university will take over part of what secondary schools are now doing (and create another problem for those schools). These younger students will be put on a track of their own that will accelerate their growth. It is estimated that academic education as we now commonly practice it is suitable for only 15 percent of the population. The remaining 35 percent will be given other kinds of educational opportunities. I believe this is one of the reforms the governor is calling for. And it will demand a radical reconstruction of the university and retraining of its faculty. Education will be much more interwoven with work.

There will be more professional schools on the model of the School of Administration that Martin will attend next year: nothing but offices, conference rooms, and consultants—no campus, no faculty, no extensive library. Professions in which this is possible—I would say administration, social work, library science, perhaps even law—will be learned mostly in practice, where most of it is learned now!

A few schools for an intellectual elite may survive; I hope they do, but whereas there are perhaps 500 liberal arts colleges that want to be, or pretend to be, Swarthmores, there may be only a few who make it on that model. The rest, if they survive, may have to reorganize themselves to be something quite different.

Then, education is tending to be more of a lifelong process and, in the future, we will not be concentrating so much of it in the age range of most of you. This will make a very different thing of the university community. The new campus of the University of Louvain in Belgium, which is now some miles outside Brussels, is not only an architectural gem, it is a new kind of community. There is no such thing as student housing. Everybody connected with the university—faculty, students, custodians, clerks, and so on—are all housed together. And there is an elementary school on the campus for the children of the families. As the age span of students becomes wider, and as university education is made suitable for a much wider range of abilities than just academic ability, the university may no longer be recognizable as we see it today. Now, most of academe will say, "Nothing like this is going to happen." And it may not. What we do not know is whether tough-minded governors who say they intend to starve the tax-supported universities into reform can survive politically. We do not know whether the marketplace value of a university degree which has supported the tremendous expansion of higher education since World War II will continue. And we do not know what student motivations will be—or how many of them there will be. But reforms of the kind I describe are, in my judgment, long overdue—and I welcome them. More of academe may join me when they get a taste of the new exciting life that is possible for them.

In your sixth question you ask, *What are your reasons for emphasis on building discrete institutions rather than on solving the larger political, social, and economic problems?*

A simple answer would be that a disproportionate share of the attention that now *is* given goes to the larger social, political, and economic problems and not enough goes directly to the quality of our institutions—one institution at a time. My effort is to try to correct that balance. But my main reason is that I believe that it is important for everybody to be concerned about the quality of the institutions of which they currently are a part, because it is through these institutions that much of the influence that determines the shape and quality of the larger society is mediated. In other words, I can do more for the total society by using my influence to build this university, or part of it, to exceptional stature than I can by trying to influence the whole world by some direct means.

We in this room are all a part of this university, so I have repeatedly stressed that we ought to work to make this the best possible university. I hope that, however you choose to be involved in the larger society later on, you will be alert to opportunities to make your influence count as a quality-building force in the institutions you are intimately related to. These are the most tangible opportunities any of us will ever have to serve.

I have also stressed this in the hope that I can offset some of the loose futurism talk we are exposed to. Surely, all of us should keep a weather eye on the future and try to anticipate requirements and opportunities. But the best preparation for the future, as I see it, is to learn to grapple effectively with the present. You will be able to build a better society in the future only if you prove that you can make better servants of the institutions you are in right now.

My feeling about the importance of learning to build better institutions—universities, businesses, hospitals, churches, social agencies—is that these are the building blocks for the larger society—city, state, nation, world. It is unrealistic, I believe, to expect the process of government to be much better than it now is as long as the many voluntary institutions that make up our society function as poorly as servants as most of them now do. What we need to learn to do is for all concerned to hold a balanced interest in the whole gamut of problems that we as a society face. And I hope that, as a result of your experience in this house, you will keep the larger social, economic, political questions high on your lifelong agendas along with your concern for all of the discrete institutions you are involved with.

I do not want to be seen as denigrating the larger social concerns, but I am willing to take that risk for the sake of helping the people in this house get their priorities in order.

Question number seven asks, *Of the nearly one hundred guests of the house in our four years, who, in your judgment, had the most important message for us?*

Each of us has her or his own gauge of importance. But to me, Dr. Broderick, the psychiatrist, made the most significant statement in response to the one question that was asked of him. You will remember that he described the two ten-year phases of his work. The first was conventional practice to try to help those who came to his office as sick people. Then he spent four years talking and writing in an effort to bring a new kind of patient, the strong, successful, healthy person—according to the usual standards—who wants to learn to be effective as a servant of society. At the end of four years one came. There was another year before the second came. Now, after five more years, his practice is largely devoted to the strong, successful, healthy people.

Three things about his talk stand out clearly in my memory of it.

First, he spent ten years in conventional practice before he started to appeal to a different kind of person. Then another ten years were spent in building the kind of practice he has today. Twenty years to find one's best work is a long time.

Second, as seen from the psychiatrist's consulting room, the strong, successful, so-called healthy people are also sick in the sense of revealing their own neediness. As I recall one of Dr. Broderick's statements, "They have been corrupted by power and have worshiped false gods who, when they came to assess their lives, had betrayed them. They have done conspicuous good works and have received honors and decorations. But there is an emptiness: *they have not been servants.*"

Then, third, and perhaps most significant, was his statement: "The hardest struggle I have with my powerful patients is to convince them that generosity and good works in other places is *not* currency with which to redeem one's neglect of one's primary opportunity": *where one wields power in the institutional structure.* The powerful serve best when they use their power to make serving institutions of those where they have influence, and to build communities in which the weak, the inept, the confused—or just the undistinguished—will be strengthened and supported in the useful roles they are able to carry out.

Dr. Broderick's statement came through with special force to me because, in this house, I have avoided trying to convert nonservants to servants. While recognizing a few notable exceptions like Mr. Lord, I had written off any possibility of making servants out of "establishment" people who have made their marks by competitive striving and who have tasted the fruits of unbridled power. But here is a man who not only takes on the task of reeducating these people to be servants, but he makes a living doing it. I was humbled by his story, and I have been rethinking my attitude toward what we do here in Jefferson House.

Your eighth question, *What do you consider the most important single learning in the Jefferson House experience?* gives me great difficulty. There is so much to be learned here. I cannot say what is or should be the most important for any of you. For me, I believe it is this: learning to use one's common sense and to live and work in community.

Time was when most humans lived in community, and they still do in some parts of the world. But in what we like to call advanced society, we have largely lost a sense of community, and I believe we are suffering for it. We need community because we are all partial people and we need the complementary qualities of others in order, as individuals, to be whole persons. "No man is an island . . . "

Although the structure of this house, as I have told you, evolved out of experience rather than according to a grand design, as I look back on it, we have been able to achieve a quite high order of community out of making *serve and be served by* our motto. There may be other ways to do it, but at this time and in this university setting, the way the work has evolved in this house seems to have built community. I will never want to be without a sense of community, that feeling of mutualism among those who are banded together because they have a yearning *to serve and be served by the present society.*

At the conclusion of twenty-four years as housemaster of Jefferson House, your ninth question asks, *can you sum up what seems important for you to say to us as a concluding observation before we go on our way?*

Before you go your several ways, I would like to share some quite intimate feelings about Jefferson House and what it means to me, something I have not expressed before. Your venture into the trustee project has brought your experience much closer to mine, and your last question has caused me to gather my thoughts from nooks and crannies of my experience where I have had only intimations. It will be difficult for me to speak to your question. Please bear with me.

Those of you who have worked with the trustee project have a view of this university that few students get. But you may not have a clear idea of what it is like to have been a member of this faculty for all of these years. Were it not for my work with students in Jefferson House, and the sense of community that you share, I would find the self-serving and competitive striving and lack of human feeling in this university unbearable. I don't know what I would have done without our house, but I doubt that I would have survived on this faculty.

You may not know it, but I am a tender person; I hurt easily. Yet the culture requires that I look and act strong and seem impervious to hurt. Otherwise I would get ground down and walked over. I have seen it happen to others here. Maybe someday I will develop enough of the power of *entheos* that Dr. Broderick talked about so that I can survive with nothing but my classes and my home to support me. But I am not yet that strong. Further, not everybody has students to teach and a home to support oneself, and even when they have them, they are not enough. There is something that Jefferson House gives me, something in the quality of life here, that nearly everyone needs—in the context of their work environment. A few seem not to have that need. They seem so tough that nothing touches them, but even they may be wearing masks, as Dr. Broderick said.

What is that something in the quality of life in this house that makes a serene life possible for persons like me? What is it? There must be something here that is deeper than the structure and programs of our house, something that may be carried to any situation. What makes community out of our relationship? It didn't just happen because we live and work together. If we know what it is, you will be helped to build community in the institutions you work with in the future. You may not be able to influence a whole institution, as we have not in our university, but you might create an island of serenity that enables some people to cope, and be a constructive leaven, in an environment that is cold and tense and hostile, conditions that mark too much of our institutional life and that will not go away easily or quickly.

Serve and be served by. As you serve by creating that constructive leaven, that haven of the spirit that benefits many, you too will be served as I am by Jefferson House.

As I mused on these ideas in preparation for tonight, the word *Mecca* came to mind. I know that Mecca is Muhammad's birthplace, that devout Muslims visit there, and that, wherever they are, they face Mecca when they kneel to pray. But it came to me as a word with a symbolic meaning, and I consulted several dictionaries for suggestions. The one that resonates with me is *birthplace of a faith.* That is what Jefferson House is for me: birthplace of a faith. What goes on here is the source of my faith—and the basis of my hope for all of our futures.

I asked myself, what gives that quality, what makes it my Mecca? And I concluded that it is a priceless blend of two powerful forces: *love* and *laughter.* Love without laughter can be grim and oppressive. Laughter without love can be derisive and venomous. Together they make for greatness of spirit. I have found both in abundance here. That is why Jefferson House is Mecca for me.

May your days be blessed with love and laughter: and, wherever you are, may you too find Mecca—community where faith is generated—as you work to create it for others.

* * *

No one spoke in response. Finally, Mr. Billings rose and stood with a warm, fond smile and looked intently from one to the other of us. Tears came to his eyes. Softly he said good night. We seniors gathered around and gave him farewell hugs as we left in silence.

LIFE'S CHOICES AND MARKERS

Part 3

LIFE'S CHOICES AND MARKERS

In the spring of 1984, I was invited to give a commencement talk at Alverno College, a Catholic Women's College in Milwaukee. I had never made a commencement talk before, but I realized that it was an occasion that was too much used for gratuitous advice. I decided that I would make a brief summary of five major ideas that had shaped the course of my work. What I wanted to convey in twenty minutes, without lecturing them about it, is that ideas nurture the human spirit that determines how one comes out of life, and that one chooses, among all the ideas one has access to, which will guide what one does with one's opportunities. And that that choice is crucial.

The text of my talk follows. It was delivered by video transmission since I no longer travel.

I welcome this opportunity to visit with my friends at Alverno College. You will recognize on the table beside me this lovely wood carving of St. Francis that was made for me many years ago by your Sister Helena Steffens-Meier. Its usual place is on my bedside table from which it watches over my sleep and greets me when I awake. I like to think that it radiates some of the spirit of St. Francis, and it is a constant reminder of pleasant days at Alverno.

What I want to share with you today is a brief summary of five ideas that have been significant markers in my past, ideas that guided choices in my work. The last four came in words. The first is distilled from early experience with my father, to whom I was very close. He was a good, intelligent man with but a fifth-grade education, and he had a life of limited opportunity. But he managed, by a prudent use of his life, to leave a little corner of the world a bit better than he found it. Many years passed before I came to a mature appreciation of him. In the perspective of considerable experience, he stands tall as a true servant. This model of servanthood deeply etched from childhood and youth was the first pivotal idea. Without it, the four ideas that came later in words might not have challenged me. And they needed to come in the order that I received them.

The second pivotal idea came in the last half of my senior year in college. I went to college with the clear vocational aim that I would become an astronomer, like a favorite uncle who encouraged me. I quickly concluded that, although I had the aptitude for science and mathematics that qualified, I did not have the temperament for an astronomer. I was not cut out for it. This conclusion did not bother me, and I laid aside the matter of vocation until after graduation. Then I assured myself I would look around and make a choice. These were the euphoric boom years of the mid-1920s, and jobs were plentiful. One had choices.

That last term I elected a course in the sociology of labor problems. The professor was old (or so he seemed to me), and he was neither a great scholar nor an exciting teacher. But he had been around, and he was wise in the ways of humans and institutions, and I was sensitive to that quality. One day in the course of a rambling lecture, he made a comment in about these words: "We are becoming a nation of large institutions; everything is getting big — business, schools, governments. There has not been before a society like ours, and these big institutions are not serving us well. Now, you can do as I do and stand outside and criticize and bring pressure, but nothing constructive will happen until someone who is inside and has her or his hands on some of the levers of power and influence decides to change something. These big institutions rarely can be changed constructively from the outside. My advice to some of you is that you make your careers inside of one of these big institutions, stay with it, and become one of those who responds to suggestions that they change for the better."

My doors of perception must have been open a bit wider than usual that day because that message came through loud and clear. Something of the servant image of my father may have opened those doors. I had a short talk with the professor, and he did not have much more to say about it. But, my career aim was settled by his advice. I would get inside the largest business that would hire me and stay there if I could. It would be a business rather than some other kind of institution because there were no professional hurdles, businesses seemed more malleable, and they may have been in greater need.

After graduation, I quickly established that American Telephone and Telegraph Company (AT&T) was the largest, and I chose it for that reason alone. In a few weeks, I was digging postholes with a line construction crew near Youngstown, Ohio. I spent thirty-eight years with the company, mostly in New York. I am not a manager by temperament, and I settled for staff work from which I might influence that vast company with ideas. Life there was not always easy or pleasant, and it needed much more help than I could give it. There were some dreary, depressing years, and a few dreadful ones that really tested my sustaining spirit. But I stayed with it; I cared intensely about the quality of the institution, and I kept a deep interest in the company's history and myth. I believe I accomplished what my old professor advised. But I did not wield enough influence to save the company from being broken up after I retired. I did try hard to save what was good about it.

The third pivotal idea came when I was twenty-five and moved to New York and quickly became devoted to the writing of E. B. White in *The New Yorker* magazine. Mr. White, I soon learned, had two gifts that are seldom possessed by one person: the ability to see things whole, or more whole than most, and the language to tell us ordinary mortals what he saw. This began what is now a fifty-five-year engagement with Mr. White's writing. Much reflection was required for me to grasp the essential idea—seeing things whole. But when I got it, it was an impressive idea. And it helped me to understand the stature of my father who also saw things whole. But my father did not have Mr. White's gift of language that makes an idea memorable.

The fourth pivotal idea came when I was about forty, when I read an article by a great radio commentator of that day, Elmer Davis. I no longer have the article, but I have a crystal-clear memory of the advice. The title of the article was, "The Uses of Old People." The gist of the article was that there are useful and necessary things to be done that are best done by old people, partly because old people have greater perspective of experience, but mostly because the things that need to be done do not fit into a career or they are too risky for young or midcareer people. He advised that younger people should look forward to old age as presenting an opportunity to be prepared for, rather than as a time to be put out to pasture when one wears out. It was a persuasive argument and, again, my doors of perception were open a bit wider than usual and that message came through loud and clear: begin now to prepare for what can best be done in old age.

The next twenty years were ones in which I was attentive to my work at AT&T, and I grew in it. Because of this preparation, I believe I was more effective in my last years there. I devoted much time to my family and to relaxation. But I was too busy for such pursuits as golf and bridge.

The details of how I spent my time are not important; I did what suited my temperament and I was governed somewhat by opportunity. But I had my eye on age sixty, when I could exercise my first retirement option at AT&T. And the day after I hung up my sword there, I took off on radically different, more venturesome, and more exciting work. My preparation between forty and sixty opened several inviting opportunities. The years between sixty and seventy-five were, in some ways, my most productive and satisfying. I am grateful for my thirty-eight years of disciplined organizational work in a huge institution. I needed that solid base of experience to be effective in my old age.

During my "retirement," I worked only on long-term consulting arrangements. Two of my clients in that period were universities during the years of student unrest and general confusion. I had close involvement with the radical students and I wondered much about the cause of this turmoil.

In the course of foundation work I was also doing in that period, I visited a number of college and university campuses, and I always looked into the campus bookstores to see what students were reading, the avocational reading. Everywhere I saw stacks and stacks of books by the contemporary German novelist Hermann Hesse. I concluded that I might better understand the students of that period if I understood Hesse. So I devoted my reading time one winter to all of the books then in translation by Hesse. I read them in the order they were written, and I read a biography that told me what was going on in Hesse's life as each was written. Hesse, for much of his life, was a tortured man, in and out of mental illness, and much of the pain in his existence is reflected in what he wrote. Since the student unrest of that period appeared to me symptomatic of massive mental illness, their lives seemed to be resonating to the turmoil Hesse wrote about. This was not a useful learning.

But my search bore fruit in another way that proved very important to me. Near the end of Hesse's life, there was a turn to the relative serenity he achieved in his old age. The turning point is marked by a book entitled, *Journey to the East*, which I found a hopeful book.

Journey to the East is an account of a mythical journey by a band of men on a search to the East, probably Hesse's own search. The central figure of the story is Leo who accompanies the party as the servant who does their menial chores, but who also sustains them with his spirit and his song. He is a person of extraordinary presence. All goes well with the journey until one day Leo disappears. Then the group falls into disarray, and the journey is abandoned. They cannot make it without the servant Leo. The narrator, one of the party, after some years of searching, finds Leo and is taken into the Order that had sponsored the search. There, he discovers that Leo, whom he had first known as a servant, was in fact, the titular head of the Order, its guiding spirit, a great and noble leader.

One can muse on what Hesse was trying to say when he wrote this story. There has been much speculation on Hesse's life and work, some of it centering on this story which critics find most puzzling. But to me this story clearly says: the greatest leader (who may be a "little" person) is seen as servant first because that is what he is deep down inside. Leadership is bestowed on the person who is, by nature, a true servant. Leadership is something given or assumed, that could be taken away. Leo's servant nature was the real person, not bestowed, not assumed, and not to be taken away. Leo was servant first. This pivotal idea was the fifth that has been a significant marker in my life.

In my private musing, it pleases me to think that Hesse, through the means whereby he created this story, recovered his sanity and moved into a serene old age. The idea of the servant as leader that I got from reading *Journey to the East* started me to writing a series of essays on this theme dealing with the nature of leadership, the structure of institutions, trusteeship, seminaries, and religious leading in general. It has been for me a truly pivotal idea. And it has kept me busy for the past fifteen years.

Shortly after the first essay, "The Servant as Leader," was published, a Catholic Sister (not a member of The School Sisters of St. Francis) came to talk about it. In the course of the conversation, she asked me where, in literature, I found the first reference to servant? My reply was, "In the Bible, all through the Bible. I checked the concordance and found 1,300 references." "Why then," was her sharp question, "do you attribute what you have written to Hermann Hesse?" "Because," I replied, "that is where I got the idea of 'The Servant as Leader.' If I had not read *Journey to the East* and seen the vivid dramatization of the servant as leader in the person of Leo, I doubt that I would ever have written on this theme. Hermann Hesse gave me that pivotal idea, not the Bible. I firmly believe that revelation is continuous; it did not end with the Bible, and we need to be listening for revelation all of the time." The good Sister changed the subject.

Concerning the student attitudes of the 1960s, they seemed to stem from a lack of hope, a lack of belief by those young people that they could live productively in the world of institutions as they then were (and still are). This was a devastating prospect for those young people to live without hope in a highly structured but imperfect society.

When I started to write on the servant-leader theme, I was trying to communicate a basis for hope—not just to students, but to everybody. I did not believe that I could communicate this directly in writing to students. But I did try to give a basis for hope to teachers, trustees, churches, and administrators in general, with the intent that their combined influence might give a greater basis for hope than is now generally available to young people, and make for a better society. Particularly, I wanted to persuade teachers to find ways to serve students as I was served by my old professor who suggested that I take on the career task of becoming a leaven in a ponderous bureaucracy.

This effort has not been a spectacular success. (My book *Teacher as Servant* was initially a commercial failure.) But there has been enough response to sustain my hope and to encourage others to hope.

As I review my experience, it has been important that I be open to ideas, all of the time — and there have been many important ones. I have named five that now seem to me to have been important in giving a sense of direction to my work. First, the servant model of my father. Then the advice of Professor Oscar Helming when I was twenty-one: Get into a big institution and stay there and help shape its character. At age twenty-five, I encountered the writing of E. B. White and was alerted to the importance of seeing things whole. I stayed with his writing for the next fifty-five years. When I was age forty, Elmer Davis advised me to start preparing for a useful old age. When I was sixty-five, Hermann Hesse gave me the idea of the servant as leader that has occupied me ever since. It seems to me, in retrospect, that responding to each of these ideas when it was offered was the ticket of admission for receiving the next one. At eighty, I am still looking and listening.

The ideas I chose to follow did not make a design for becoming either rich or famous or for wielding a world-shaping influence. I doubt that I had it in me to achieve either of these anyway. These ideas did make an interesting and rewarding life and I am glad that I chose to respond to these five.

To the graduating seniors, I would say the pivotal ideas that have guided me in my work may not be the ideas that you choose to guide you in your work. But I am sure that you will choose either consciously or by default. And to make good choices I have found it helpful to be open to ideas, to be expectant, to be hopeful. But this is risky; you just might get a great idea.

Let me close with Aldous Huxley's little poem on choice:

> The choice is always ours. Then let me choose
> The longest art, the hard Promethian way
> Cherishingly to tend and feed and fan
> That inward fire, whose small precarious flame,
> Kindled or quenched, creates
> The noble or the ignoble folk we are,
> The worlds we live in and the very fates,
> Our bright or muddy star.

GREENLEAF BIBLIOGRAPHY

"Abraham Joshua Heschel: Build a Life Like a Work of Art." *Friends Journal*, 1973, 19(15), 459–460.

Advices to Servants. Indianapolis: The Greenleaf Center, 1991.

"The Art of Knowing." *Friends Journal*, 1974, 20(17).

"Business Ethics—Everybody's Problem." *New Catholic World*, 1980, 223, 275–278.

"Choose the Nobler Belief." *AA Grapevine*, 1966, 23(5), 27–31.

"Choosing Greatness." *AA Grapevine*, 1966, 23(4), 26–30.

"Choosing to be Aware." *AA Grapevine*, 1966, 23(1), 26–28.

"Choosing to Grow." *AA Grapevine*, 1966, 23(2), 11–13.

"Community as Servant and Nurturer of the Human Spirit." *Resources for Community-Based Economic Development*, 1986, 4, 9–11.

Education and Maturity. Indianapolis: The Greenleaf Center, 1988.

Have You a Dream Deferred? Indianapolis: The Greenleaf Center, 1988.

The Institution as Servant. Indianapolis: The Greenleaf Center, 1976.

The Leadership Crisis. Indianapolis: The Greenleaf Center, 1978.

Life's Choices and Markers. Indianapolis: The Greenleaf Center, 1986.

Mission in a Seminary: A Prime Trustee Concern. Indianapolis: The Greenleaf Center, 1981.

My Debt to E. B. White. Indianapolis: The Greenleaf Center, 1987.

Old Age: The Ultimate Test of Spirit. Indianapolis: The Greenleaf Center, 1987, 2003.

On Becoming a Servant Leader. San Francisco: Jossey-Bass, 1996.

"Overcome Evil with Good." *Friends Journal*, 1977, 23(10), 292–302.

Robert Frost's "Directive" and the Spiritual Journey. Boston: Nimrod Press, 1963.

Seeker and Servant. San Francisco: Jossey-Bass, 1996.

Seminary as Servant. Indianapolis: The Greenleaf Center, 1988.

Servant Leadership. New York: Paulist Press, 1977, 2002.

The Power of Servant Leadership. San Francisco: Berrett-Koehler, 1998.

The Servant as Leader. Indianapolis: The Greenleaf Center, 1991.

"The Servant as Leader." *Journal of Religion and the Applied Behavioral Sciences*, Winter 1982, 3, 7–10.

The Servant as Religious Leader. Indianapolis: The Greenleaf Center, 1983.

Servant: Retrospect and Prospect. Indianapolis: The Greenleaf Center, 1980.

251

Spirituality as Leadership. Indianapolis: The Greenleaf Center, 1988.

Teacher as Servant: A Parable. Indianapolis: The Greenleaf Center, 1987.

"The Trustee and the Risks of Persuasive Leadership." *Hospital Progress*, 1978, 50–52, 88.

"Trustee Traditions and Expectations." In *The Good Steward: A Guide to Theological School Trusteeship*. Washington, D.C.: Association of Governing Boards of Universities and Colleges, n.d.

Trustees as Servants. Indianapolis: The Greenleaf Center, 1990.

"Two More Choices." *AA Grapevine*, 1966, 23(3), 22–23.

INDEX

253

ABOUT THE EDITORS
AND THE GREENLEAF CENTER
FOR SERVANT-LEADERSHIP

DR. HAMILTON BEAZLEY is scholar-in-residence at St. Edward's University, Austin, Texas. His major fields of expertise are organizational behavior, organizational culture, leadership, and spirituality in organizations. Before launching an academic career, he served in the for-profit and not-for-profit sectors. His wide range of talents led him to co-create a television series entitled *Secrets Out* on the BBC; to found a successful consulting firm; and to hold the position of president for the National Council on Alcoholism and Drug Dependence, Inc.

JULIE YANCICH BEGGS is a former staff member of the Greenleaf Center. Her professional career began in higher education as the assistant director of campus activities for Butler University in Indianapolis, Indiana. While at Butler, she helped to create "The Hampton House," a special-interest housing facility where student servant-leaders can live and learn together. The Hampton House is one of only four housing models in the country based on Robert K. Greenleaf's book *Teacher as Servant*.

LARRY C. SPEARS is a writer, editor, and president/CEO of The Greenleaf Center for Servant-Leadership. He is the editor of seven previous books: *Servant Leadership (25th Anniversary Edition)*, 2002; *Focus on Leadership* (with Michele Lawrence), 2002; *The Power of Servant-Leadership*, 1998; *Insights on Leadership*, 1998; *On Becoming a Servant-Leader* (with Don Frick), 1996; *Seeker and Servant* (with Anne Fraker), 1996; and *Reflections on Leadership*, 1995. His essays are also included in the books: *Cutting Edge: Leadership 2000*, 2000; *Stone*

Soup for the Soul, 1998; and *Leadership in a New Era*, 1994. He is series editor for the *Voices of Servant-Leadership Essay Series* (published by The Greenleaf Center) and the founder and senior editor of The Greenleaf Center's quarterly newsletter, *The Servant-Leader*. Spears has also published over 400 articles, essays, and book reviews.

THE GREENLEAF CENTER FOR SERVANT-LEADERSHIP, headquartered in Indianapolis, Indiana, is an international nonprofit educational organization that seeks to encourage the understanding and practice of servant-leadership. It has offices in Australia/New Zealand, Canada, Europe, Japan, Korea, the Philippines, Singapore, South Africa, and the United Kingdom. The center's mission is to improve the caring and quality of all institutions through servant-leadership.

The Greenleaf Center's programs and resources include the worldwide publication and sale of books, essays, and videotapes on servant-leadership; an annual International Conference on Servant-Leadership held each June in Indianapolis; a variety of programs, institutes, retreats, and speakers; a membership program; consultative services; and other activities focused on servant-leadership.

Servant-leadership is being practiced today by many individuals and organizations. For more information about servant-leadership and The Greenleaf Center, contact:

The Greenleaf Center for Servant-Leadership
921 East 86th Street, Suite 200
Indianapolis, IN 46240
Phone (317) 259-1241; Fax (317) 259-0560
E-mail: info@greenleaf.org
Website: www.greenleaf.org